MATCH OF THE DAY

BBC

THE OFFICIAL 2008 ANNUAL

CONTENTS

MATCH OF THE DAY ANNUAL 2008

EDITOR Chris Hunt (www.ChrisHunt.biz) **ART DIRECTOR** David Houghton **CONTRIBUTORS** Will Lincoln, Patrick Mascall, Luke Nicoli, Adam Paget **DATA** © Warner Leach Ltd **RANKINGS** © Interact Publishing & Warner Leach Ltd **DESIGN PRODUCTION** Cambridge Publishers Ltd (www.cpl.biz) **PHOTOGRAPHY** © Getty Images **PROJECT MANAGER AT INTERACT** Terry Pratt **RANDOM HOUSE COMMISSIONING EDITOR** Lorna Russell **PRODUCTION CONTROLLER** Antony Heller

A 'MILE AWAY CLUB' PRODUCTION by Chris Hunt & David Houghton for Interact Publishing Ltd

Published in 2007 by BBC Books, an imprint of Ebury Publishing. A Random House Group Company. The Random House Group Limited Reg. No. 954009. Addresses for companies within the Random House Group can be found at www.randomhouse.co.uk. A CIP catalogue record for this book is available from the British Library. The Random House Group Limited supports The Forest Stewardship Council (FSC), the leading international forest certification organisation. All our titles that are printed on Greenpeace approved FSC certified paper carry the FSC logo. Our paper procurement policy can be found at www.rbooks.co.uk/environment.

Printed in Germany **ISBN** 978 1 846 07345 8

TEN REASONS
WHY THIERRY HENRY
SHOULD HAVE STAYED AT ARSENAL

1. Barcelona don't need another world class player.

2. The number of French players at the club is dropping dangerously low.

3. Would your sister really want a picture of Emmanual Adebayor on her wall?

4. The Gunners will soon plummet down the league without his vital 'va-va-voom'.

5. Arsene Wenger won't splash the cash to replace him.

6. It will be too hot to wear gloves while playing in Spain.

7. Walcott may be the next Henry but he's English – and everyone knows that Arsenal don't field English players.

8. You can't see Jens Lehmann replacing him in the Renault ad.

9. He's too good looking to be a Barcelona striker.

10. Oh yeah, he did score 174 goals for the club in his eight years in London.

A LAUGH A MINUTE WITH ALAN & GARY!

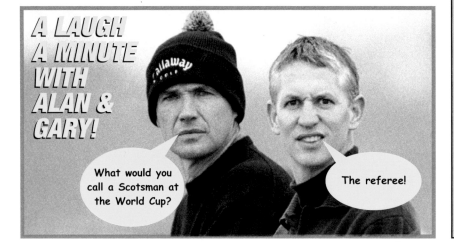

What would you call a Scotsman at the World Cup?

The referee!

THE BEST

What did some of your favourite *Match Of The Day* commentators and pundits rate as their highlights of last season...

SIMON BROTHERTON

"I did over 90 games last season and the one that stands out was the Champions League semi-final between AC Milan and Man United at the San Siro. It was fantastic to cover a big game on that stage. In terms of English games I did West Ham v Spurs with Motty, the 4-3 one when Tevez got his first goal and jumped into the crowd. That was a memorable moment.

"It's not all about the big games. I was at the second leg of the League One play-off semi between Yeovil and Forest. It was a fantastic game – 5-2 in extra time and was possibly in my top three games of the season."

ALAN HANSEN

"I watched Wigan's match at Sheffield United and it was one of the great games, in terms of tension and excitement. Paul Jewell did an amazing job to get Wigan fired up for that match. You could argue that those sort of games are even bigger than the title-deciders and what they went through, especially in the last 20 minutes… it was like the Alamo. Sheffield were pummeling them and Wigan only had ten men.

"Eight weeks before the end of the campaign my player of the season was Drogba but Cristiano Ronaldo made it a very close call. Drogba's goals were unbelievable and if you took them away from Chelsea they would have really struggled. If you took Ronaldo's from United I still think they would achieved what they have."

OF THE YEAR!

JONATHAN PEARCE

"My favourite moments of last season include Man United v Everton, when the Everton keeper Turner dropped the ball and John O'Shea scored. That was the moment when the whole title race changed because Chelsea were winning at home to Bolton at the time, and then Bolton pulled back to 2-2. It was all so significant. I've also enjoyed watching the development of Blackburn Rovers and Mark Hughes as a manager too. I always go to a game and see something. I really enjoy occasions like Weymouth v Bury every bit as much as I enjoy grabbing Didier Drogba on the pitch after the FA Cup final at Wembley. I'm really lucky to be in the position I am and I never forget that."

LES FERDINAND

"For my best moment it's hard to look beyond that West Ham v Tottenham game to be honest. I was watching it live while we were working on *Match Of The Day 2* and my co-pundit Lee Dixon was giving me a lot of stick because he knows I'm a Spurs fan. But I said, 'Don't worry, we'll come through in the end'. If you were a neutral watching that game, you'd have been thoroughly entertained.

"The player of last season has to be a toss up between Cristiano Ronaldo and Didier Drogba. I think they were both exceptional. As for manager of the season, I think Alex Ferguson rose to the challenge that was set."

STEVE WILSON

"I must have commentated on 80 games last season. Although I was commentating when Rooney scored for United against Bolton following that incredible break away with Ronaldo, which got Goal Of The Season, I'd ve to say that my own personal highlight was Robin Van Persie's al for Arsenal against Charlton. It was a fantastic volley."

QUESTION TIME

England and Tottenham goalkeeper Paul Robinson answers the questions…

WHO DID YOU SUPPORT AS A KID?
"Leeds was the biggest and nearest club but my grandad used to take me to see Hull City play. I remember one time at Christmas there was a lot of snow and the club advertised for people to go and clear the snow and they would get a free ticket. I went there with my snow shovel."

WHAT'S THE FUNNIEST TERRACE CHANT YOU CAN REMEMBER?
"I liked the one that the Spurs fans sang to the Fulham fans: 'You must have come in a taxi', because there were only about four of them there. I also like the one to the Chelsea fans: "Next year you'll be supporting Man U."

WHAT WOULD YOU HAVE DONE IF YOU HADN'T BEEN A FOOTBALLER?
"There was never anything else I wanted to do. They used to ask me at school what I wanted to be and I always said, 'I am going to be a footballer'. That was it. There really was no back up plan."

WHOSE POSTER DID YOU HAVE ON YOUR WALL?
"Everton keeper Neville Southall was always my

hero. He was so unorthodox. It was either his way or the highway. He was a great all round goalkeeper. That's where I get the black kit from. He was the first keeper I ever saw wearing a black goalkeeper's shirt and we talked about that when we were designing my black Spurs kit."

WHAT MUSIC WOULD YOU LIKE PLAYED AT YOUR FUNERAL?
"I think I would chose Bon Jovi's 'Blaze Of Glory' — I'm going to be cremated you see!"

WHAT'S THE WORST HOLIDAY YOU'VE HAD?
"It was a caravan holiday with my parents when I was a kid to a place called Silleth!"

WHAT DID YOU DO WITH YOUR FIRST PAY CHEQUE?
"Nothing that memorable to be honest. In fact, I probably paid my mum and dad back some of the money that I owed them!"

WHAT IS YOUR POSITION ON FACIAL HAIR?
"Absolutely fine on males!"

EVER HAD A REALLY RUBBISH CAR?
"Yes, I'd have to say my first car. It was a mint green Renault 5."

KICK-OFF!

GOALS GOALS GOAL!
GOALS OF THE MONTH 2006-07

There were a lot of cracking goals scored last season, and just a few of them were honoured with the *Match Of The Day* Goal Of The Month Award…

MARCH
WAYNE ROONEY

Manchester United v Bolton
First goal, March 17

There were many wonderful strikes to choose from in the 2006-07 season, but the much-coveted *Match Of The Day* accolade was awarded to Wayne Rooney for his delicate chip following a skilful dribble from Cristiano Ronaldo. The goal was the first of a brace for the England superstar in the match. Ronaldo started the move after picking up the ball from a wasted Wanderers corner, exchanging passes with Rooney as they sprinted up the pitch at full speed. With the Bolton defence unable to keep pace, Ronaldo slotted the ball through to Rooney, who rounded off the move with a perfect chip that left Jussi Jaaskaleinen with no chance.

MATCH OF THE DAY'S GOAL OF THE SEASON

OCTOBER
GARETH BARRY

Aston Villa v Tottenham
October 14

Despite stiff competition from Leighton Baines and Seol Ki-Hyeon, it was a Gareth Barry effort that the pundits chose as October's Goal Of The Month. With only ten minutes of the match left and Villa 1-0 down, Barry kept a cool head as he curled in a 20-yard strike to give his side a share of the points.

MAY
CRAIG GARDNER

Bolton v Aston Villa
May 13

The young Aston Villa midfielder received *MOTD*'s final monthly award. With his side trailing by a single goal, a terrific strike levelled the score to keep Villa in the game.

FEBRUARY
DENNY LANDZAAT

Arsenal v Wigan *February 11*

Wigan may have lost 2-1, but Dutch international Landzaat at least left his team-mates with something to smile about, scoring a stunning 30-yard drive. Only the second goal the midfielder had scored in English football, he would be hard pressed to score a better one.

DECEMBER
PAUL SCHOLES

Aston Villa v Manchester United *December 23*

Described as "arguably the best Goal Of The Month competition ever", the shortlist for December was packed with net-busting gems. It took a spectacular long-range volley from Paul Scholes to tip the scales for the pundits, while Scholes himself admitted that it was the best goal he had ever scored

SEPTEMBER
ROBIN VAN PERSIE

Charlton v Arsenal
September 29

After the Dutch striker netted an airborne volley from the edge of the box, Arsene Wenger described the shot as "technically perfect". The *MOTD* pundits selected this effort ahead of goals from Cristiano Ronaldo and Xabi Alonso.

APRIL
JAMES McFADDEN
Everton v Charlton April 15

First class strikes from Dimitar Berbatov and Gavin Mahon were beaten to the April Goal Of The Month award by a dramatic late blast from Everton forward James McFadden. With the game delicately poised at 1-1 McFadden produced the goods in the 90th minute to steal all the points.

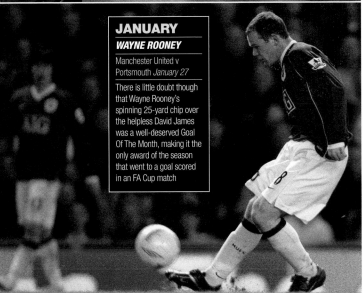

JANUARY
WAYNE ROONEY
Manchester United v Portsmouth January 27

There is little doubt though that Wayne Rooney's spinning 25-yard chip over the helpless David James was a well-deserved Goal Of The Month, making it the only award of the season that went to a goal scored in an FA Cup match

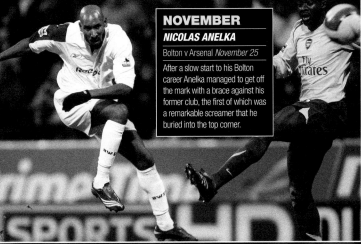

NOVEMBER
NICOLAS ANELKA
Bolton v Arsenal November 25

After a slow start to his Bolton career Anelka managed to get off the mark with a brace against his former club, the first of which was a remarkable screamer that he buried into the top corner.

AUGUST
DAN AGGER
Liverpool v West Ham August 26

This may have been the Danish centre-back's first goal for Liverpool, but it's unlikely he'll ever score a better one. It was the perfect way to introduce himself to the Merseyside faithful as he smashed home a 35-yard curler into the net in front of the Kop, sealing a 2-1 win.

---

4 REASONS WHY DOES THE IVORY COAST PRODUCE SUCH GREAT FOOTBALLERS...

We ask the stars of the Premiership...

IVORY COAST

Where: West Africa
Language: French
Population: 17 million (est)
Largest city: Abidjan

Didier Drogba Chelsea

Kolo Toure Arsenal

Salomon Kalou Chelsea

Didier Zokora Spurs

1. THE STANDARD OF FOOTBALL JUST KEEPS PROGRESSING

DIDIER ZOKORA: "Football has progressed a lot in the Ivory Coast – you can see that with the kind of clubs our players are joining when they come to the Premiership. There is a great generation of footballers being produced at the moment."

DIDIER DROGBA: "Before there was always one African team close to the European level, but now there are more and more coming through to that level, which means an African team has a greater chance of winning something."

2. THE TOP PLAYERS ARE VERY CLOSE

DIDIER ZOKORA: "We're like brothers. They're like family to me. Having said that, it's difficult to see each other regularly because of games and training, so we speak a lot on the phone."

KOLO TOURE: "I really believe in this current Ivory Coast team. We are all good players, playing at a high level in Europe, but we also all grew up playing together and have known each other for a long time, so we have a really strong mentality."

DIDIER DROGBA: "Big experiences like we had in the last couple of years really bring you together as people. As a team, the players who represent the Ivory Coast are very close. That's our mentality and that's where we come from."

3. MANY OF THE PLAYERS WENT TO THE SAME TOP FOOTBALL ACADEMY

KOLO TOURE: "It was set up by an ex-France player called Jean Marc Gillou and it's had such an unbelievable impact on football in the Ivory Coast. It has changed things completely for us. It gave us the opportunity to become better players and to change our lives. It was a very strict education but it gave us the belief that we could make it."

SALOMON KALOU: "They choose only the best players in the country so of course it is hard to get into the academy. The levels are very high so you have to give your absolute best to get in."

DIDIER ZOKORA: "I went there at 11 and spent seven magnificent years there, and all the players from my generation there have ended up moving to big clubs. All of our national team, apart from Didier Drogba, went to the Academy, so it's really had a huge impact."

4. THE WORLD CUP GAVE THEM A LOT OF VALUABLE EXPERIENCE

DIDIER ZOKORA: "We were the first generation of players to take Ivory Coast to the World Cup, which says everything. It was a childhood dream. We played some big teams – just in our group we played Holland and Argentina. But even though we didn't make it past the group stage, everybody learnt things and we grew in maturity from the experience."

SALOMON KALOU: "Everyone dreams about playing for their national team, and when you pull on the shirt you feel very proud."

KOLO TOURE: "We hope that one day we will win the World Cup."

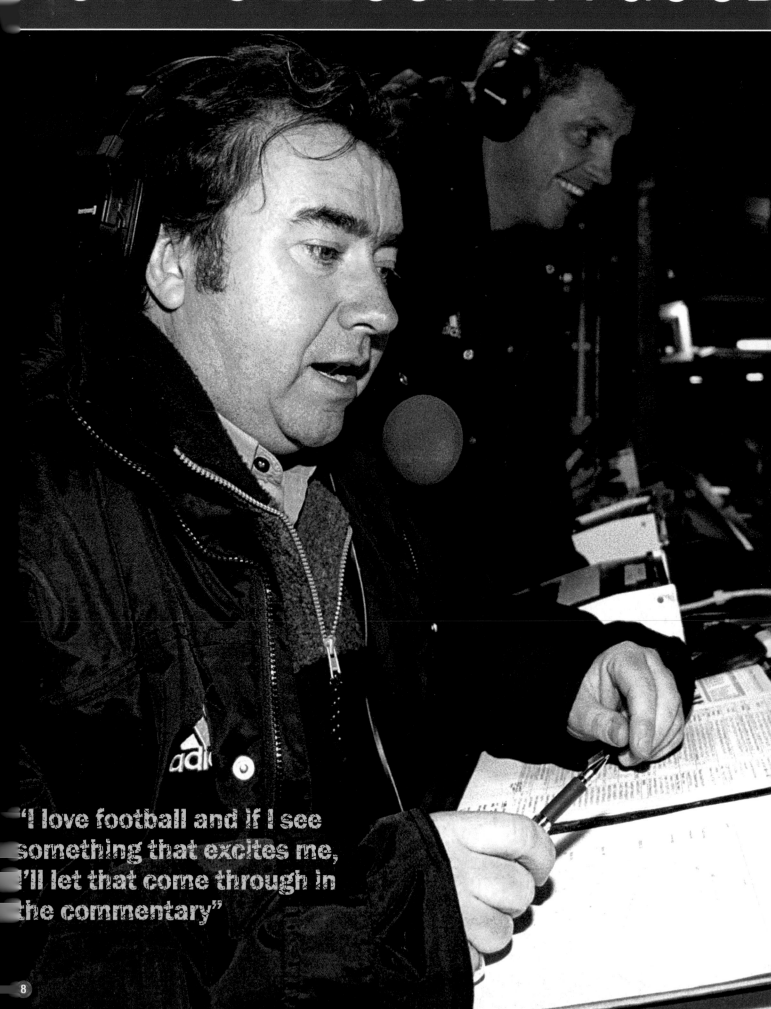

"I love football and if I see something that excites me, I'll let that come through in the commentary"

COMMENTATOR

Ever wanted to work on *Match Of The Day*? Some of the BBC's top voices explain what it takes to become a great commentator.

"SOME PEOPLE ARE ON THE PITCH! THEY THINK IT'S ALL OVER… IT IS NOW!" SO ENDED THE 1966 World Cup Final – in the words of the BBC's Kenneth Wolstenholme. His commentary has become as much a part of that famous game as Geoff Hurst's hat-trick and it just goes to show how the words that roll off the tongue in the heat of the moment can be etched into history forever. Decades later we are more reliant than ever on the reassuring voices of our commentators to bring the action from the stadiums into our front rooms. There's no question that it's a highly skilled art involving dedication, talent and a lot of hard work. But thanks to the advice of some of MOTD's finest, here's our 11-step guide to a career behind the mic…

STEP ONE: DO YOUR HOMEWORK

You can't become a really good commentator unless you know what you're talking about.

Simon Brotherton: "Going to the games and doing the commentating is the exciting part. You have to do a lot of work that isn't that exciting to prepare."

Jonathan Pearce: "You've got to know your stats and background but the most important thing is knowing your players. I've built up a library of videos covering everything from World Cup and European Championship games to UEFA Cup and Champions League matches, and even things like the Copa America. You have to know the teams as a whole too. If you were doing Chelsea you need to know that they switch from attacking with a two to a three quite regularly. If you can, speaking to the managers can be a great benefit but is becoming harder and harder to do so these days."

John Motson: "If you are going to be doing an England game against someone like Azerbaijan you have got to work very hard to know about the opposing players and that is where going to a training session almost invariably comes into play. It also helps going to the team hotel and trying to spot players as they walk through the foyer, and things like going to press conferences so that you can get the drift of what the opposing manager is thinking."

STEP TWO: DON'T USE ALL YOUR STATS

You may know everything, but you don't need to say everything!

Steve Wilson: "You'll probably only use a tiny percentage of your prep but you never quite know which bit you may need to use. If a player gets a serious knee injury, and six years before he'd missed a season with a cruciate problem, you need to be able to call on that knowledge because it's suddenly relevant. But you have to edit yourself as you go along – it's so important to only use what's relevant."

Simon Brotherton: "Only include stats or facts if you think they're necessary at that exact moment. Don't read stats off a sheet just to prove you've done your homework. Stats should only be used to add to the picture. The info you have on a sheet is like a comfort blanket – it's there if you need it but you shouldn't use all of it. And if you're going to come out with a stat make sure it's correct or don't bother using it. Using a stat that's wrong is worse than using none at all."

STEP THREE: KNOW YOUR HISTORY

A wide knowledge of the history of the game helps to understand the modern game.

Jonathan Pearce: "Interpreting the game accurately requires an in-depth historical knowledge of football.

Steve Wilson says that research is essential to support a good match commentary.

If something sensational happens in a game and you have that knowledge, you can place it properly into context more easily."

Steve Wilson: "Football didn't start in 1992 with the Premiership! Who won the league in 1973? You need to know these things because even though you may be commentating on a game today, it may have a connection to a famous incident 30 years ago. You have to be totally steeped in football past and present."

Simon Brotherton: "The more you know historically, the better you'll be at putting things in context. You could easily get carried away saying a particular game or goal is the greatest ever when clearly it's not."

STEP FOUR: STAY IMPARTIAL

Don't go cheering when one team scores, as the viewers won't trust you any more.

Steve Wilson: "Being English, you wouldn't be human if you were commentating on an England game and didn't want England to win. That said, you can't be obviously biased. You still need to remain objective – you're not a cheerleader!"

John Motson: "It's only when a game is over I might think to myself, 'Oh, they were a bit unlucky'. I have never gone into a match thinking, 'I hope so and so wins'. I've never found it a problem staying impartial. I'm totally preoccupied in calling the game, identifying the players and interpreting the decisions."

STEP FIVE: HAVE AN OPINION

Football is all about opinions, so if you've got one, let people know.

Steve Wilson: "If you have a summariser, they are probably an ex-player or manager and will be in a good position to offer a particular insight. But commentators shouldn't restrict themselves to just describing situations. There has to be more to it than that. Maybe the finer technical aspects of the game are better left to the summariser, but we still have to offer an opinion."

Simon Brotherton: "You have to have the confidence that you know the rules and that you can offer an insight into key incidents. Not everyone watching is an expert on football and they need someone to guide them. They don't have to agree with all you say but they need to believe you're credible."

Jonathan Pearce: "While I might describe something as a bad miss, you'll never hear me say that someone can't play the game or that the manager shouldn't have picked a player. I'm appalled when I hear that. I don't have a UEFA coaching badge after all."

STEP SIX: DON'T TALK TOO MUCH

Remember that silence speaks volumes, when used at the right time.

Steve Wilson: "Brian Moore – who was a brilliant commentator – once said that the best piece of commentary he ever did was during a World Cup qualifier when Holland beat England, preventing England going to the 1994 World Cup. England couldn't afford to lose and were a goal down when Holland scored again. As a commentator, you could scream at that moment and start coming out with all sorts. But Brian Moore said nothing for about 20 seconds – an eternity to a commentator. He felt that silence summed up the magnitude of the moment better than anything he could say. In a 50-year career the piece of commentary he was most proud of was

"You have to be able to ad lib and deal with any kind of situation that may arise, even if it's humourous"

when he said nothing for 20 seconds. It's a really good lesson for us all."

Simon Brotherton: "It's important to let the pictures speak for themselves. If a goal goes in and the crowd goes wild, you don't have to fill every second of that celebration. Sometimes it's better to let the viewer feel that atmosphere unfold before them."

Jonathan Pearce: "I don't like the modern style of commentary where there are constant conversations over the pictures, where the commentary team just talk non-stop, and often not even about the events on the pitch either. In television you need to let the pictures tell their own story to a degree."

STEP SEVEN: EXPECT THE UNEXPECTED

You can be caught by surprise but a good commentator is prepared for these moments.

Jonathan Pearce: "You have to be able to ad lib and deal with any situation that may arise. If it's a funny situation then I don't think there's anything wrong in letting the humour come out. Didn't a squirrel come on to the pitch at Highbury a couple of years ago?"

Steve Wilson: "I did a play-off semi-final between Millwall and Derby at the New Den a few years ago. There was a massive pitch invasion when Derby scored which meant the players were taken off for 25 minutes, so Frank McLintock and I had to fill that time. Eventually the game resumed but with 20 minutes to go Derby scored another and it happened again. We'd already said everything there is to say about pitch invasions, so that was a bit of a struggle. But it shows that you've got to be ready for the unexpected."

John Motson: "You've got to be prepared to react to things. People use the word commentator an awful lot but being a good broadcaster is something slightly different. You can give someone a microphone and they can call themselves a commentator but it doesn't necessarily make them a good broadcaster."

STEP EIGHT: DON'T GET TOO EXCITED

You don't have to scream your head off to let the viewers know something exciting has happened.

Steve Wilson: "You need to sound enthusiastic but there's nothing to be gained from screaming your head off. You're a commentator, not a fan. That doesn't mean to say you shouldn't sound excited – you have convey the atmosphere in the stadium and the action and drama on the pitch but screaming like mad when a goal goes in doesn't make for great commentary."

Simon Brotherton: "It's important to give yourself somewhere to go. Don't commentate on overdrive from the off. If you speak at a hundred decibels and at 100mph throughout, how are you ever going to convey the great moments in the game? You also need to be able to stay in control of your voice. If your voice cracks

Steve Wilson and his Outside Broadcast Unit!

Simon Brotherton (left) and Steve Wilson (right) head into the stadium with the director.

"You've got to stay impartial when you're commentating," says Motty.

Steve Wilson tries not to get too excited when he's commentating on *Match Of The Day.*

and wobbles, you'll be harder to understand and it will sound like you're yodelling."

Jonathan Pearce: "You've got to reflect the mood of people watching. If they're watching an England game in a World Cup and the country is in a great excitement and you're sounding bored, they'll turn over and watch it on another station. It's an entertainment business and we're part of that. I love football and if I see something that excites me, I'll let that excitement come through in the commentary."

STEP NINE: KEEP YOUR WITS ABOUT YOU

Make sure you always know what's happening, both on and off the pitch.

Steve Wilson: "As a commentator, I'm looking at a small screen showing everything that the viewer can see, but I'm also looking at the game and there is little point discussing something the viewer can't see. I can obviously have a conversation with the director off mic and alert him to something I may have spotted, but you have to make sure he's showing what you want to talk about and you're talking about what he wants to show."

Simon Brotherton: "Checking your monitor is the same as checking in the rear view mirror when driving: you know what's in it but you're not obviously looking in it all the time. You have to commentate live from what you're seeing rather than off the monitor but you need to know what the people on TV are seeing. At corners the cameras will often pick up the central defenders heading to the box, so there's no point talking about Wayne Rooney when the viewers are getting a waist up view of Rio Ferdinand."

STEP TEN: GET SOME EXPERIENCE

Commentating is a skill and there's nothing to stop you gaining some experience of your own.

Steve Wilson: "Journalism is a traditional route in to commentary but it's about more than just that. You have to set yourself apart from the rest and that's why I'd always advise working for local or hospital radio or even a local newspaper while you're still at college. You've got to be willing to give your weekends up to work for nothing because that's what it takes."

Simon Brotherton: "I started working in local radio when I was 15, ringing around to get the local football scores. After that I did some sports bulletins that led to match reports and eventually to commentary."

Jonathan Pearce: "I got a job covering Bristol City for BBC Radio Bristol. I worked for them through university and then went to the National Broadcasting School. I'd recommend getting involved in hospital and local radio but some journalistic training is essential too."

STEP ELEVEN: DON'T WORRY ABOUT ACCENTS

You don't have to speak like a newsreader, but viewers have to understand what you're saying.

Steve Wilson: "I'm from Merseyside so if you had to speak the Queen's English I wouldn't have got very far. Five Live's John Murray is from the North East and is a great commentator so your accent has nothing to do with it. If everybody sounded the same it would be a bit boring, but you have to have a voice that people can understand otherwise what's the point of being there."

Simon Brotherton: "An accent can be a benefit as it makes you sound different. Alan Green on Five Live is from Northern Ireland and has an accent that is very distinctive, as does Adrian Chiles on *MOTD 2*."

THE WORLD'S TOP 50

The MOTD computer eats stats for breakfast and spits out lists of the world's best strikers

OVER THE LAST 12 MONTHS WE'VE FOLLOWED 5,000 OF THE BEST PLAYERS IN world football to check on their form. Every game, goal, booking and substitution, every minute of action and every point earned is entered into the *Match Of The Day* computer. Then we tell it to find the very best players in each position. This section gives you the Top 50 Strikers in the world.

We show how each player rates in their division. For instance, **Zlatan Ibrahimovic** ranks as the fifth best striker in Italy's Serie A. We also give them an Overall World Ranking, which combines all players regardless of position. So **Francesco Totti** is the World's Best Striker and the seventh best player overall when we include other positions. To make our Top 50 strikers chart, you have to be scoring goals, playing regularly, sparking the team's attack and winning. One of the key stats we use is Strike Rate – how many minutes it takes them to score a goal on average. **Peter Crouch** is penalised for playing only 1511 minutes for Liverpool (less than half a league season) but gets into the top 50 because he has a Strike Rate of a goal every 168 minutes. It also helps that Crouch is in top scoring form in the Champions League and for England.

STRIKERS WHO DIDN'T MAKE THE TOP 50

There are some big names strikers missing from our Top 50 chart. Here we look at some of the goalscorers who just didn't deliver over the last 12 months…

FERNANDO TORRES ranks only number 62. He had a good season for Atletico Madrid with 15 goals (only 13 the previous season) at a Strike Rate of 206, but Atletico only finished mid-table, didn't feature in Europe and Torres lost his place in the Spanish side.

THIERRY HENRY was 72nd despite having one of the best Strike Rates in the world (147) but he played less than a half a league season and only scored once in Europe.

MARK VIDUKA had a brilliant end to the season but was injured for a spell. He didn't play in European competition and he barely featured for Australia. He was 76th in our chart.

ROBBIE KEANE seemed on fire, hitting 22 goals, but suffers from not being a regular. He rated only 60th having played over 1,000 league minutes less than team-mate **Dimitar Berbatov**. His average points per game record was also well down on other Spurs players.

ADRIANO only scored five goals for Inter Milan last season and admits to a lack of form. He faces more competition from new Inter signing David Suazo this season.

UNDERSTANDING THE GRAPH

To work out the world's best players, we have awarded points to each player for their performances through the season. **The Players Graph** shows the competitions where they are earning points through the year. We have used the Werder Bremen and German midfield star **Torsten Frings** to demonstrate exactly how the graph works.

Torsten Frings' Playing Record

	League rating	European Cups	Internationals
Aug			
Sep			
Oct			
Nov			
Dec			
Jan			
Feb			
Mar			
Apr			
May			
June			

Total points for year ▪ 256,142 ▪ 777,50 ▪ 49458

Points: at the bottom of the graph is a note of the points awarded to the player for his performances in each element of his season. They take into account winning, scoring, strengh of opposition, bookings and so on. Frings scored highly in all three areas.

Orange bars: the orange bars show Frings' league activity for Werder Bremen over ten months without injury. The Bundesliga finished in mid May with Bremen in contention until the end.

Yellow bars: the yellow bar shows cup games in Europe. Bremen played initially in the Champions League, finishing third in their group and transferring to the UEFA Cup where they reached the semis.

Green bars: the green bar shows games where Frings played for Germany in internationals. He played ten internationals in Germany's race to the top of Euro 2008 Qualifying Group G.

1 **Francesco Totti**

Age: 30 · *Best striker in Italian League* · Overall World Ranking: 7

Roma manager Luciano Spalletti uses the 4-2-3-1 system but his 'one' is club hero Francesco Totti. He made his debut as a 16-year old and 14 years on he is Roma's undisputed star. His 25 Serie A goals make him Italy's top scorer and winner of the European Golden Boot. He hit 125 shots in 35 games, led Roma to second in the league and to a famous Coppa Italia final triumph, 6-2 over Inter.

Season 2006-07 record

National Team: Italy
Apps: 0 **Goals:** 0 **Cards:** 0 **0**

Club: Roma
Apps: 35 **Goals:** 25 **Cards:** 2 **1**
Strike rate: Goal every 120 mins
Mins played: 3010 **Ave mins:** 86

Europe: Champions League quarter-finals
Mins: 799 **Goals:** 4 **Cards:** 2 **0**

League rating   European Cups   Internationals

Aug
Sep
Oct
Nov
Dec
Jan
Feb
Mar
Apr
May
June

Total points for year   312,868   64,240   0

STRIKERS

2 Didier Drogba

Age: 29 › *Best striker in Premiership* › **Overall World Ranking: 8**

Didier Drogba spear-headed Chelsea's famous assault on four trophies. He scored 20 in the league as they pushed United all the way; three and four respectively in FA and Carling Cup triumphs and six in a run to the Champions League semi-finals. Club record signing Andriy Shevchenko struggled alongside him, but Drogba's third season in the Premiership showed why the club paid £24m for him in 2004.

Season 2006-07 record

National Team: Ivory Coast
Apps: 5 **Goals:** 2 **Cards:** 0 0

Club: Chelsea
Apps: 36 **Goals:** 20 **Cards:** 9 0
Strike rate: 147
Mins played: 2944 **Ave mins:** 82

Europe: Champions League semi-finals
Mins: 1051 **Goals:** 6 **Cards:** 2 0

	League rating	European Cups	Internationals
Aug			
Sep			
Oct			
Nov			
Dec			
Jan			
Feb			
Mar			
Apr			
May			
June			

Total points for year   265,758   106,113   48,13

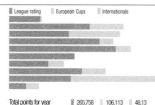

3 David Villa

Age: 25 › *Best striker in Spanish Liga* › **Overall World Ranking: 9**

David Villa has emerged from the shadow of Fernando Torres to become Raul's successor as Spain's main striker. The Valencia forward currently plays up front alone for his country and started every one of Spain's 11 games last season, scoring seven goals. He hit 15 La Liga goals plus five in the Champions League for Valencia, following on from a 25 goal haul in his first season with the club.

Season 2006-07 record

National Team: Spain
Apps: 11 **Goals:** 7 **Cards:** 1 0

Club: Valencia
Apps: 36 **Goals:** 15 **Cards:** 5 0
Strike rate: Goal every 196 mins
Mins played: 2934 **Ave mins:** 82

Europe: Champions League quarter-finals
Mins: 695 **Goals:** 4 **Cards:** 0 0

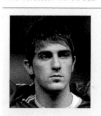

	League rating	European Cups	Internationals
Aug			
Sep			
Oct			
Nov			
Dec			
Jan			
Feb			
Mar			
Apr			
May			
June			

Total points for year   240,249   61,943   74,425

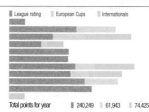

4 Wayne Rooney

Age: 21 › *2nd best striker in Premiership* › **Overall World Ranking: 10**

Wayne Rooney fired into the top corner of David Seaman's goal to end Arsenal's 30-match unbeaten run. He was just 16 and it made him the Premiership's youngest-ever scorer. At 17 he became the youngest England scorer and he began his United career with a hat-trick. He was eclipsed by team-mate Cristiano Ronaldo last season but still top-scored with 23 goals in all competitions and a league title.

Season 2006-07 record

National Team: England
Apps: 5 **Goals:** 1 **Cards:** 2 1

Club: Manchester United
Apps: 35 **Goals:** 14 **Cards:** 5 0
Strike rate: Goal every 209 mins
Mins played: 2926 **Ave mins:** 84

Europe: Champions League semi-finals
Mins: 1060 **Goals:** 4 **Cards:** 1 0

	League rating	European Cups	Internationals
Aug			
Sep			
Oct			
Nov			
Dec			
Jan			
Feb			
Mar			
Apr			
May			
June			

Total points for year   276,230   96,375   14,190

5 Ruud van Nistelrooy

Age: 31 › *2nd best striker in Spanish Liga* › **Overall World Ranking: 33**

When Ruud van Nistelrooy fell out with Sir Alex Ferguson at United it was felt that a legendary goalscorer was in decline. Instead his £10m transfer to Real Madrid was made to look a ridiculous bargain as his 25 Liga goals fired Real to the league title. In the Champions League he scored six in seven starts for Real to take his record in Europe to an astonishing 53 goals in just 64 appearances for three clubs.

Season 2006-07 record

National Team: Holland
Apps: 0 **Goals:** 0 **Cards:** 0 0

Club: Real Madrid
Apps: 37 **Goals:** 25 **Cards:** 5 0
Strike rate: Goal every 127 mins
Mins played: 3179 **Ave mins:** 86

Europe: Champions League last 16
Mins: 581 **Goals:** 6 **Cards:** 0 0

	League rating	European Cups	Internationals
Aug			
Sep			
Oct			
Nov			
Dec			
Jan			
Feb			
Mar			
Apr			
May			
June			

Total points for year   227,212   53,630   0

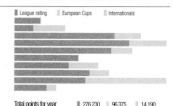

6 Dimitar Berbatov

Age: 26 • *3rd best striker in the Premiership* • **Overall World Ranking: 34**

Martin Jol is a real student of the European game and spotted Dimitar Berbatov twice hitting 20-plus goals for little Bayer Leverkusen to finish in the top three scorers in the Bundesliga. He signed him for Spurs for £10.9m and the rest of the Premiership soon woke up to his talent. The Bulgarian is 1.89m tall but it was his deft footwork that saw him hit 23 goals (plus 13 assists) in all competitions last season.

Season 2006-07 record

National Team: Bulgaria
Apps: 8 **Goals:** 2 **Cards:** 0 0

Club: Tottenham
Apps: 33 **Goals:** 12 **Cards:** 1 0
Strike rate: Goal every 226 mins
Mins played: 2716 **Ave mins:** 82

Europe: UEFA Cup quarter-finals
Mins: 693 **Goals:** 7 **Cards:** 2 0

League rating — European Cups — Internationals

Aug
Sep
Oct
Nov
Dec
Jan
Feb
Mar
Apr
May
June

Total points for year: 258,404 | 56,021 | 9,078

7 Miroslav Klose

Age: 29 • *Best striker in the Bundesliga* • **Overall World Ranking: 44**

Jurgen Klinsmann revitalised Germany's struggling team for the 2006 World Cup by playing two Poles up front! He teamed the youth of Lukas Podolski with the guile of Werder Bremen's Miroslav Klose. It was Klose who became the tournament's top scorer with five goals and took his form back to the Bundesliga, top-scoring with 13 as Bremen narrowly failed in a bid for the league title and UEFA Cup.

Season 2006-07 record

National Team: Germany
Apps: 7 **Goals:** 4 **Cards:** 2 0

Club: Werder Bremen
Apps: 31 **Goals:** 13 **Cards:** 0 0
Strike rate: Goal every 207 mins
Mins played: 2692 **Ave mins:** 87

Europe: UEFA Cup semi-finals
Mins: 857 **Goals:** 2 **Cards:** 1 1

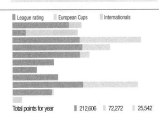

League rating — European Cups — Internationals

Aug
Sep
Oct
Nov
Dec
Jan
Feb
Mar
Apr
May
June

Total points for year: 212,606 | 72,272 | 25,542

8 Ronaldinho

Age: 27 • *3rd best striker in Spanish Liga* • **Overall World Ranking: 51**

Ronaldinho was feted as the world's best player for two years but one poor tournament – the World Cup – led to claims that he was past his best. He answered these by leading Barcelona's near miss (they would have been champs under UK rules) on La Liga title. Without strike partner Samuel Eto'o, Ronaldinho scored 21 league goals in a top-ten European Strike Rate of one every 130 minutes.

Season 2006-07 record

National Team: Brazil
Apps: 7 **Goals:** 2 **Cards:** 0 0

Club: Barcelona
Apps: 32 **Goals:** 21 **Cards:** 8 1
Strike rate: Goal every 130 mins
Mins played: 2733 **Ave mins:** 85

Europe: Champions League last 16
Mins: 720 **Goals:** 2 **Cards:** 0 0

League rating — European Cups — Internationals

Aug
Sep
Oct
Nov
Dec
Jan
Feb
Mar
Apr
May
June

Total points for year: 208,803 | 59,825 | 32,925

9 Benni McCarthy

Age: 29 • *4th best striker in Premiership* • **Overall World Ranking: 71**

The best bit of business in Mark Hughes's astute management career was signing Benni McCarthy for just £2.5m. He hit 20 goals in just 23 games for Porto to win the 2003 Golden Boot in Portugal and his goals knocked out Manchester United on route to the 2004 Champions League title. He scores from distance, poaches and has a terrific leap. Only Didier Drogba hit more Premier goals last season.

Season 2006-07 record

National Team: South Africa
Apps: 0 **Goals:** 0 **Cards:** 0 0

Club: Blackburn Rovers
Apps: 36 **Goals:** 18 **Cards:** 8 0
Strike rate: Goal every 169 mins
Mins played: 3049 **Ave mins:** 85

Europe: UEFA Cup last 32
Mins: 293 **Goals:** 1 **Cards:** 0 0

League rating — European Cups — Internationals

Aug
Sep
Oct
Nov
Dec
Jan
Feb
Mar
Apr
May
June

Total points for year: 266,820 | 20,041 | 0

10 ▲ Dirk Kuyt

Age: 27 › *5th best striker in Premiership* › **Overall World Ranking: 77**

Dirk Kuyt first came to our attention in 2004-05 when he hit 20 goals for Feyenoord. The following season he was Europe's top-scorer with 29 goals for the Dutch club. After scoring a further 22 in the following season, Rafa Benitez pounced and took the hard-working Dutch international to Anfield. It wasn't a total success but he top-scored with 12 goals, sharing striking duties with Craig Bellamy and Peter Crouch.

Season 2006-07 record

National Team: Holland
Apps: 9 **Goals:** 1 **Cards:** 0 **0**

Club: Liverpool
Apps: 34 **Goals:** 12 **Cards:** 0 **0**
Strike rate: Goal every 215 mins
Mins played: 2577 **Ave mins:** 76

Europe: Champions League finalists
Mins: 928 **Goals:** 1 **Cards:** 3 **0**

■ League rating   ■ European Cups   ■ Internationals

Aug
Sep
Oct
Nov
Dec
Jan
Feb
Mar
Apr
May
June

Total points for year   ■ 155,929   ■ 97,671   ■ 30,984

---

11 ▲ Adrian Mutu

Age: 28 › *2nd best striker in Italian league* › **Overall World Ranking: 79**

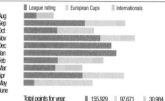

Adrian Mutu's 16 goals for Parma in Serie A tempted Roman Abramovich to sign him for Chelsea for £15.8m in 2003. Ten goals was seen as a poor return, then he fell out with Jose Mourinho, failed a drugs test and was banned for seven months. Now he's back and matching Luca Toni with 16 league goals for Fiorentina in Serie A. The Romanian vice-captain also struck five times for his country last season.

Season 2006-07 record

National Team: Romania
Apps: 8 **Goals:** 5 **Cards:** 1 **0**

Club: Fiorentina
Apps: 33 **Goals:** 16 **Cards:** 13 **0**
Strike rate: Goal every 176 mins
Mins played: 2813 **Ave mins:** 85

Europe: Did not play
Mins: 0 **Goals:** 0 **Cards:** 0 **0**

■ League rating   ■ European Cups   ■ Internationals

Aug
Sep
Oct
Nov
Dec
Jan
Feb
Mar
Apr
May
June

Total points for year   ■ 270,188   ■ 0   ■ 14,265

---

12 ▲ Frederic Kanoute

Age: 29 › *4th best striker in Spanish Liga* › **Overall World Ranking: 98**

Fredi Kanoute was a favourite at West Ham and promised much at Spurs but neither sets of fans expected he had 30 goals a season in him. But that's what he has achieved in La Liga in a stellar campaign where Seville managed a rare defence of the UEFA Cup, mounted a credible challenge for the league title and won Spain's Copa del Rey, with Kanoute scoring the only goal in the final.

Season 2006-07 record

National Team: Mali
Apps: 2 **Goals:** 1 **Cards:** 1 **1**

Club: Seville
Apps: 32 **Goals:** 22 **Cards:** 2 **0**
Strike rate: Goal every 117 mins
Mins played: 2576 **Ave mins:** 81

Europe: UEFA Cup winners
Mins: 768 **Goals:** 3 **Cards:** 2 **0**

■ League rating   ■ European Cups   ■ Internationals

Aug
Sep
Oct
Nov
Dec
Jan
Feb
Mar
Apr
May
June

Total points for year   ■ 207,766   ■ 58,563   ■ 3,400

---

13 ▲ Rolando Bianchi

Age: 24 › *3rd best striker in Italian League* › **Overall World Ranking: 105**

In Britain, only Manchester City fans would have heard of Rolando Bianchi before this season started, when new manager Sven-Göran Eriksson insisted Bianchi was the man to solve City's abysmal goals record. The 24-year-old had risen to fourth in the Serie A scoring table, where his 18 goals for Reggina came at a Strike Rate of one every 173 minutes. He has previously hit seven goals for Italy's Under-21s.

Season 2006-07 record

National Team: Italy
Apps: 0 **Goals:** 0 **Cards:** 0 **0**

Club: Reggina
Apps: 37 **Goals:** 18 **Cards:** 6 **0**
Strike rate: Goal every 173 mins
Mins played: 3114 **Ave mins:** 84

Europe: Did not play
Mins: 0 **Goals:** 0 **Cards:** 0 **0**

■ League rating   ■ European Cups   ■ Internationals

Aug
Sep
Oct
Nov
Dec
Jan
Feb
Mar
Apr
May
June

Total points for year   ■ 267,271   ■ 0   ■ 0

14 ▲ Jefferson Farfan

Age: 22 ∘ *Best striker in Dutch League* ∘ **Overall World Ranking: 119**

Jefferson Farfan is the latest striker to win the Dutch league title for PSV Eindhoven. First it was Mateja Kezman and Arjen Robben (both sold to Chelsea) then Jan Vennegoor (sold to Celtic) before the young Peruvian hit form, scoring 21 league goals in both the last two seasons. Formerly a title winner with Alianza Lima in Peru, he made his national debut in 2003 and had 13 goals at the start of this season.

Season 2006-07 record

National Team: Peru
Apps: 3 **Goals:** 1 **Cards:** 0 **0**

Club: PSV Eindhoven
Apps: 30 **Goals:** 21 **Cards:** 3 **0**
Strike rate: Goal every 122 mins
Mins played: 2560 **Ave mins:** 85

Europe: Champions League quarter-finals
Mins: 644 **Goals:** 0 **Cards:** 0 **0**

	League rating	European Cups	Internationals
Aug			
Sep			
Oct			
Nov			
Dec			
Jan			
Feb			
Mar			
Apr			
May			
June			

Total points for year | 209337 | 47717 | 2747

15 ▲ Alfonso Alves

Age: 26 ∘ *2nd best striker in Dutch League* ∘ **Overall World Ranking: 124**

Two Brazilians called Alves made their mark last season. Daniel (no relation) won the UEFA Cup with Seville, while Alfonso came within a point of pipping Francesco Totti to the European Golden Boot. Alves top scored for Heerenveen with 34 goals but Totti won it as Serie A is the tougher league. Brazil gave him his first cap in May of this year and it had become five by the end of the Copa America.

Season 2006-07 record

National Team: Brazil
Apps: 7 **Goals:** 0 **Cards:** 1 **0**

Club: Heerenveen
Apps: 31 **Goals:** 34 **Cards:** 0 **0**
Strike rate: Goal every 80 mins
Mins played: 2707 **Ave mins:** 87

Europe: UEFA Cup last 32
Mins: 360 **Goals:** 1 **Cards:** 2 **0**

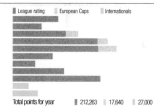

	League rating	European Cups	Internationals
Aug			
Sep			
Oct			
Nov			
Dec			
Jan			
Feb			
Mar			
Apr			
May			
June			

Total points for year | 212,263 | 17,640 | 27,000

16 ▲ Kevin Kuranyi

Age: 25 ∘ *2nd best striker in German League* ∘ **Overall World Ranking: 125**

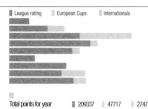

Kevin Kuranyi proves that football is the most international business there is. Born in Rio to a Hungarian dad and Panamanian mum, he plays for Germany. He hit 50 goals in three seasons for Stuttgart before a high-profile move to Schalke 04 in 2005. As he adapted, the goals decreased and he was dropped from Germany's World Cup squad. A year on, he's back top-scoring for both Schalke and his adopted country.

Season 2006-07 record

National Team: Germany
Apps: 5 **Goals:** 4 **Cards:** 0 **0**

Club: Schalke 04
Apps: 34 **Goals:** 15 **Cards:** 4 **0**
Strike rate: Goal every 193 mins
Mins played: 2889 **Ave mins:** 85

Europe: Did not play
Mins: 0 **Goals:** 0 **Cards:** 0 **0**

	League rating	European Cups	Internationals
Aug			
Sep			
Oct			
Nov			
Dec			
Jan			
Feb			
Mar			
Apr			
May			
June			

Total points for year | 231,174 | 0 | 25,384

17 ▲ Tommaso Rocchi

Age: 29 ∘ *4th best striker in Italian League* ∘ **Overall World Ranking: 127**

Tommaso Rocchi isn't a well-known name outside of Italy but each season he adds to a reputation as a striker. First at Empoli, where his 11 goals for the relegation-bound Tuscan club gained Lazio's interest; then he hit 16 for the Rome club. He repeated the feat over 36 games last season and it took Lazio up to an unexpected third spot. It earned him a call-up to the Azzurri against Croatia in 2006.

Season 2006-07 record

National Team: Italy
Apps: 3 **Goals:** 0 **Cards:** 0 **0**

Club: Lazio
Apps: 36 **Goals:** 16 **Cards:** 3 **1**
Strike rate: Goal every 189 mins
Mins played: 3019 **Ave mins:** 84

Europe: Did not play
Mins: 0 **Goals:** 0 **Cards:** 0 **0**

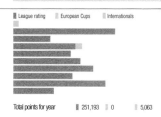

	League rating	European Cups	Internationals
Aug			
Sep			
Oct			
Nov			
Dec			
Jan			
Feb			
Mar			
Apr			
May			
June			

Total points for year | 251,193 | 0 | 5,063

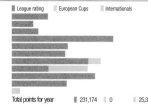

18   Nicola Zigic

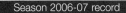

Age: 26 • *5th best striker in Spanish Liga* • **Overall World Ranking: 128**

The towering height of Nikola Zigic who measures 2.02m, makes him the Peter Crouch of Serbia. He broke into their squad just before the World Cup but was then left out for the first two group games before starting and scoring in the third. This season he's made the striker's spot his own with four goals and made the move from Red Star Belgrade to Racing Santander in Spain, scoring ten goals and getting 13 cards.

Season 2006-07 record

National Team: Serbia
Apps: 6 **Goals:** 4 **Cards:** 0 **1**

Club: Racing Santander
Apps: 32 **Goals:** 10 **Cards:** 12 **1**
Strike rate: Goal every 260 mins
Mins played: 2863 **Ave mins:** 87

Europe: Did not play
Mins: 0 **Goals:** 0 **Cards:** 0 **0**

Aug Sep Oct Nov Dec Jan Feb Mar Apr May June

■ League rating   ■ European Cups   ■ Internationals

Total points for year   ■ 247,116   ■ 0   ■ 9,108

---

19   Obafemi Martins

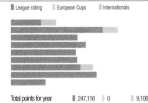

Age: 22 • *6th best striker in Premiership* • **Overall World Ranking: 131**

Obafemi Martins was an occasional performer for top Italian side Inter Milan. He played in only 88 games over four seasons but scored 28 goals. Facing another season of playing second fiddle behind a quartet of Ibrahimovic, Adriano, Crespo and Cruz; Martins accepted a move to replace the injured Michael Owen at Newcastle. With 11 league goals and six more in cups he soon won over the fans.

Season 2006-07 record

National Team: Nigeria
Apps: 2 **Goals:** 0 **Cards:** 0 **0**

Club: Newcastle
Apps: 33 **Goals:** 11 **Cards:** 1 **0**
Strike rate: Goal every 260 mins
Mins played: 2863 **Ave mins:** 87

Europe: Uefa Cup last 16
Mins: 306 **Goals:** 2 **Cards:** 0 **0**

Aug Sep Oct Nov Dec Jan Feb Mar Apr May June

■ League rating   ■ European Cups   ■ Internationals

Total points for year   ■ 209,499   ■ 19,632   ■ 1,600

---

20   Roy Makaay

Age: 32 • *3rd best striker in German League* • **Overall World Ranking: 154**

Roy Makaay is an ever-present in our top 25 strikers and has been a scoring phenomenon since winning Europe's Golden Boot in 2002-03 for his 38 league and cup goals with Deportivo. He moved to Bayern the following season and won two Bundesliga titles, scoring 78 league goals in four seasons. He has never carried that success into the Dutch side but moved back to Holland and Feyenoord in the summer.

Season 2006-07 record

National Team: Holland
Apps: 0 **Goals:** 0 **Cards:** 0 **0**

Club: Bayern Munich
Apps: 33 **Goals:** 16 **Cards:** 2 **0**
Strike rate: Goal every 162 mins
Mins played: 2598 **Ave mins:** 79

Europe: Champions League quarter-finals
Mins: 646 **Goals:** 2 **Cards:** 0 **0**

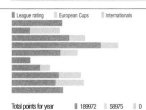

Aug Sep Oct Nov Dec Jan Feb Mar Apr May June

■ League rating   ■ European Cups   ■ Internationals

Total points for year   ■ 189972   ■ 58975   ■ 0

---

21   Zlatan Ibrahimovic

Age: 25 • *5th best striker in Italian League* • **Overall World Ranking: 158**

Inter Milan used the Serie A match-fixing scandal as a chance to snatch striking Swede, Zlatan Ibrahimovic, from relegated rivals Juventus. He became their top scorer as they won the league comprehensively. The 1.92m tall forward caught Arsene Wenger's eye at Malmo but moved instead to Ajax, scoring 46 goals in 73 games before signing for Juve for £13m. Two red cards show the other side of his temperament.

Season 2006-07 record

National Team: Sweden
Apps: 3 **Goals:** 0 **Cards:** 1 **0**

Club: Inter Milan
Apps: 27 **Goals:** 15 **Cards:** 6 **2**
Strike rate: Goal every 144 mins
Mins played: 2167 **Ave mins:** 80

Europe: Champions League last 16
Mins: 552 **Goals:** 0 **Cards:** 2 **1**

Aug Sep Oct Nov Dec Jan Feb Mar Apr May June

■ League rating   ■ European Cups   ■ Internationals

Total points for year   ■ 204,499   ■ 39,412   ■ 2,520

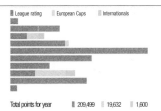

22 Diego Forlan

Age: 28 • *6th best striker in Spanish Liga* • **Overall World Ranking: 161**

The Old Trafford crowd cheered Diego Forlan, but for his effort, not his goals – he scored only ten in 63 games. In 2004 Villarreal signed the blond Uruguayan and suddenly it clicked. He hit 24 goals for them in his first season, propelling the 'Yellow Submarines' into the Champions League. A further 19 goals led to speculation that he was wanted by Liverpool but instead, Atletico Madrid pounced for £14m.

Season 2006-07 record

National Team: Uruguay
Apps: 4 **Goals:** 0 **Cards:** 0 **0**

Club: Villarreal
Apps: 36 **Goals:** 19 **Cards:** 2 **0**
Strike rate: Goal every 159 mins
Mins played: 3013 **Ave mins:** 84

Europe: Did not play
Mins: 0 **Goals:** 0 **Cards:** 0 **0**

League rating | European Cups | Internationals
Total points for year ▌237,838 ▌0 ▌7,665

23 Jan Vennegoor

Age: 28 • *Best striker in Scottish Premier League* • **Overall World Ranking: 174**

The man with the longest name in football came to Britain last season and immediately impressed football-mad Glasgow. He scored 14 league goals for Celtic and worked hard in a Champions League run only ended in extra-time by Kaka for the eventual winners, AC Milan. Jan Vennegoor of Hesselink top-scored for the title-winning Bhoys. His name refers to the linking of two farms. In Dutch the 'of' means 'or'.

Season 2006-07 record

National Team: Holland
Apps: 4 **Goals:** 1 **Cards:** 0 **0**

Club: Celtic
Apps: 21 **Goals:** 14 **Cards:** 3 **1**
Strike rate: Goal every 118 mins
Mins played: 1656 **Ave mins:** 79

Europe: Champions League last 16
Apps: 390 **Goals:** 1 **Cards:** 0 **0**

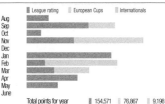

League rating | European Cups | Internationals
Total points for year ▌154,571 ▌76,867 ▌9,198

24 Robinho

Age: 23 • *7th best striker in Spanish Liga* • **Overall World Ranking: 181**

Real Madrid's Robson da Souza, better known as Robinho, was eclipsed by Ruud van Nistelrooy this season. He scored six league goals in 32 appearances. The previous season he hit eight, which is not living up to the promise of his £15m transfer. However, he is in great form for Brazil, top scoring with six goals as they won the Copa America – he was the player of the tournament.

Season 2006-07 record

National Team: Brazil
Apps: 13 **Goals:** 6 **Cards:** 2 **0**

Club: Real Madrid
Apps: 32 **Goals:** 6 **Cards:** 3 **1**
Strike rate: Goal every 327 mins
Mins played: 1959 **Ave mins:** 61

Europe: Champions League last 16
Mins: 349 **Goals:** 1 **Cards:** 0 **0**

League rating | European Cups | Internationals
Total points for year ▌141,207 ▌30,146 ▌67,474

25 Peter Crouch

Age: 26 • *7th best striker in Premiership* • **Overall World Ranking: 187**

Season 2006-07 record

National Team: England
Apps: 8 **Goals:** 6 **Cards:** 2 **0**

Club: Liverpool
Apps: 32 **Goals:** 9 **Cards:** 2 **0**
Strike rate: Goal every 168 mins
Mins played: 1511 **Ave mins:** 47

Europe: Champions League finalists
Mins: 664 **Goals:** 6 **Cards:** 0 **0**

Peter Crouch seems to be fighting a prejudice against his height. He only played 1511 league minutes for Liverpool last season, yet scored nine goals at a Strike Rate better than Benni McCarthy's. He top-scored overall with 18 goals at the club. Over the last two seasons he is easily England's best scorer but everyone assumes he'll be stood down once Michael Owen and Wayne Rooney are both fit.

League rating | European Cups | Internationals
Total points for year ▌136,258 ▌80,413 ▌20,832

---

26 Diego Milito
Age: 28 • *8th best striker in Spanish Liga* •
Overall World Ranking: 192
National Team: Argentina Caps: 2 Goals: 1
Club: Real Zaragoza Mins: 3136 Goals: 23
Europe: Did not play

27 Arouna Kone
Age: 23 • *3rd best striker in Dutch League* •
Overall World Ranking: 196
National Team: Ivory Coast Caps: 3 Goals: 3
Club: PSV Eindhoven Mins: 2689 Goals: 10
Europe: Ch Lge quarter-finals Mins: 690 Goals: 2

28 Gabriel Agbonlahor
Age: 20 • *8th best striker in Premiership* •
Overall World Ranking: 209
National Team: England Caps: 0 Goals: 0
Club: Aston Villa Mins: 3325 Goals: 9
Europe: Did not play

29 Nicolas Anelka
Age: 28 • *9th best striker in Premiership* •
Overall World Ranking: 209
National Team: France Caps: 7 Goals: 3
Club: Bolton Mins: 3010 Goals: 11
Europe: Did not play

30 Andriy Shevchenko
Age: 30 • *10th best striker in Premiership* •
Overall World Ranking: 209
National Team: Ukraine Caps: 3 Goals: 2
Club: Chelsea Mins: 1797 Goals: 4
Europe: Ch Lge semi-finals Mins: 762 Goals: 3

31 Nicola Amoruso
Age: 32 • *6th best striker in Italian League* •
Overall World Ranking: 213
National Team: Italy Caps: 0 Goals: 0
Club: Reggina Mins: 2578 Goals: 17
Europe: Did not play

32 David Suazo
Age: 27 • *7th best striker in Italian League* •
Overall World Ranking: 217
National Team: Honduras Caps: 0 Goals: 0
Club: Cagliari Mins: 3209 Goals: 14
Europe: Did not play

33 Alberto Gilardinho
Age: 25 • *8th best striker in Italian League* •
Overall World Ranking: 220
National Team: Italy Caps: 3 Goals: 1
Club: AC Milan Mins: 2093 Goals: 12
Europe: Ch Lge winners Mins: 489 Goals: 2

34 Raul
Age: 30 • *9th best striker in Spanish Liga* •
Overall World Ranking: 231
National Team: Spain Caps: 3 Goals: 0
Club: Real Madrid Mins: 2709 Goals: 7
Europe: Ch Lge last 16 Mins: 601 Goals: 5

35 Luiz Garcia Fernandez
Age: 26 • *10th best striker in Spanish Liga* •
Overall World Ranking: 236
National Team: Spain Caps: 0 Goals: 0
Club: Espanyol Mins: 2656 Goals: 10
Europe: UEFA Cup finalists Mins: 773 Goals: 5

36 Klaas jan Huntelaar
Age: 23 • *4th best striker in Dutch League* •
Overall World Ranking: 239
National Team: Holland Caps: 7 Goals: 2
Club: Ajax Mins: 2685 Goals: 21
Europe: Uefa Cup last 32 Mins: 292 Goals: 4

37 Hernan Crespo
Age: 32 • *9th best striker in Italian League* •
Overall World Ranking: 241
National Team: Argentina Caps: 3 Goals: 2
Club: Inter Milan Mins: 1902 Goals: 14
Europe: Ch Lge last 16 Mins: 355 Goals: 1

38 Igor Budan
Age: 27 • *10th best striker in Italian League* •
Overall World Ranking: 243
National Team: Croatia Caps: 0 Goals: 0
Club: Parma Mins: 2704 Goals: 12
Europe: UEFA Cup last 32 Mins: 225 Goals: 3

39 Raul Tamudo
Age: 29 • *11th best striker in Spanish Liga* •
Overall World Ranking: 244
National Team: Spain Caps: 0 Goals: 0
Club: Espanyol Mins: 2389 Goals: 15
Europe: UEFA Cup finalists Mins: 356 Goals: 2

40 Fernando Baiano
Age: 28 • *12th best striker in Spanish Liga* •
Overall World Ranking: 256
National Team: Brazil Caps: 0 Goals: 0
Club: Celta Vigo Mins: 2993 Goals: 15
Europe: UEFA Cup last 32 Mins: 304 Goals: 1

41 Kennedy Bakircioglu
Age: 26 • *5th best striker in Dutch League* •
Overall World Ranking: 258
National Team: Sweden Caps: 3 Goals: 0
Club: Twente Mins: 2972 Goals: 15
Europe: Did not play

42 Ayegbeni Yakubu
Age: 24 • *11th best striker in Premiership* •
Overall World Ranking: 259
National Team: Nigeria Caps: 1 Goals: 0
Club: Middlesbrough Mins: 3164 Goals: 12
Europe: Did not play

43 Andrew Johnson
Age: 26 • *12th best striker in Premiership* •
Overall World Ranking: 271
National Team: England Caps: 5 Goals: 0
Club: Everton Mins: 2711 Goals: 11
Europe: Did not play

44 Luca Toni
Age: 30 • *11th best striker in Italian League* •
Overall World Ranking: 277
National Team: Italy Caps: 3 Goals: 3
Club: Fiorentina Mins: 2311 Goals: 16
Europe: Did not play

45 Kevin Doyle
Age: 23 • *13th best striker in Premiership* •
Overall World Ranking: 282
National Team: Rep of Ireland Caps: 4 Goals: 2
Club: Reading Mins: 2469 Goals: 13
Europe: Did not play

46 Miguel Angel Angulo
Age: 30 • *13th best striker in Spanish Liga* •
Overall World Ranking: 290
National Team: Spain Caps: 0 Goals: 0
Club: Valencia Mins: 2124 Goals: 6
Europe: Ch Lge quarter-finals Mins: 575 Goals: 0

47 Blaise N'Kufo
Age: 32 • *6th best striker in Dutch League* •
Overall World Ranking: 293
National Team: Switzerland Caps: 0 Goals: 0
Club: Twente Mins: 2958 Goals: 22
Europe: Did not play

48 Theofanis Gekas
Age: 27 • *4th best striker in German League* •
Overall World Ranking: 297
National Team: Greece Caps: 4 Goals: 1
Club: Bochum Mins: 2778 Goals: 21
Europe: Did not play

49 Brian McBride
Age: 35 • *14th best striker in Premiership* •
Overall World Ranking: 311
National Team: United States Caps: 0 Goals: 0
Club: Fulham Mins: 2897 Goals: 9
Europe: Did not play

50 Pauleta
Age: 34 • *Best striker in French League* •
Overall World Ranking: 315
National Team: Portugal Caps: 0 Goals: 0
Club: Paris St Germain Mins: 2588 Goals: 15
Europe: UEFA Cup last 32 Mins: 461 Goals: 5

FOOTBALL CHALLENGE — QUIZ 1

Do you know your football?

THINK YOU'RE A FOOTY KNOW-IT-ALL? TEST YOUR KNOWLEDGE ON THE FOUR QUIZ PAGES IN THIS ANNUAL.
FILL IN YOUR ANSWERS ON PAGE 94 AND SEE HOW MANY YOU SCORED OUT OF 200!

NAME THE YEAR

They were all voted World Player Of The Year, but can you name the year?

1 LUIS FIGO

2 FABIO CANNAVARO

3 RIVALDO

4 ROBERTO BAGGIO

5 ROMARIO

GOAL OF THE MONTH *WORD SEARCH*

Find the 35 scorers who were nominated for Match Of The Day's Goal Of The Month!

S	C	A	S	H	E	V	C	H	E	N	K	O	N	P	B	A	C	V
O	A	G	G	E	R	E	P	J	A	G	I	E	L	K	A	E	T	A
L	L	O	U	N	I	C	R	O	U	C	H	C	O	L	I	T	U	N
B	O	U	A	Z	Z	A	A	T	S	E	Y	H	J	P	O	N	V	P
A	N	O	U	M	A	M	U	M	C	D	E	F	O	E	N	A	G	E
R	S	A	M	A	R	A	S	O	P	I	O	M	H	F	G	S	I	R
R	O	B	A	I	S	R	T	L	Z	O	N	Q	N	X	O	C	L	S
Y	E	R	K	N	L	A	M	P	A	R	D	R	S	A	I	H	L	I
A	R	T	E	T	A	R	I	E	C	M	O	E	O	S	T	O	E	E
S	C	H	L	A	M	T	A	D	S	P	I	O	N	R	U	L	S	L
E	V	H	E	S	K	E	Y	E	L	S	O	D	N	R	G	E	P	I
A	N	E	L	K	A	R	A	R	D	P	I	T	O	E	A	S	I	S
R	O	B	E	L	E	T	A	S	C	R	R	E	K	Q	Y	O	E	C
Z	S	H	E	V	E	C	H	E	N	K	O	T	N	B	R	I	D	A
R	O	B	I	N	S	O	N	N	U	B	N	G	O	R	D	A	L	M
O	C	H	R	A	T	I	M	O	T	E	A	R	B	A	I	N	E	S
B	A	R	T	P	V	L	W	T	A	Y	L	O	R	A	W	H	I	E
S	E	C	H	K	F	G	E	R	O	N	D	I	S	T	A	I	N	L
K	R	A	N	C	J	A	R	Y	O	U	O	W	A	R	D	O	E	T

AGGER	BOUAZZA	ESSIEN	KRANCJAR	ROONEY
ALONSO	CAMARA	GILLESPIE	LAMPARD	SAMARAS
ANELKA	CAMPO	HESKEY	MAKELELE	SCHOLES
ARTETA	CROUCH	KI-HYEON	MIDO	SHEVECHENKO
BAINES	DEFOE	JAGIELKA	PEDERSEN	TAYLOR
BARRY	DISTAIN	JOHNSON	ROBINSON	TUGAY
BENTLEY	DROGBA	KING	RONALDO	VAN PERSIE

HOW MUCH CAN YOU REMEMBER ABOUT THE 2006-07 SEASON?

1. Name the manager who led Watford last season?

2. Who became England captain?

3. The City Of Manchester Stadium had the fourth largest Premiership capacity. Name the three bigger grounds?

4. Which winger's middle names are George Best?

5. Arsenal moved to a new stadium. Can you name it?

6. True or false, star of *The Apprentice* Alan Sugar was still a shareholder in Tottenham last season?

7. Who was Manchester United's vice captain?

8. Dan Agger scored *Match Of The Day's* first Goal Of The Month last season. Who for?

9. In which division were Stenhousemuir playing?

10. After swapping his tracksuit for a suit, which manager said: "My wife told me it looked as if I knew what I was doing a bit more"?

11. Who knocked Spurs out of the UEFA Cup?

12. Name the team beaten 7-1 by Manchester United in the European Cup quarter final?

GUESS THE PUNDIT

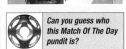

Can you guess who this Match Of The Day pundit is?

WHO CAPTAINS WHO?

Match the 2006-07 captains to their clubs...

1. LUKE YOUNG	A. CHELSEA
2. KEVIN NOLAN	B. CHARLTON
3. KEVIN GALLEN	C. RANGERS
4. JOHN TERRY	D. TOTTENHAM
5. SCOTT PARKER	E. QPR
6. STEVEN GERRARD	F. BOLTON WANDERERS
7. LEDLEY KING	G. NEWCASTLE
8. BARRY FERGUSON	H. LIVERPOOL

GETTING SHIRTY

Can you name the players who last season wore the following shirt numbers for their clubs...

1	MANCHESTER UNITED	**7** _____
2	EVERTON	**9** _____
3	CHELSEA	**10** _____
4	READING	**12** _____
5	ARSENAL	**14** _____
6	TOTTENHAM	**26** _____

21

STEVEN GERRARD

He's won almost everything there is to win in club football, it's Liverpool captain STEVIE G!

THERE ARE FEW PLAYERS who could walk into any team in the world – and Steven Gerrard is one of them. He's a powerhouse in midfield and his fearsome tackling, pinpoint passing and his awesome shooting make him just about the most complete midfielder on the planet.

When Stevie G walks onto the pitch you know what you are going to get. He is focussed, determined and his leadership qualities inspire those around him. Other clubs, most notably Chelsea, have tried to lure him away from Liverpool, but Gerrard's heart belongs to Anfield and all the club's recent triumphs have had their skipper's hallmark stamped on them.

FA Cup, League Cup, UEFA Cup and Champions League victories have come

Liverpool's way in recent seasons and Gerrard has delivered with a goal in each final, making him the only player to have achieved such a feat.

Recognition has come in the form of PFA Player Of The Year and Young Player Of The Year awards, likewise a Most Valuable Player award by UEFA following Liverpool's Champions League success in 2005.

The Queen has been equally impressed, handing Stevie an MBE for his services to football earlier this year, but his contribution is best summed up by his manager Rafa Benitez, who says: "He is a fantastic player and a nice person as well. If I play him on the right, he plays well. If I play him in the middle, he plays well and if I play him on the left, he will probably play well.

"Whatever you ask him to do, you get 100 per cent and there is more to come. He can be an even better player."

DEBUT BOY

Gerrard made his Liverpool bow on November 29, 1998, as a last-minute substitute in the 2-0 win against Blackburn Rovers at Anfield. His full debut came just nine days later in a UEFA Cup tie against Celta Vigo. The Reds lost the home tie 1-0 but Gerrard was widely praised for his combative performance. It was an impressive contribution for an 18-year-old to make.

GERRARD SAID: *"To play for Liverpool is a dream come true, an amazing feeling. It is my ambition to become as good as Vieira and Keane, then to hopefully become even better."*

MAKE MINE A TREBLE!

Young Player Of The Year Gerrard picked up his first three major honours in just one season. He first tasted success beating Birmingham in the Worthington Cup, before returning to the Millennium Stadium to help Liverpool overcome Arsenal 2-1 in the FA Cup final. The hat-trick of cups was complete with a 5-4 golden goal victory against Alaves in the UEFA Cup, a game that saw Gerrard score.

GERRARD SAID: *"It's the best game I've ever played in and, as a local lad, to put Liverpool back on the European map is fantastic. To win three cups is amazing. I was very emotional."*

WORLD CUP JOY AND PAIN

Gerrard was one of three Liverpool players to score in the 5-1 World Cup qualifying win against Germany in Munich but having suffered with injuries throughout his early career, he was forced to miss the finals after picking up a re-occurrence of a groin problem on the final day of the season. Following an operation and treatment on his back by French osteopath Philippe Boixel, his problems soon disappeared.

GERRARD SAID: *"To miss the World Cup is a disappointment. However I wouldn't have been able to do myself or the team justice. But I'm confident this surgery means I'll be involved in the future."*

UNITED WE STAND

The Millennium Stadium was proving a happy hunting ground as Steven Gerrard's 39th minute goal helped Liverpool to a 2-0 Worthington Cup win against arch-rivals Manchester United. He opened the scoring when a 25-yard effort took a deflection off David Beckham, and then Michael Owen made the game safe for Liverpool in the second-half.

GERRARD SAID: *"That goal ranks as one of my best because of the way I felt when it went in. It's up there with the goal against Germany. It's an unbelievable feeling to score like that in a final."*

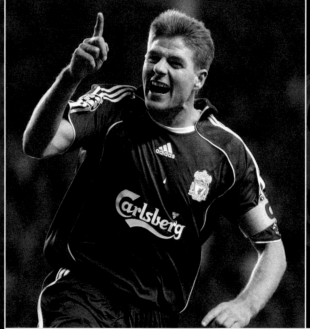

"He is the only player to have scored in the final of the FA Cup, League Cup, UEFA Cup and the Champions League"

SWEDE AND SOUR

Gerrard was given his England debut by Kevin Keegan against Ukraine in May 2000 and 21 caps later he captained the side for the first time in a friendly against Sweden. In David Beckham's absence, Steven led an under-strength team, which included debutants Jermain Defoe, Alan Thompson and Anthony Gardner, and he ended up on the losing side for the first time as the game ended 1-0.

GERRARD SAID: *"I was disappointed with the scoreline but very proud to captain my country. My undefeated record has gone, which is a shame, but it's better that it went in a friendly."*

EURO KINGS

Gerrard became the second youngest skipper to lift the Champions League trophy, following a dramatic penalty shoot-out victory against AC Milan. The Italians stromed to a 3-0 half-time lead, but with Gerrard pushed forward he set the tone by heading home on 53 minutes. Liverpool were level inside six minutes and they made it European Cup win number five by snatching victory 3-1 on penalties.

GERRARD SAID: *"It is the greatest night of my life. I thought there were going to be tears but we were a completely different team after the break."*

BLUE IS THE COLOUR?

Following the arrival of Roman Abramovich, Gerrard was linked with Chelsea in the summer of 2004. He was persuaded to stay by family and new manager Rafa Benitez, but the lure of London would not go away. "How can I leave after a night like this?" he had said after the Champions League win, but on July 5 he stated that he wanted to move. Incredibly, within 24 hours he had changed his mind again.

GERRARD SAID: *"There was confusion and doubt in my mind. I don't want to get into attaching blame but if I blame anyone, it's myself. Now I know how much the club wants me."*

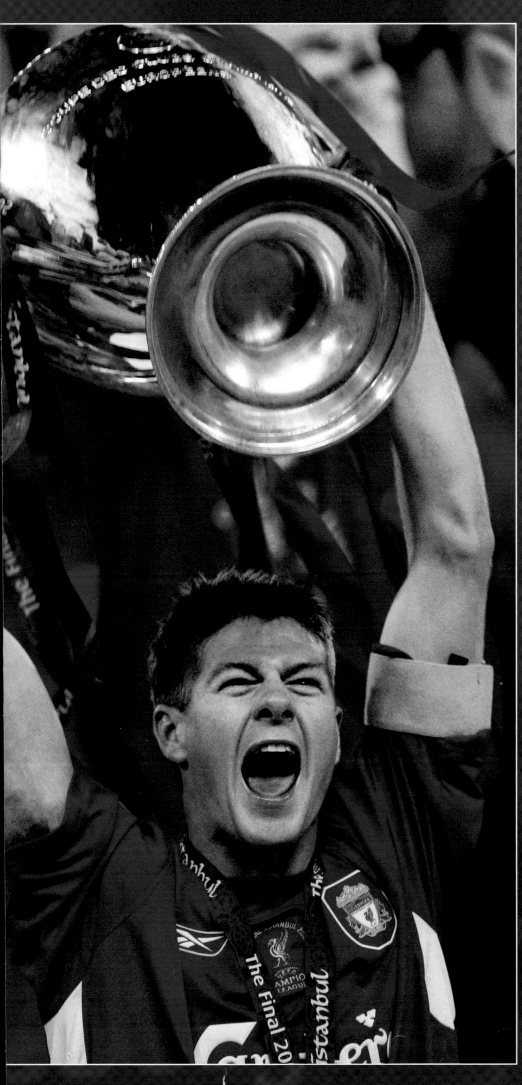

MAY 2006

GETTING HAMMERED!

 The Liverpool skipper turned in the greatest game of his career in the 2006 FA Cup Final against West Ham, who raced into a 2-0 lead. Gerrard lashed home a 54th minute equaliser, but Konchesky put the Hammers ahead again until Gerrard let fly with a 35-yard injury-time goal, voted *Match Of The Day*'s Goal Of The Season. Liverpool won on penalties in a game known as 'The Gerrard Final'.

GERRARD SAID: *"West Ham were brilliant but we had that never-say-die attitude in the final. My second goal really was a dream goal on a dream day."*

MARCH 2007

TEA WITH HER MAJ

 Having led Liverpool to their European Cup success and played such a prominent role in the FA Cup win against West Ham, Gerrard was awarded an MBE in the Queen's New Year honours list for his services to football. Zara Phillips and Rod Stewart were also grateful recipients on the day Gerrard made his trip to Buckingham Palace with fiancée Alex Curran.

GERRARD SAID: *"I'd like to accept this on behalf of all those people who have been so supportive throughout my career. I've played in special games but never experienced anything like this."*

MAY 2007

MILAN MISERY

 Milan took their Champions League revenge on Liverpool by winning the showpiece final in Athens. Rafa Benitez changed his formation, playing Gerrard just behind main striker Dirk Kuyt, but it was AC Milan who took the lead. Gerrard missed a great chance to grab an equaliser before Inzaghi made the game safe eight minutes from time, leaving Gerrard disappointed.

GERRARD SAID: *"My heart is in two pieces. It's the lowest point of my career and the feeling is truly awful, the complete opposite of the final in Istanbul in 2005."*

25

THE WORLD'S TOP 50

MIDF

The MOTD computer never stops its quest to discover the game's best midfield stars

OVER THE LAST 12 MONTHS WE'VE FOLLOWED 5,000 OF THE BEST PLAYERS IN world football to check on their form. Are they playing for teams that win and progress in important competitions? When they play do they make a difference to how goals are scored or conceded? We've turned the info into a chart of the world's best strikers, midfielders, defenders and keepers.

This is the Top 50 midfielders. The midfield is the engine room of a team and needs players who can take the wear and tear of defending one moment and launching an attack the next. The midfield has to win possession, control possession, turn it into goals and have the highest energy levels on the pitch.

As well as listing the Top 50, the computer also ranks them within their division, for example **Cesc Fabregas** is the sixth best midfielder in the Premiership on current form. It also works out their Overall World Ranking, reagrdless of position or league. It checks how much a team relies on a particular player over the 12 months.

Chelsea manager Jose Mourinho rates some of his players as 'Untouchables'. He knows if they are injured or suspended then Chelsea won't function as well as they should. Scoring and making goals are important but we also look just as closely at midfield ball-winners such as **Gennaro Gattuso** and how they tighten a defence.

Who's missing? Most big names made the Top 50 but surprisingly **Lionel Messi**, **Tomas Rosicky** and **Patrick Vieira** didn't cut it, all playing less than 2,000 league minutes for their club sides.

HOW WE MEASURE THE PLAYERS

We analyse a player whenever they are on the pitch for club and country. Do they start in the big games? Do they stay fit? Yellow and red cards are also very important as they can lead to suspensions, as Joey Barton found out. How much do their club rely on them?

We use the European cups as a guide to the quality of the leagues over the season and rank players higher if they are in a tougher league. The Premiership comes out highest with three semi-finalists in the Champions League. France performed least well.

We count games they play in league matches but not domestic cups, where big clubs rest their stars. We use Champions League games from the Group stages onwards and Uefa Cup games after the first qualifying round. We also rate the players in internationals.

Our Rankings aren't based on opinions, only on the facts: games played, substitutions, goals scored by the individual and by the team when he was on the pitch, the quality of the opposition, the results and whether a side has a better record when that player is playing.

UNDERSTANDING THE GRAPH

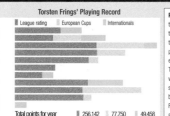

To work out the world's best players, we have awarded points to each player for their performances through the season. **The Players Graph** shows the competitions where they are earning points through the year. We have used the Werder Bremen and German midfield star **Torsten Frings** to demonstrate how the graph works.

Torsten Frings' Playing Record

■ League rating ■ European Cups ■ Internationals

Aug
Sep
Oct
Nov
Dec
Jan
Feb
Mar
Apr
May
June

Total points for year ■ 256,142 ■ 77,750 ■ 49,458

Points: at the bottom of the graph is a note of the points awarded to the player for his performances in each element of his season. They take into account winning, scoring, strengh of opposition, bookings and so on. Frings scored highly in all three areas.

Orange bars: the orange bars show Frings' league activity for Werder Bremen over ten months without injury. The Bundesliga finished in mid May with Bremen in contention until the end.

Yellow bars: the yellow bar shows cup games in Europe. Bremen played initially in the Champions League, finishing third in their group and transferring to the UEFA Cup, where they reached the semis.

Green bars: the green bar shows games where Frings played for Germany in internationals. He played ten internationals in Germany's race to the top of Euro 2008 Qualifying Group G.

1   Frank Lampard

Age: 29 ◦ *Best midfielder in the Premiership* ◦ **Overall World Ranking: 1**

At 5,356 minutes Frank Lampard played double the time that some of the players in our Top 25's did. Jose Mourinho calls him an 'untouchable' and only one other top league player has such a good scoring record from midfield in recent years – Michael Ballack. When you put them together in the same side, Ballack hits seven goals in all competitions; Lampard scores three times that number – 21 goals and 12 assists!

Season 2006-07 record

National Team: England
Apps: 10   **Goals:** 1   **Cards:** 0   0

Club: Chelsea
Apps: 37   **Goals:** 11   **Cards:** 2   0
Strike rate: Goal every 295 mins
Mins played: 3243   **Ave mins:** 88

Europe: Champions League semi-finals
Mins: 1019   **Goals:** 1   **Cards:** 3   0

	League rating	European Cups	Internationals
Aug			
Sep			
Oct			
Nov			
Dec			
Jan			
Feb			
Mar			
Apr			
May			
June			

Total points for year   ■ 296,009   ■ 114,388   ■ 30,018

2 Kaka

Age: 25 · *Best midfielder in Italian League* · **Overall World Ranking: 2**

Ronaldinho may have lost the FIFA World Player Of The Year crown but there's another brilliant Brazilian ready to take over – Kaka. The AC Milan attacking midfielder plays just as intuitively and this season he romped to the top of the Champions League scoring charts with ten strikes and he hit another eight in the league. He destroyed Manchester United in both legs of their semi-final to set-up the final decider.

Season 2006-07 record

National Team: Brazil
Apps: 9 **Goals:** 4 **Cards:** 0 0

Club: AC Milan
Apps: 32 **Goals:** 8 **Cards:** 1 0
Strike rate: Goal every 332 minutes
Mins played: 2653 **Ave mins:** 83

Europe: Champions League winners
Mins: 1142 **Goals:** 10 **Cards:** 1 0

■ League rating ■ European Cups ■ Internationals

Aug Sep Oct Nov Dec Jan Feb Mar Apr May June

Total points for year ■ 221,234 ■ 138,994 ■ 49,755

3 Steven Gerrard

Age: 27 · *2nd best midfielder in Premiership* · **Overall World Ranking: 3**

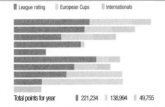

Steven Gerrard is England vice-captain and a leader on the pitch when things get tough. As the boos rang out for Steve McClaren against Andorra, it was Gerrard who led England's performance. He led by example in the tight Champions League semi against Chelsea and can change a match with an accurate cross, a raking pass, a deft header or a blast from distance. Not a bad tackler either!

Season 2006-07 record

National Team: England
Apps: 10 **Goals:** 3 **Cards:** 2 0

Club: Liverpool
Apps: 36 **Goals:** 7 **Cards:** 1 0
Strike rate: Goal every 439 mins
Mins played: 3076 **Ave mins:** 85

Europe: Champions League finalists
Mins: 859 **Goals:** 3 **Cards:** 0 0

■ League rating ■ European Cups ■ Internationals

Aug Sep Oct Nov Dec Jan Feb Mar Apr May June

Total points for year ■ 270,421 ■ 105,642 ■ 33,268

4 Cristiano Ronaldo

Age: 22 · *3rd best midfielder in Premiership* · **Overall World Ranking: 4**

Most pundits' selection as the top Premiership midfielder, Ronaldo has added the goals and final pass to the step-overs. He has blistering pace and is good with either foot or in the air. The stats tell the story: he broke the Premiership midfield scoring record with 17; United were most likely to score when he or Ryan Giggs were on the pitch and he led the Premiership assists charts with 15. He's also scoring for Portugal.

Season 2006-07 record

National Team: Portugal
Apps: 5 **Goals:** 5 **Cards:** 2 1

Club: Manchester United
Apps: 34 **Goals:** 17 **Cards:** 2 0
Strike rate: Goal every 164 mins
Mins played: 2783 **Ave mins:** 82

Europe: Champions League semi-finals
Mins: 957 **Goals:** 2 **Cards:** 1 0

■ League rating ■ European Cups ■ Internationals

Aug Sep Oct Nov Dec Jan Feb Mar Apr May June

Total points for year ■ 270,168 ■ 90,691 ■ 49,755

5 Torsten Frings

Age: 30 · *Best midfielder in German League* · **Overall World Ranking: 6**

Now in his second spell with Werder Bremen, Torsten Frings has taken over from Michael Ballack as the midfield star of the Bundesliga. He played alongside Ballack for a season at Bayern Munich in 2004-05, winning the league title but left for Bremen and raised their game in both league and Europe. Frings hit a scorcher in the first game of the World Cup as he and Ballack ran the best centre midfield on show.

Season 2006-07 record

National Team: Germany
Apps: 10 **Goals:** 3 **Cards:** 0 0

Club: Werder Bremen
Apps: 33 **Goals:** 1 **Cards:** 8 0
Strike rate: Goal every 2970 mins
Mins played: 2970 **Ave mins:** 90

Europe: UEFA Cup semi-finals
Mins: 1065 **Goals:** 1 **Cards:** 2 0

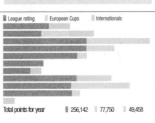

■ League rating ■ European Cups ■ Internationals

Aug Sep Oct Nov Dec Jan Feb Mar Apr May June

Total points for year ■ 256,142 ■ 77,750 ■ 49,458

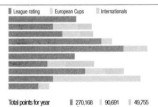

6 Diego Ribas da Cunha

Age: 22 · 2nd best midfielder in German League · **Overall World Ranking: 16**

Driving the Bremen midfield with Torsten Frings is the young Brazilian known as Diego. He joined from Porto in the summer of 2006, having previously played at Pelé's club, Santos in Brazil, alongside Robinho. Unlike Frings, Diego is a natural scorer and hit 13 goals in 33 games, making him joint top scorer at the club with Miroslav Klose. He was voted top Bundesliga player and also reunited with the Brazil squad.

Season 2006-07 record

National Team: Brazil
Apps: 7 **Goals:** 1 **Cards:** 0 0

Club: Werder Bremen
Apps: 33 **Goals:** 13 **Cards:** 9 0
Strike rate: Goal every 226 mins
Mins played: 2935 **Ave mins:** 89

Europe: UEFA Cup semi-finals
Mins: 1036 **Goals:** 2 **Cards:** 1 0

■ League rating ■ European Cups ■ Internationals

Aug
Sep
Oct
Nov
Dec
Jan
Feb
Mar
Apr
May
June

Total points for year ■ 264,067 ■ 78,420 ■ 14,109

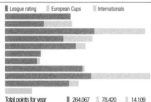

7 Michael Essien

Age: 24 · 4th best midfielder in Premiership · **Overall World Ranking: 17**

8 Gilberto Silva

Age: 30 · 5th best midfielder in Premiership · **Overall World Ranking: 20**

Gilberto Silva has not basked in the limelight like many Brazil stars. He's secure rather than flamboyant but he's vital for Arsenal and Brazil and fans of both teams know it. He came to prominence when 'Phil' Scolari pulled him into Brazil's midfield, first to rescue a poor qualification campaign and ultimately to win the 2002 World Cup. He signed for Arsenal straight after and captained the side for much of the season.

Season 2006-07 record

National Team: Brazil
Apps: 11 **Goals:** 0 **Cards:** 1 0

Club: Arsenal
Apps: 34 **Goals:** 10 **Cards:** 2 1
Strike rate: Goal every 293 mins
Mins played: 2933 **Ave mins:** 86

Europe: Champions League last 16
Mins: 630 **Goals:** 1 **Cards:** 1 0

■ League rating ■ European Cups ■ Internationals

Aug
Sep
Oct
Nov
Dec
Jan
Feb
Mar
Apr
May
June

Total points for year ■ 238,538 ■ 46,390 ■ 63,296

The energy and pace of Michael Essien have persuaded Jose Mourinho to tip him for great things. Last season, his all-round talents included filling in at centre-half, right-back and across the midfield. He started at the back for Bastia but it was when he moved to midfield that his career took off with Lyon, before a £24m move to Chelsea – making him the most expensive African player ever.

Season 2006-07 record

National Team: Ghana
Apps: 3 **Goals:** 1 **Cards:** 0 0

Club: Chelsea
Apps: 33 **Goals:** 2 **Cards:** 5 0
Strike rate: Goal every 1485 mins
Mins played: 2970 **Ave mins:** 90

Europe: Champions League semi-finals
Mins: 930 **Goals:** 2 **Cards:** 3 0

■ League rating ■ European Cups ■ Internationals

Aug
Sep
Oct
Nov
Dec
Jan
Feb
Mar
Apr
May
June

Total points for year ■ 267,349 ■ 85,925 ■ 2,300

9 Cesc Fabregas

Age: 20 · 6th best midfielder in Premiership · **Overall World Ranking: 21**

Alongside Gilberto shines the talent of Cesc Fabregas. His 14 assists sum up Arsenal's style – driving forward in attacking waves. But only two goals in 38 league starts reflects the team's current problem – scoring goals. Arsene Wenger nurtured the talent he tempted away from Barça's youth team and turned Fabregas into one of the best midfield passers in the game. And he's still only 20!

Season 2006-07 record

National Team: Spain
Apps: 8 **Goals:** 0 **Cards:** 1 0

Club: Arsenal
Apps: 38 **Goals:** 2 **Cards:** 7 0
Strike rate: Goal every 1591 mins
Mins played: 3182 **Ave mins:** 84

Europe: Champions League last 16
Mins: 717 **Goals:** 0 **Cards:** 1 0

■ League rating ■ European Cups ■ Internationals

Aug
Sep
Oct
Nov
Dec
Jan
Feb
Mar
Apr
May
June

Total points for year ■ 277,422 ■ 61,525 ■ 9,178

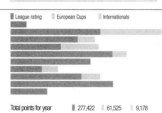
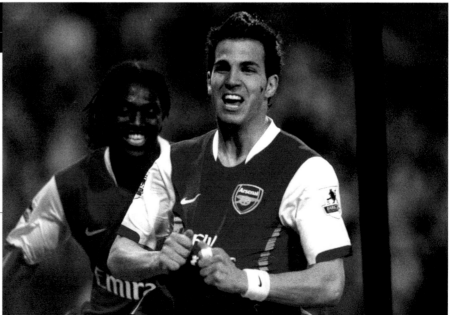

10 Andrea Pirlo

Age: 28 · 2nd best midfielder in Italian League · Overall World Ranking: 29

While Kaka prompts the AC Milan attack from just behind a lone striker, Andrea Pirlo dictates play from in front of their back four. The 'Maestro' only saw 22 games in three seasons at Inter, being loaned to Reggina and Brescia before Milan signed him in 2001. He has won Serie A, a World Cup and two Champions Leagues titles, hitting the free-kick that deflected in for the first goal in last season's final.

Season 2006-07 record

National Team: Italy
Apps: 7 **Goals:** 0 **Cards:** 1 0

Club: AC Milan
Apps: 34 **Goals:** 2 **Cards:** 5 1
Strike rate: A goal every 1389 minutes
Mins played: 2778 **Ave mins:** 82

Europe: Champions League winners
Mins: 1038 **Goals:** 1 **Cards:** 0 0

	League rating	European Cups	Internationals
Aug			
Sep			
Oct			
Nov			
Dec			
Jan			
Feb			
Mar			
Apr			
May			
June			

Total points for year 222,280 98,811 11,368

11 Raul Albiol

Age: 21 · Best midfielder in Spanish Liga · Overall World Ranking: 30

Valencia spotted defensive midfielder Raul Albiol's talent when he played against their youth team, aged just nine. He came up through their ranks and was loaned to Getafe in 2004. He only made 17 La Liga appearances but topped the club's points' average and had their best midfield stats. Valencia put him in their team for 2005-06 and he started 46 league and European games last season.

Season 2006-07 record

National Team: Spain
Apps: 0 **Goals:** 0 **Cards:** 0 0

Club: Valencia
Apps: 36 **Goals:** 1 **Cards:** 6 0
Strike rate: Goal every 3185 mins
Mins played: 3185 **Ave mins:** 88

Europe: Champions League quarter-finals
Mins: 880 **Goals:** 0 **Cards:** 0 0

	League rating	European Cups	Internationals
Aug			
Sep			
Oct			
Nov			
Dec			
Jan			
Feb			
Mar			
Apr			
May			
June			

Total points for year 253,204 77,918 0

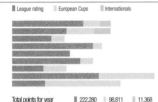

12 Shunsuke Nakamura

Age: 29 · Best midfielder in Scottish Premier · Overall World Ranking: 32

The Scottish PFA quite rightly voted Nakamura their player of the year, as the Japanese international scored more goals than any other midfielder at the club and set up more than any other player. The free-kick maestro scored nine goals in the league and deceived the Manchester United defence home and away, with his second goal putting Celtic into the knock-out stages of the Champions League for the first time.

Season 2006-07 record

National Team: Japan
Apps: 1 **Goals:** 0 **Cards:** 0 0

Club: Celtic
Apps: 37 **Goals:** 9 **Cards:** 2 0
Strike rate: Goal every 358 mins
Mins played: 3219 **Ave mins:** 87

Europe: Champions League last 16
Mins: 616 **Goals:** 2 **Cards:** 0 0

	League rating	European Cups	Internationals
Aug			
Sep			
Oct			
Nov			
Dec			
Jan			
Feb			
Mar			
Apr			
May			
June			

Total points for year 269,930 77,944 2,022

13 Paul Scholes

Age: 32 · 7th best midfielder in Premiership · Overall World Ranking: 37

Scholes retired from international football after Euro 2004 and lost half of the 2005-06 season to blurred vision. It looked as if a fine career was on the wane. Instead the modest play-maker returned to United's midfield and prompted them back to a Premiership title, his seventh. The 32-year-old scored on his 500th appearance for the club in a Man Of The Match performance against Liverpool.

Season 2006-07 record

National Team: England
Apps: 0 **Goals:** 0 **Cards:** 0 0

Club: Manchester United
Apps: 30 **Goals:** 6 **Cards:** 8 1
Strike rate: Goal every 432 mins
Mins played: 3293 **Ave mins:** 87

Europe: Champions League semi-finals
Mins: 825 **Goals:** 1 **Cards:** 3 1

	League rating	European Cups	Internationals
Aug			
Sep			
Oct			
Nov			
Dec			
Jan			
Feb			
Mar			
Apr			
May			
June			

Total points for year 248,432 73,532 0

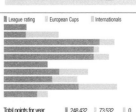
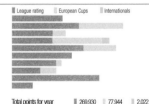

14 Xabi Alonso

Age: 25 ◦ *8th best midfielder in Premiership* ◦ **Overall World Ranking: 38**

Xabi Alonso is a deep-lying playmaker who can break up attacks, keep possession and hit penetrating passes. He also has a reputation for scoring from distance after twice netting from inside his own half for Liverpool, first against Luton in the FA Cup and repeating the feat against Newcastle last season. He is a regular in the Spanish squad and hit their first goal in the 2006 World Cup.

Season 2006-07 record

National Team: Spain
Apps: 8 **Goals:** 0 **Cards:** 1 0

Club: Liverpool
Apps: 32 **Goals:** 4 **Cards:** 9 0
Strike rate: Goal every 666 mins
Mins played: 2662 **Ave mins:** 83

Europe: Champions League finalists
Mins: 924 **Goals:** 0 **Cards:** 1 0

■ League rating ■ European Cups ■ Internationals

Aug
Sep
Oct
Nov
Dec
Jan
Feb
Mar
Apr
May
June

Total points for year ■ 211,035 ■ 93,014 ■ 14,326

15 Danielle De Rossi

Age: 23 ◦ *3rd best midfielder in Italian League* ◦ **Overall World Ranking: 40**

Francesco Totti provides Roma's finesse but Daniele De Rossi provides the steel in midfield. He has also taken over his team-mate's number ten shirt with the Italian national side, since Totti retired from the Azzurri. De Rossi earned a red card for a dreadful elbow on Brian McBride in a World Cup game against the USA but returned from suspension to score a penalty in the final's deciding shoot-out.

Season 2006-07 record

National Team: Italy
Apps: 7 **Goals:** 1 **Cards:** 0 0

Club: Roma
Apps: 36 **Goals:** 2 **Cards:** 7 0
Strike rate: Goal every 1472 mins
Mins played: 2944 **Ave mins:** 82

Europe: Champions League quarter-finals
Mins: 879 **Goals:** 2 **Cards:** 2 0

■ League rating ■ European Cups ■ Internationals

Aug
Sep
Oct
Nov
Dec
Jan
Feb
Mar
Apr
May
June

Total points for year ■ 230,109 ■ 70,105 ■ 13,323

16 Michael Carrick

Age: 26 ◦ *9th best midfielder in Premiership* ◦ **Overall World Ranking: 42**

Wallsend Boys Club in Newcastle has produced England stars such as Alan Shearer and Peter Beardsley. Now it can add Manchester United playmaker Michael Carrick to that list. He began his career at West Ham alongside Joe Cole and was relegated in 2003. Spurs signed him in 2004 and he gained rave reviews in helping them gain a UEFA Cup spot before an £18.6m transfer to United and a league title.

Season 2006-07 record

National Team: England
Apps: 6 **Goals:** 0 **Cards:** 0 0

Club: Manchester United
Apps: 33 **Goals:** 3 **Cards:** 2 0
Strike rate: Goal every 835 mins
Mins played: 2505 **Ave mins:** 76

Europe: Champions League semi-finals
Mins: 1027 **Goals:** 2 **Cards:** 1 0

■ League rating ■ European Cups ■ Internationals

Aug
Sep
Oct
Nov
Dec
Jan
Feb
Mar
Apr
May
June

Total points for year ■ 208,679 ■ 84,913 ■ 19,074

17 Florent Malouda

Age: 27 ◦ *Best midfielder in French League* ◦ **Overall World Ranking: 48**

Chelsea can afford to buy only the best and all of French football is convinced that they have continued that policy with Florent Malouda. A former team-mate of Didier Drogba at little Guingamp and of Michael Essien in a dominant Lyon side, Malouda is left winger who attacks at pace but defends well. He was part of the midfield that took France to the World Cup final. He has 25 goals in 138 games for Lyon.

Season 2006-07 record

National Team: France
Apps: 11 **Goals:** 1 **Cards:** 0 0

Club: Lyon
Apps: 35 **Goals:** 10 **Cards:** 6 0
Strike rate: Goal every 259 mins
Mins played: 2588 **Ave mins:** 74

Europe: Champions League last 16
Mins: 630 **Goals:** 2 **Cards:** 3 0

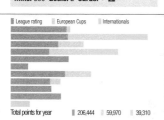

■ League rating ■ European Cups ■ Internationals

Aug
Sep
Oct
Nov
Dec
Jan
Feb
Mar
Apr
May
June

Total points for year ■ 206,444 ■ 59,970 ■ 39,310

18 Clarence Seedorf

Age: 31 ~ *4th best midfielder in Italian League* ~ **Overall World Ranking: 52**

Clarence Seedorf was part of the great Ajax side that won the Dutch title twice in the mid '90s before claiming the Champions League in 1995. Playing alongside Edgar Davids, the two Suriname Dutch midfielders played for both Ajax and Holland. Seedorf went on to repeat his Champions League triumphs with Real Madrid in 1997-98 and AC Milan twice, scoring against United in last season's semi-final.

Season 2006-07 record

National Team: Holland
Apps: 4 **Goals:** 0 **Cards:** 1 **0**

Club: AC Milan
Apps: 32 **Goals:** 7 **Cards:** 2 **0**
Strike rate: Goal every 324 mins
Mins played: 2269 **Ave mins:** 71

Europe: Champions League winners
Mins: 967 **Goals:** 2 **Cards:** 1 **0**

■ League rating ■ European Cups ■ Internationals

Aug
Sep
Oct
Nov
Dec
Jan
Feb
Mar
Apr
May
June

Total points for year ■ 181,560 ■ 100,731 ■ 18,714

19 Timmy Simons

Age: 30 ~ *Best midfielder in Dutch League* ~ **Overall World Ranking: 53**

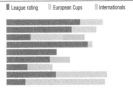

Belgium football is in the doldrums and looking to Timmy Simons to lead them out of it. Like most top Belgian stars, Simons plays outside his home league and has won two Dutch league titles with PSV. He played centre-midfield alongside the veteran Phillip Cocu last season as PSV clinched the title by one goal over Ajax on the last day of league action. He started the 2007-08 season with 47 Belgian caps.

Season 2006-07 record

National Team: Belgium
Apps: 8 **Goals:** 1 **Cards:** 1 **0**

Club: PSV Eindhoven
Apps: 34 **Goals:** 5 **Cards:** 1 **0**
Strike rate: Goal every 612 mins
Mins played: 3060 **Ave mins:** 90

Europe: Champions League quarter-finals
Mins: 900 **Goals:** 1 **Cards:** 0 **0**

■ League rating ■ European Cups ■ Internationals

Aug
Sep
Oct
Nov
Dec
Jan
Feb
Mar
Apr
May
June

Total points for year ■ 222,703 ■ 72,100 ■ 4,880

20 Gennaro Gattuso

Age: 29 ~ *5th best midfielder in Italian League* ~ **Overall World Ranking: 54**

Gennaro Gattuso is the hardman of Italian football; a snarling bundle of energy who hunts down opponents and wins the ball for Kaka and Andrea Pirlo. His partnership with team-mate Pirlo was key to winning the World Cup for Italy. He started his career with Perugia and played at Rangers before blossoming at AC Milan with an impressive Man Of The Match performance in the 2003 Champions League final.

Season 2006-07 record

National Team: Italy
Apps: 6 **Goals:** 0 **Cards:** 3 **0**

Club: AC Milan
Apps: 30 **Goals:** 1 **Cards:** 9 **0**
Strike rate: Goal every 2173 mins
Mins played: 2173 **Ave mins:** 72

Europe: Champions League winners
Mins: 864 **Goals:** 0 **Cards:** 3 **0**

■ League rating ■ European Cups ■ Internationals

Aug
Sep
Oct
Nov
Dec
Jan
Feb
Mar
Apr
May
June

Total points for year ■ 191,932 ■ 96,073 ■ 11,520

21 Bernd Schneider

Age: 33 ~ *3rd best midfielder in German League* ~ **Overall World Ranking: 55**

With the little 22,500 capacity BayArena stadium, Bayer Leverkusen punch above their weight in the Bundesliga, despite regularly selling their stars. One it has hung onto is the versatile Bernd Schneider. He is primarily a right midfielder, but also plays in central midfield and even in defence when called upon. 'Schnix' was the best German player in the 2002 World Cup final and has over 75 caps.

Season 2006-07 record

National Team: Germany
Apps: 7 **Goals:** 2 **Cards:** 2 **0**

Club: Bayer Leverkusen
Apps: 31 **Goals:** 6 **Cards:** 6 **0**
Strike rate: Goal every 457 mins
Mins played: 2743 **Ave mins:** 88

Europe: UEFA Cup quarter-finals
Mins: 719 **Goals:** 2 **Cards:** 1 **0**

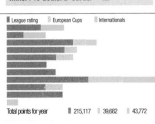

■ League rating ■ European Cups ■ Internationals

Aug
Sep
Oct
Nov
Dec
Jan
Feb
Mar
Apr
May
June

Total points for year ■ 215,117 ■ 39,682 ■ 43,772

22 David Silva

 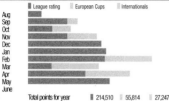

Age: 21 • 2nd best midfielder in Spanish Liga • **Overall World Ranking: 57**

David Silva is part of the exciting all-Spanish midfield at Valencia. Like Raul Albiol he came through the club's youth team and was hardened in loan spells with SD Eibar and Celta Vigo before returning to grace the Mestalla Stadium last season. He plays on the left and scored a wonder goal against Chelsea at Stamford Bridge. He also played in Spain's 1-0 defeat of England last February.

Season 2006-07 record

National Team: Spain
Apps: 5 **Goals:** 0 **Cards:** 0 **0**

Club: Valencia
Apps: 36 **Goals:** 4 **Cards:** 6 **1**
Strike rate: Goal every 664 mins
Mins played: 2654 **Ave mins:** 74

Europe: Champions League quarter-finals
Mins: 592 **Goals:** 2 **Cards:** 1 **0**

League rating   European Cups   Internationals

Aug / Sep / Oct / Nov / Dec / Jan / Feb / Mar / Apr / May / June

Total points for year   214,510   55,814   27,247

23 Dejan Stankovic

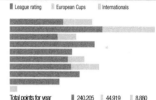

Age: 28 • 6th best midfielder in Italian League • **Overall World Ranking: 65**

Serbian captain Dejan Stankovic was destined for great things from his first appearance with Red Star Belgrade as a 16-year-old. He can play anywhere in the midfield and proved it, getting into a star-studded midfield at Lazio as a 20-year-old after a £7.5m move. He was the midfield star of Inter's Serie A triumph last season, out-performing Luis Figo and Patrick Vieira and scoring six goals.

Season 2006-07 record

National Team: Serbia
Apps: 8 **Goals:** 1 **Cards:** 3 **0**

Club: Inter Milan
Apps: 34 **Goals:** 6 **Cards:** 9 **0**
Strike rate: Goal every 454 mins
Mins played: 2721 **Ave mins:** 80

Europe: Champions League last 16
Apps: 616 **Goals:** 0 **Cards:** 1 **0**

League rating   European Cups   Internationals

Aug / Sep / Oct / Nov / Dec / Jan / Feb / Mar / Apr / May / June

Total points for year   240,205   44,919   8,880

24 Claude Makelele

Age: 34 • 10th best midfielder in Premiership • **Overall World Ranking: 72**

Students of football understand the value of Claude Makelele. The top midfielder in this chart last year and the best ball-winner in Europe again last season, he has a unique gift for breaking up attacks and proved it at Real Madrid. While he played they dominated La Liga and won the Champions League; when they sold him to Chelsea, they hit a three year slump. He was 'the engine' of the side, according to Zinedine Zidane.

Season 2006-07 record

National Team: France
Apps: 8 **Goals:** 0 **Cards:** 0 **0**

Club: Chelsea
Apps: 29 **Goals:** 1 **Cards:** 5 **0**
Strike rate: Goal every 2268 mins
Mins played: 2268 **Ave mins:** 78

Europe: Champions League semi-finals
Mins: 703 **Goals:** 0 **Cards:** 1 **0**

 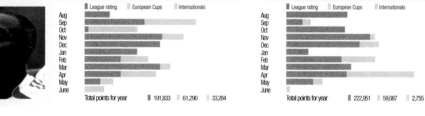

League rating   European Cups   Internationals

Aug / Sep / Oct / Nov / Dec / Jan / Feb / Mar / Apr / May / June

Total points for year   191,833   61,290   33,284

25 Ryan Giggs

Age: 33 • 11th best midfielder in Premiership • **Overall World Ranking: 74**

Season 2006-07 record

National Team: Wales
Apps: 8 **Goals:** 1 **Cards:** 0 **0**

Club: Manchester United
Apps: 30 **Goals:** 4 **Cards:** 5 **0**
Strike rate: Goal every 576 mins
Mins played: 2303 **Ave mins:** 77

Europe: Champions League semi-finals
Mins: 600 **Goals:** 2 **Cards:** 1 **0**

The secret of United winning back the Premiership title was as much about having Ryan Giggs and Paul Scholes fit to dominate possession as it was about Cristiano Ronaldo. In fact, only Giggs matched Ronaldo in terms of goals scored by United when an individual is on the pitch. They managed a goal every 39 minutes when Giggs played. He set up 12 goals and has the best assists record in recent years.

League rating   European Cups   Internationals

Aug / Sep / Oct / Nov / Dec / Jan / Feb / Mar / Apr / May / June

Total points for year   222,951   59,087   2,755

---

26 Christian Poulsen
Age: 27 • 3rd best midfielder in Spanish Liga •
Overall World Ranking: 78
National Team: Denmark **Caps:** 0 **Goals:** 0
Club: Seville **Mins:** 2467 **Goals:** 1
Europe: UEFA Cup winners **Mins:** 984 **Goals:** 0

27 Morten Gamst Pedersen
Age: 25 • 12th best midfielder in Premiership •
Overall World Ranking: 81
National Team: Norway **Caps:** 7 **Goals:** 2
Club: Blackburn **Mins:** 3104 **Goals:** 6
Europe: UEFA Cup last 32 **Mins:** 277 **Goals:** 0

28 David Bentley
Age: 22 • 13th best midfielder in Premiership •
Overall World Ranking: 82
National Team: England **Caps:** 0 **Goals:** 0
Club: Blackburn **Mins:** 3069 **Goals:** 4
Europe: UEFA Cup last 32 **Mins:** 360 **Goals:** 1

29 John Arne Riise
Age: 26 • 14th best midfielder in Premiership •
Overall World Ranking: 85
National Team: Norway **Caps:** 8 **Goals:** 1
Club: Liverpool **Mins:** 2582 **Goals:** 1
Europe: Ch League finalists **Mins:** 981 **Goals:** 2

30 Xavi Hernandez
Age: 27 • 4th best midfielder in Spanish Liga •
Overall World Ranking: 90
National Team: Spain **Caps:** 7 **Goals:** 3
Club: Barcelona **Mins:** 2864 **Goals:** 3
Europe: Ch League last 16 **Mins:** 396 **Goals:** 0

31 Andres Iniesta
Age: 23 • 5th best midfielder in Spanish Liga •
Overall World Ranking: 91
National Team: Spain **Caps:** 9 **Goals:** 2
Club: Barcelona **Mins:** 2696 **Goals:** 3
Europe: Ch League last 16 **Mins:** 482 **Goals:** 2

32 Clemens Fritz
Age: 28 • 4th best midfielder in German League •
Overall World Ranking: 95
National Team: Germany **Caps:** 7 **Goals:** 1
Club: Werder Bremen **Mins:** 2813 **Goals:** 1
Europe: UEFA Cup semis **Mins:** 990 **Goals:** 1

33 Gareth Barry
Age: 26 • 15th best midfielder in Premiership •
Overall World Ranking: 97
National Team: England **Caps:** 0 **Goals:** 0
Club: Aston Villa **Mins:** 3119 **Goals:** 8
Europe: Did not play

34 Michael Ballack
Age: 30 • 16th best midfielder in Premiership •
Overall World Ranking: 100
National Team: Germany **Caps:** 7 **Goals:** 4
Club: Chelsea **Mins:** 2016 **Goals:** 4
Europe: Ch League semis **Mins:** 884 **Goals:** 2

35 Lee Carsley
Age: 33 • 17th best midfielder in Premiership •
Overall World Ranking: 102
National Team: Rep of Ireland **Caps:** 5 **Goals:** ?
Club: Everton **Mins:** 3375 **Goals:** 1
Europe: Did not play

36 Francisco Casquero
Age: 30 • 6th best midfielder in Spanish Liga •
Overall World Ranking: 104
National Team: Spain **Caps:** 0 **Goals:** 0
Club: Getafe **Mins:** 3015 **Goals:** 5
Europe: Did not play

37 Deco
Age: 29 • 7th best midfielder in Spanish Liga •
Overall World Ranking: 108
National Team: Portugal **Caps:** 7 **Goals:** 0
Club: Barcelona **Mins:** 2479 **Goals:** 1
Europe: Ch League last 16 **Mins:** 720 **Goals:** 2

38 Simone Perrotta
Age: 29 • 7th best midfielder in Italian League •
Overall World Ranking: 110
National Team: Italy **Caps:** 5 **Goals:** 1
Club: Roma **Mins:** 2747 **Goals:** 8
Europe: Ch League quarters **Mins:** 691 **Goals:** 1

39 Fabio Liverani
Age: 31 • 8th best midfielder in Italian League •
Overall World Ranking: 113
National Team: Italy **Caps:** 1 **Goals:** 0
Club: Fiorentina **Mins:** 2611 **Goals:** 1
Europe: Did not play

40 Giacomo Tedesco
Age: 31 • 9th best midfielder in Italian League •
Overall World Ranking: 123
National Team: Italy **Caps:** 0 **Goals:** 0
Club: Reggina **Mins:** 3116 **Goals:** 2
Europe: Did not play

41 Mikel Arteta
Age: 25 • 18th best midfielder in Premiership •
Overall World Ranking: 134
National Team: Spain **Caps:** 0 **Goals:** 0
Club: Everton **Mins:** 3134 **Goals:** 9
Europe: Did not play

42 Steven Sidwell
Age: 24 • 19th best midfielder in Premiership •
Overall World Ranking: 136
National Team: England **Caps:** 0 **Goals:** 0
Club: Reading **Mins:** 3092 **Goals:** 4
Europe: Did not play

43 Pavel Pardo
Age: 31 • 5th best midfielder in German League •
Overall World Ranking: 139
National Team: Mexico **Caps:** 0 **Goals:** 0
Club: Stuttgart **Mins:** 2970 **Goals:** 1
Europe: Did not play

44 Luciano Zauri
Age: 29 • 10th best midfielder in Italian League •
Overall World Ranking: 144
National Team: Italy **Caps:** 0 **Goals:** 0
Club: Lazio **Mins:** 3239 **Goals:** 0
Europe: Did not play

45 Bastian Schweinsteiger
Age: 23 • 6th best midfielder in German League •
Overall World Ranking: 145
National Team: Germany **Caps:** 8 **Goals:** 4
Club: Bayern Munich **Mins:** 2242 **Goals:** 4
Europe: Ch League quarters **Mins:** 450 **Goals:** 0

46 Mahamadou Diarra
Age: 6 • 8th best midfielder in Spanish Liga •
Overall World Ranking: 148
National Team: Mali **Caps:** 0 **Goals:** 0
Club: Real Madrid **Mins:** 2841 **Goals:** 3
Europe: Ch League last 16 **Mins:** 586 **Goals:** 0

47 David Albelda
Age: 29 • 9th best midfielder in Spanish Liga •
Overall World Ranking: 153
National Team: Spain **Caps:** 9 **Goals:** 0
Club: Valencia **Mins:** 2013 **Goals:** 0
Europe: Ch League quarters **Mins:** 450 **Goals:** 0

48 James Harper
Age: 26 • 20th best midfielder in Premiership •
Overall World Ranking: 155
National Team: England **Caps:** 0 **Goals:** 0
Club: Reading **Mins:** 3199 **Goals:** 3
Europe: Did not play

49 Phillip Cocu
Age: 36 • 2nd best midfielder in Dutch League •
Overall World Ranking: 157
National Team: Holland **Caps:** 0 **Goals:** 0
Club: PSV Eindhoven **Mins:** 2706 **Goals:** 7
Europe: Ch League quarters **Mins:** 630 **Goals:** 0

50 Fabio Celestini
Age: 31 • 10th best midfielder in Spanish Liga •
Overall World Ranking: 159
National Team: Switzerland **Caps:** 0 **Goals:** 0
Club: Getafe **Mins:** 2984 **Goals:** 1
Europe: Did not play

FOOTBALL CHALLENGE QUIZ 2

Do you know your football?

THINK YOU'RE A FOOTY KNOW-IT-ALL? TEST YOUR KNOWLEDGE ON THE FOUR QUIZ PAGES IN THIS ANNUAL. FILL IN THE ANSWERS ON PAGE 94 AND SEE HOW MANY YOU SCORED OUT OF 200!

FOREIGN LEGION

None of them are English but can you name the countries these Arsenal stars com from?

1 CESC FÀBREGAS

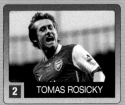
2 TOMAS ROSICKY

3 ALIAKSANDR HLEB

4 ROBIN VAN PERSIE

5 KOLO TOURÉ

THE CARDIFF CUPS

How much can you remember about the FA Cup finals played at the Millenium Stadium? Here are ten tough-tackling questions to test your knowledge.

1 Only one own-goal was scored in a Cardiff FA Cup final. Who scored it?

2 Which team won the last FA Cup final to be played at the old Wembley?

3 The 2006 FA Cup final went to penalties. Who won it?

4 One penalty was scored while the FA Cup final was in Cardiff. Who scored it?

5 The 2002 FA Cup final was contested between two London clubs, but who won?

6 Who scored the only goal of the 2003 FA Cup Final?

7 Millwall got to the final of the 2004 FA Cup. Who defeated them?

8 Name the Liverpool player who scored two goals in the 2001 FA Cup final.

9 Who scored the stoppage time goal that took the 2006 final to extra time?

10 What teams contested the first FA Cup final at the new Wembley Stadium?

GUESS THE PRESENTER

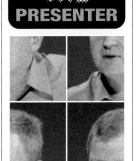

Can you guess the Match Of The Day presenter?

HOW HIGH CAN YOU GO?

Match the Premiership players with their height?

1. STUART DOWNING	A. 6ft 7in
2. CRAIG BELLAMY	B. 6ft 2in
3. SOL CAMPBELL	C. 6ft 1in
4. ALAN SMITH	D. 5ft 11in
5. PETER CROUCH	E. 5ft 10in
6. AARON LENNON	F. 5ft 9in
7. CRISTIANO RONALDO	G. 5ft 8in
8. MICHAEL OWEN	H. 5ft 6in

UNLUCKY 13

Name the players who wore their clubs Number 13 shirt last season...

1	MANCHESTER UNITED
	_____
2	WIGAN
	_____
3	ARSENAL
	_____
4	CHELSEA
	_____
5	TOTTENHAM
	_____
6	EVERTON
	_____

HOW MUCH CAN YOU REMEMBER ABOUT THE 2006-07 SEASON?

1 England's captain and vice captain share a middle name. What name unites John Terry and Steven Gerrard?

2 Name Sheffield United's shirt sponsor last season?

3 Who knocked Gretna out of the second qualifying round of the UEFA Cup?

4 Who was manager of Rangers at the start of the last campaign?

5 With which club was Nigerian international Danny Shittu playing?

6 Who scored the first competitive goal at the Emirates Stadium?

7 Which England player scored an own goal playing away in Croatia?

8 Who did Chelsea play on the season's final day?

9 True or false, last season was Alex Ferguson's 20th in charge of Manchester United?

10 Who finished bottom of the Football League Championship?

11 Who did Liverpool beat to reach the Champions League final?

12 How many times did Arsenal play Tottenham during the season?

KINGS OF

BARCLAYS

ENGLAND

SINCE THE PREMIER LEAGUE WAS FORMED IN 1992, only one club can truly class themselves as the footballing Kings of England… Manchester United.

With nine league titles behind them, United can also boast one European Cup crown, four FA Cup victories and a solitary League Cup success. During this time, the United fans have seen some of the world's finest players wear the fabled red shirt, on an Old Trafford stage that has evolved into one of Europe's finest sporting arenas.

Ryan Giggs, Eric Cantona, Roy Keane and David Beckham are just four of the many superstars to have made a big contribution to the United success story, none

of which would have been possible without the leadership qualities of their one and only manager, Sir Alex Ferguson.

Regarded by many as the greatest British manager of all time, the wily old Scot has built successful United sides, only to dismantle them soon afterwards, yet he has always managed to maintain the conveyor belt of trophies which are envied the country over.

Even the financial might of Chelsea couldn't live with Fergie's men last season and with the likes of Cristiano Ronaldo, Wayne Rooney and Owen Hargreaves likely to star for many years to come, it seems that the good times are set to roll on and on…

2007

HOW IT FINISHED

	P	W	D	L	F	A	PTS
MAN UNITED	38	28	5	5	83	27	89
CHELSEA	38	24	11	3	64	24	83
LIVERPOOL	38	20	8	10	57	27	68

PLAYER OF THE SEASON: Cristiano Ronaldo

TITLE WON: May 5 (with 3 games left)

BIGGEST WIN: 5-1 v Fulham (h)

BIGGEST DEFEAT: 1-2 v Arsenal (a)

RECORD AGAINST RUNNERS-UP: 1-1 (h) and 0-0 (a)

OTHER TROPHIES WON: None

TEAM OF THE SEASON: Van der Sar, G Neville, Ferdinand, Vidic, Evra, Giggs, Scholes, Carrick, Ronaldo, Rooney, Saha

 Ryan Giggs stated that this title win was the best of the record nine he has picked up. Not just because United had returned to the stylish football that has often set them apart from the opposition, but because they managed to wrestle the title back from the power and financial might of Chelsea. The Londoners looked to have a vice-like grip on the Premiership following successive victories and when they signed Michael Ballack and Andrei Shevchenko it looked odds-on they'd make it three. But United, inspired by Cristiano Ronaldo, had other ideas and it was their exciting football (they scored 19 goals more than Jose Mourinho's men) that saw them home by six points.

2003

United picked up their eighth title in 11 years but were helped, in no small part, by a late-season collapse by rivals Arsenal. The Gunners led the Premiership by eight points at the beginning of March, but a series of draws let United back into the race. Sir Alex's men won five of their final six games and victory was confirmed when Arsenal lost 3-2 at home to struggling Leeds in their penultimate home game of the season.

HOW IT FINISHED

	P	W	D	L	F	A	PTS
MAN UNITED	38	25	8	5	74	34	83
ARSENAL	38	23	9	6	85	42	78
NEWCASTLE	38	21	6	11	63	48	69

PLAYER OF THE SEASON: Ruud van Nistelrooy

TITLE WON: May 11 (with 1 game left)

BIGGEST WIN: 6-2 v Newcastle United (a)

BIGGEST DEFEAT: 1-3 v Middlesbrough (a), 1-3 v Man City (a)

RECORD AGAINST RUNNERS-UP: 2-0 (h) and 2-2 (a)

OTHER TROPHIES WON: None

TEAM OF THE SEASON: Barthez, G Neville, Brown, Ferdinand, Silvestre, Giggs, O'Shea, Scholes, Veron, Solskjaer, van Nistelrooy

2001

Sir Alex Ferguson became the first manager in English football history to win three successive titles and such was United's domination, bookmakers had stopped taking bets by Christmas. Having lost just one of their opening 17 league games, they showed their domination with a 6-1 demolition of nearest rivals Arsenal on February 25. Six weeks later the title was won amid rumours that Sir Alex would quit the next season.

HOW IT FINISHED

	P	W	D	L	F	A	PTS
MAN UNITED	38	24	8	6	79	31	80
ARSENAL	38	20	10	8	63	38	70
LIVERPOOL	38	20	9	9	71	39	69

PLAYER OF THE SEASON: Teddy Sheringham

TITLE WON: April 14 (with 5 games left)

BIGGEST WIN: 6-0 v Bradford (h)

BIGGEST DEFEAT: 3-1 v Tottenham (a)

RECORD AGAINST RUNNERS-UP: 6-1 (h) and 0-1 (a)

OTHER TROPHIES WON: None

TEAM OF THE SEASON: Barthez, P Neville, G Neville, Brown, Irwin, Beckham, Butt, Scholes, Giggs, Sheringham, Solskjaer

2000

United courted controversy when they pulled out of the FA Cup to play in the World Club Championship in Brazil, but few could criticise their performances in the Premiership, which they won by an emphatic 18-point margin. As the new millennium dawned, United were second in the table to Leeds but having gone into overdrive, they won their final 11 league games, clinching the title with a 3-1 win at Southampton.

HOW IT FINISHED

	P	W	D	L	F	A	PTS
MAN UNITED	38	28	7	3	97	45	91
ARSENAL	38	22	7	9	73	43	73
LEEDS UNITED	38	21	6	11	58	43	69

PLAYER OF THE SEASON: Roy Keane

TITLE WON: April 22 (with 4 games left)

BIGGEST WIN: 7-1 v West Ham (h)

BIGGEST DEFEAT: 0-5 v Chelsea (a)

RECORD AGAINST RUNNERS-UP: 1-1 (h) and 2-1 (a)

OTHER TROPHIES WON: None

TEAM OF THE SEASON: Bosnich, G Neville, Stam, Silvestre, Irwin, Giggs, Keane, Butt, Beckham, Scholes, Yorke

1999

The season will go down in United folklore as they picked up a unique treble of the Premiership, FA Cup and Champions League. The title appeared to have slipped from their grasp as they drew with Liverpool while Arsenal beat Tottenham with just three games left. However, the Gunners then lost at Leeds to ensure the race went to the final game and United's 2-1 win against Spurs saw them home by a single point.

HOW IT FINISHED

	P	W	D	L	F	A	PTS
MAN UNITED	38	22	13	3	80	37	79
ARSENAL	38	22	12	4	59	17	78
CHELSEA	38	20	15	3	57	30	75

PLAYER OF THE SEASON: Paul Scholes

TITLE WON: May 16 (final game)

BIGGEST WIN: 8-1 v Nott'm Forest (a)

BIGGEST DEFEAT: 0-3 v Arsenal (a)

RECORD AGAINST RUNNERS-UP: 1-1 (h) and 0-3 (a)

OTHER TROPHIES WON: FA Cup, Champions League

TEAM OF THE SEASON: Schmeichel, G Neville, Stam, Johnsen, Irwin, Beckham, Butt, Scholes, Giggs, Yorke, Cole

United's title in 2003 was their eighth since the start of the Premiership, but they would not win it again until 2007.

1993

Crowned champions of the newly-formed Premier League after a wait of 26 years, United had looked anything but contenders when five draws in a row saw them occupying tenth place by mid-November. But the arrival of Eric Cantona from Leeds prove to be the catalyst and eight wins from ten league games after Christmas put them in the driving seat. United were confirmed as the champions on May 2 when Villa lost at home to Oldham.

HOW IT FINISHED

	P	W	D	L	F	A	PTS
MAN UNITED	42	24	12	6	67	31	84
ASTON VILLA	42	21	11	10	57	40	74
NORWICH	42	21	9	12	61	65	72

PLAYER OF THE SEASON: Eric Cantona

TITLE WON: May 2 (with 2 games left)

BIGGEST WIN: 5-0 v Coventry City (h)

BIGGEST DEFEAT: 0-3 v Everton (h)

RECORD AGAINST RUNNERS-UP: 1-1 (h) and 0-1 (a)

OTHER TROPHIES WON: None

TEAM OF THE SEASON: Schmeichel, Parker, Bruce, Pallister, Irwin, Ince, McClair, Sharpe, Giggs, Cantona, Hughes

1994

United became only the fourth team of the century to complete the League and FA Cup 'double' and their dominance was such that they led the Premiership table from the fourth game of the season and had a 16-point lead in the table by January. Bolstered by the arrival of Roy Keane at the heart of midfield, the season belonged to Eric Cantona, whose 25 goals won him the PFA Player Of The Year award.

HOW IT FINISHED

	P	W	D	L	F	A	PTS
MAN UNITED	42	27	11	4	80	38	92
BLACKBURN	42	25	9	8	63	36	84
NEWCASTLE	42	23	8	11	82	41	77

PLAYER OF THE SEASON: Eric Cantona

TITLE WON: May 2 (with 2 games left)

BIGGEST WIN: 5-0 v Sheffield Wednesday (h)

BIGGEST DEFEAT: 0-2 v Blackburn (a)

RECORD AGAINST RUNNERS-UP: 1-1 (h) and 0-2 (a)

OTHER TROPHIES WON: FA Cup

TEAM OF THE SEASON: Schmeichel, Parker, Bruce, Pallister, Irwin, Kanchelskis, Giggs, Keane, Ince, Hughes, Cantona

1997

United lifted their fourth title in five seasons but it didn't look likely when they conceded 13 goals after losing consecutive games against Newcastle (5-0), Southampton (6-3) and Chelsea (2-1) early on. Yet they bounced back emphatically and by the end of the campaign were hailing new striker Ole Gunnar Solskjaer, who netted 18 Premiership goals, while the fans said a tearful au revoir to retiring legend Eric Cantona.

HOW IT FINISHED

	P	W	D	L	F	A	PTS
MAN UNITED	38	21	12	5	76	44	75
NEWCASTLE	38	19	11	8	73	40	68
ARSENAL	38	19	11	8	62	32	68

PLAYER OF THE SEASON: David Beckham

TITLE WON: May 4 (with 3 games left)

BIGGEST WIN: 4-0 v Leeds United (a), 4-0 v Nott'm Forest (a)

BIGGEST DEFEAT: 0-5 v Newcastle (a)

RECORD AGAINST RUNNERS-UP: 0-0 (h) and 0-5 (a)

OTHER TROPHIES WON: None

TEAM OF THE SEASON: Schmeichel, G Neville, Pallister, Johnsen, Irwin, Beckham, Keane, Butt, Giggs, Cantona, Solskjaer.

1996

Alan Hansen declared "You'll never win anything with kids" following an opening day defeat at Aston Villa. United looked lost after the sale of Ince, Kanchelskis and Hughes, and they trailed Newcastle by ten points at the New Year. But 'Fergie's Fledglings' regrouped as the gaffer's mind games began. Rival boss Kevin Keegan took the bait with his "I'd love it" rant and the title was clinched at Middlesbrough on the final day.

HOW IT FINISHED

	P	W	D	L	F	A	PTS
MAN UNITED	38	25	7	6	73	35	82
NEWCASTLE	38	24	6	8	66	37	78
LIVERPOOL	38	20	11	7	70	34	71

PLAYER OF THE SEASON: Eric Cantona

TITLE WON: May 5 (final games)

BIGGEST WIN: 6-0 v Bolton (a)

BIGGEST DEFEAT: 4-1 v Tottenham (a)

RECORD AGAINST RUNNERS-UP: 2-0 (h) and 1-0 (a)

OTHER TROPHIES WON: FA Cup

TEAM OF THE SEASON: Schmeichel, G Neville, Bruce, Pallister, Irwin, Keane, Beckham, Butt, Giggs, Cantona, Cole

THE WORLD'S TOP 50

DEFE

The MOTD computer has the job of tackling the world's 50 meanest defenders

OVER THE LAST 12 MONTHS WE'VE FOLLOWED 5,000 OF THE BEST PLAYERS in world football to check on their form. This section gives you the 50 Top Defenders, based on their ability to win games, stay fit and stop opponents from scoring. A great defender reads the game exceptionally well.

We show where each is ranked in their own division. For example, Real Madrid's **Sergio Ramos** rates as the seventh best defender in Spain's La Liga. We also show their Overall World Ranking – where they rank in our list against the world's finest players, regardless of position. The first job of a defender is to stop the opposition scoring. We work out how often their international and club sides concede a goal when they are on the pitch. We count the clean sheets where opponents' score-lines were blank. We check out how often teams win or lose when they play. By dividing their minutes played by the goals they conceded, each player gets a Defensive Rating, shown on the charts as a 'Concede Rate'. For example, PSV only concede one goal every 168 minutes when **Alex** played. They conceded one every 55 minutes when he is injured!

THE WORLD'S TOP 100 PLAYERS BY COUNTRY

While working out the Top 50 in every position, the MOTD computer also compiled the **Hot 100** – the best 100 players in the world, regardless of position. This year Brazil has the most entries with 15, although players from 30 different countries feature. Spain is second due to the strength of La Liga and England comes third with 12, including four centre-halves and four central midfielders. The USA has three, all keepers.

	Top Clubs	No of players
1	BRAZIL	15
2	SPAIN	13
3	ENGLAND	12
4	GERMANY	8
5	ITALY	7
6	HOLLAND	6
7	FRANCE	5
8	ARGENTINA	4
9	PORTUGAL	3
=	UNITED STATES	3

UNDERSTANDING THE GRAPH

To work out the world's best players, we have awarded points to each player for their performances through the season. **The Players Graph** shows the competitions where they are earning points through the year. We have used the Werder Bremen and German midfield star **Torsten Frings** to demonstrate how the graph works.

Torsten Frings' Playing Record

	League rating	European Cups	Internationals
Aug			
Sep			
Oct			
Nov			
Dec			
Jan			
Feb			
Mar			
Apr			
May			
June			

Total points for year ■ 256,142 77,750 49,458

Points: at the bottom of the graph is a note of the points awarded to the player for his performances in each element of his season. They take into account winning, scoring, strength of opposition, bookings and so on. Frings scored highly in all three areas.

Orange bars: the orange bars show Frings' league activity for Werder Bremen over ten months without injury. The Bundesliga finished in mid May with Bremen in contention until the end.

Yellow bars: the yellow bar shows cup games in Europe. Bremen played initially in the Champions League, finishing third in their group and transferring to the Uefa Cup where they reached the semis.

Green bars: the green bar shows games where Frings played for Germany in internationals. He played ten internationals in Germany's race to the top of Euro 2008 Qualifying Group G.

1 ▲ Jamie Carragher

Age: 29 • *Best defender in the Premiership* • **Overall World Ranking: 5**

Jamie Carragher found himself in a media spat after announcing that he was thinking of pulling out of England squads. Maybe he feels ill-used because he's had such a great year at club level. He played 51 games and 4,374 minutes for Liverpool last season – the most used outfield player – to give them the second best defensive record in Europe and yet another Champions League final date.

Season 2006-07 record

National Team: England
Apps: 5 **Goals conceded:** 3 **Cards:** 1 0

Club: Liverpool
Apps: 35 **Goals conceded:** 22 **Cards:** 4 0
Concede rate: Goal every 99 mins
Mins played: 2978 **Ave mins:** 85

Europe: Champions League finalist
Mins: 1110 **Goals conceded:** 10 **Cards:** 1 0

■ League rating　　■ European Cups　　■ Internationals

Aug
Sep
Oct
Nov
Dec
Jan
Feb
Mar
Apr
May
June

Total points for year ■ 255,050 ■ 126,510 ■ 15,748

2 Rio Ferdinand

Age: 28 ^ *2nd best defender in Premiership* ^ **Overall World Ranking: 14**

It wasn't much of a surprise when the computer spat out Rio Ferdinand as the second best defender in the world when you consder the facts. Only Inter had a better points record than United and only Chelsea had a better defensive record. Ferdinand (with Wayne Rooney) played the most outfield games for them and Rio was out for both legs of the Champions League semi-final defeat against AC Milan.

Season 2006-07 record

National Team: England
Apps: 7 **Goals conceded:** 4 **Cards:** 1 0

Club: Manchester United
Apps: 33 **Goals conceded:** 23 **Cards:** 2 0
Concede rate: Goal every 127mins
Mins played: 2925 **Ave mins:** 89

Europe: Champions League semi-finalists
Mins: 765 **Goals conceded:** 8 **Cards:** 1 0

■ League rating ■ European Cups ■ Internationals

Aug
Sep
Oct
Nov
Dec
Jan
Feb
Mar
Apr
May
June

Total points for year ■ 262,820 ■ 69,420 ■ 30,810

3 Ricardo Carvalho

Age: 29 ^ *3rd best defender in Premiership* ^ **Overall World Ranking: 15**

Jose Mourinho was quick to praise the efforts of his Portuguese compatriot Ricardo Carvalho in holding Chelsea's injury-hit defence together last season. With Petr Cech and John Terry out for crucial periods, the centre-back with UEFA Cup and Champions League winners medals played 51 games, conceding only 35 goals. He has also frustrated England in their last two international tournaments.

Season 2006-07 record

National Team: Portugal
Apps: 7 **Goals conceded:** 4 **Cards:** 1 0

Club: Chelsea
Apps: 31 **Goals conceded:** 19 **Cards:** 6 0
Concede rate: Goal every 139 mins
Mins played: 2630 **Ave mins:** 85

Europe: Champions League semi-finals
Mins: 900 **Goals conceded:** 7 **Cards:** 0 0

■ League rating ■ European Cups ■ Internationals

Aug
Sep
Oct
Nov
Dec
Jan
Feb
Mar
Apr
May
June

Total points for year ■ 231,808 ■ 97,175 ■ 31,613

4 Javier Zanetti

Age: 33 ^ *Best defender in Italian League* ^ **Overall World Ranking: 18**

Inter Milan's Il Capitano Javier Zanetti finally won the Serie A championship last season. No one in football deserves it more. Inter are one of the top three Italian clubs but they hadn't won the league title on the pitch since 1989. The Argentinian right-back has consistently been one of the best (and most versatile) players in the league since he joined Inter 12 years ago.

Season 2006-07 record

National Team: Argentina
Apps: 3 **Goals conceded:** 2 **Cards:** 0 0

Club: Inter Milan
Apps: 37 **Goals conceded:** 31 **Cards:** 2 0
Concede rate: Goal every 101 mins
Mins played: 3133 **Ave mins:** 85

Europe: Champions League last 16
Mins: 641 **Goals conceded:** 6 **Cards:** 1 0

■ League rating ■ European Cups ■ Internationals

Aug
Sep
Oct
Nov
Dec
Jan
Feb
Mar
Apr
May
June

Total points for year ■ 264,265 ■ 48,795 ■ 37,725

5 Roberto Ayala

Age: 34 ^ *Best defender in Spanish Liga* ^ **Overall World Ranking: 22**

Another ex-Argentina captain with a similarly unruffled style to Javier Zanetti is the classy Roberto Ayala. This season it's all change for 'Raton' (Mouse). The quietly effective centre-half has tidied things up at the back for Valencia since 2000 and for Argentina since 1994, but he left his club for Real Zaragoza at the end of last season and retired from national duty (on 115 caps) after the Copa America.

Season 2006-07 record

National Team: Argentina
Apps: 4 **Goals conceded:** 4 **Cards:** 1 0

Club: Valencia
Apps: 29 **Goals conceded:** 31 **Cards:** 10 1
Concede rate: Goal every 83 mins
Mins played: 2272 **Ave mins:** 89

Europe: Champions League quarter-finals
Mins: 720 **Goals conceded:** 10 **Cards:** 5 0

■ League rating ■ European Cups ■ Internationals

Aug
Sep
Oct
Nov
Dec
Jan
Feb
Mar
Apr
May
June

Total points for year ■ 238,682 ■ 64,935 ■ 42,585

6 Naldo

Age: 24 • *Best defender in German League* • **Overall World Ranking: 23**

Described as 'probably the most talented defender in Brazil' by his club manager Thomas Schaaf. The Werder Bremen defender broke into the national team last season after a heavy playing schedule which saw him miss just two league games and one UEFA Cup game in Bremen's best season for years. His height isn't his only talent though as he scored a hat-trick for the club against Eintracht Frankfurt.

Season 2006-07 record

National Team: Brazil
Apps: 2 **Goals conceded:** 1 **Cards:** 0 0

Club: Werder Bremen
Apps: 32 **Goals conceded:** 38 **Cards:** 5 0
Concede rate: Goal every 76 mins
Mins played: 2875 **Ave mins:** 90

Europe: UEFA Cup semi-finals
Mins: 1080 **Goals conceded:** 11 **Cards:** 2 0

■ League rating ■ European Cups ■ Internationals

Aug Sep Oct Nov Dec Jan Feb Mar Apr May June

Total points for year   ■ 243,155 ■ 78,420 ■ 20,175

7 Daniel Alves

Age: 24 • *2nd best defender in Spanish Liga* • **Overall World Ranking: 24**

Daniel Alves is the attack-minded Seville right-back who marshalled Stewart Downing so effectively in the 2006 UEFA Cup Final. He starred again as the Spanish club repeated the feat last summer and also challenged Madrid and Barcelona for La Liga title until the very last game of the season. The Brazilian, who tends to attract yellows cards, played against England at Wembley but didn't have one of his better games.

Season 2006-07 record

National Team: Brazil
Apps: 2 **Goals conceded:** 0 **Cards:** 0 0

Club: Seville
Apps: 34 **Goals conceded:** 32 **Cards:** 16 0
Concede rate: Goal every 94 mins
Mins played: 3015 **Ave mins:** 89

Europe: UEFA Cup winner
Mins: 1015 **Goals conceded:** 10 **Cards:** 0 0

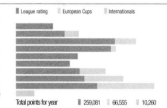

■ League rating ■ European Cups ■ Internationals

Aug Sep Oct Nov Dec Jan Feb Mar Apr May June

Total points for year   ■ 259,081 ■ 66,555 ■ 10,260

8 Steve Finnan

Age: 31 • *4th best defender in Premiership* • **Overall World Ranking: 25**

Steve Finnan is another vital cog in the Liverpool defence that threatens clean sheets records seemingly every season. The Republic of Ireland right-back first played for his country in 2000, when he was with Fulham. He moved to Liverpool in 2003 but suffered initially from a spate of injuries. He has been free of injuries and is now a regular, with only Jamie Carragher playing more in the Reds defence last season.

Season 2006-07 record

National Team: Republic of Ireland
Apps: 8 **Goals conceded:** 11 **Cards:** 0 0

Club: Liverpool
Apps: 33 **Goals conceded:** 22 **Cards:** 2 0
Concede rate: Goal every 131 mins
Mins played: 2889 **Ave mins:** 86

Europe: Champions League finalist
Mins: 927 **Goals conceded:** 6 **Cards:** 1 0

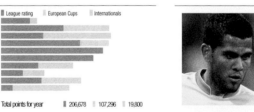

■ League rating ■ European Cups ■ Internationals

Aug Sep Oct Nov Dec Jan Feb Mar Apr May June

Total points for year   ■ 206,678 ■ 107,296 ■ 19,800

9 John Terry

Age: 26 • *5th best defender in Premiership* • **Overall World Ranking: 26**

The public debate over whether John Terry or Steven Gerrard would take over the England captaincy from David Beckham was settled in the Chelsea man's favour. Terry is a strong character, using his few public scrapes to come back stronger. He's a natural leader and scored in his first game as England captain repeating the feat against giants Brazil in the nation's first game at Wembley.

Season 2006-07 record

National Team: England
Apps: 10 **Goals conceded:** 3 **Cards:** 0 0

Club: Chelsea
Apps: 28 **Goals conceded:** 14 **Cards:** 2 1
Concede rate: Goal every 172 mins
Mins played: 2413 **Ave mins:** 86

Europe: Champions League semi-finals
Mins: 852 **Goals conceded:** 8 **Cards:** 3 0

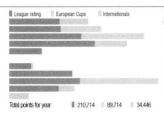

■ League rating ■ European Cups ■ Internationals

Aug Sep Oct Nov Dec Jan Feb Mar Apr May June

Total points for year   ■ 210,714 ■ 89,714 ■ 34,446

10 Philipp Lahm

Age: 23 › *2nd best defender in German League* › **Overall World Ranking: 27**

Philipp Lahm struck the first goal of the 2006 World Cup to rapturous applause from his home crowd in the Allianz Arena in Munich. Cutting in from his left flank, a fierce shot curled in off Costa Rica's far post. An adventurous left-back, Lahm is fast, able to drift past challenges but never neglects his defensive duties. He was a nominee for the FIFA World Player Of The Year award for 2006 but lost out to Fabio Cannavaro.

Season 2006-07 record

National Team: Germany
Apps: 9 **Goals conceded:** 5 **Cards:** 0 0

Club: Bayern Munich
Apps: 34 **Goals conceded:** 40 **Cards:** 3 0
Concede rate: Goal every 76 mins
Mins played: 3022 **Ave mins:** 89

Europe: Champions League quarter-finals
Mins: 810 **Goals conceded:** 9 **Cards:** 0 0

	League rating	European Cups	Internationals
Aug			
Sep			
Oct			
Nov			
Dec			
Jan			
Feb			
Mar			
Apr			
May			
June			
Total points for year	201,833	80,055	52,620

11 Daniel Agger

Age: 22 › *6th best defender in Premiership* › **Overall World Ranking: 31**

Liverpool had a mammoth task replacing Sami Hyypia at the heart of the Liverpool defence but Rafa Benitez put full faith in Daniel Agger, a player he signed from Brondby for £5.8m in 2006. He bedded into the side over 18 months, and finished last season with the best defensive record in Europe. The club only conceded a goal every 197 minutes when Agger played. He also has an eye for spectacular goals.

Season 2006-07 record

National Team: Denmark
Apps: 9 **Goals conceded:** 4 **Cards:** 0 0

Club: Liverpool
Apps: 27 **Goals conceded:** 11 **Cards:** 1 0
Concede rate: Goal every 197 mins
Mins played: 2167 **Ave mins:** 80

Europe: Champions League finalist
Mins: 1007 **Goals conceded:** 10 **Cards:** 2 0

	League rating	European Cups	Internationals
Aug			
Sep			
Oct			
Nov			
Dec			
Jan			
Feb			
Mar			
Apr			
May			
June			
Total points for year	187,614	101,450	41,910

12 Daniel Jarque

Age: 24 › *3rd best defender in Spanish Liga* › **Overall World Ranking: 35**

Espanyol are used to living in Barcelona's shadow as the city's second team, but emerged to claim Spain's Copa del Rey in 2006. A young centre-back, Daniel Jarque made 33 appearances in that season. One season on and Espanyol outlasted Barça in Europe, reaching the final of the UEFA Cup with Jarque playing every minute of the campaign and adding 36 league appearances.

Season 2006-07 record

National Team: Spain
Apps: 0 **Goals conceded:** 0 **Cards:** 0 0

Club: Espanyol
Apps: 36 **Goals conceded:** 49 **Cards:** 5 1
Concede rate: Goal every 62 mins
Mins played: 3035 **Ave mins:** 84

Europe: UEFA Cup finalist
Mins: 930 **Goals conceded:** 7 **Cards:** 2 0

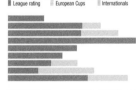

	League rating	European Cups	Internationals
Aug			
Sep			
Oct			
Nov			
Dec			
Jan			
Feb			
Mar			
Apr			
May			
June			
Total points for year	247,391	75,160	0

13 Michael Dawson

Age: 23 › *7th best defender in Premiership* › **Overall World Ranking: 39**

Spurs trio of top strikers were banging in the goals last season but the defence was trying out different combinations around the absence of Ledley King. Fifth place in the league and a run to the quarter-finals of the UEFA Cup showed they mainly got it right. Michael Dawson, with 58 appearances in a long season, was one of the key reasons why and he's now around the fringes of the England squad.

Season 2006-07 record

National Team: England
Apps: 0 **Goals conceded:** 0 **Cards:** 0 0

Club: Tottenham
Apps: 32 **Goals conceded:** 52 **Cards:** 6 0
Concede rate: Goal every 63 mins
Mins played: 3283 **Ave mins:** 89

Europe: UEFA Cup quarter-finals
Mins: 720 **Goals conceded:** 10 **Cards:** 1 0

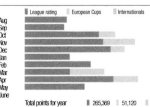

	League rating	European Cups	Internationals
Aug			
Sep			
Oct			
Nov			
Dec			
Jan			
Feb			
Mar			
Apr			
May			
June			
Total points for year	265,369	51,120	0

14 Carlos Puyol

Age: 29 • *4th best defender in Spanish Liga* • **Overall World Ranking: 41**

Carlos Puyol topped our defender list last season, having lifted both the Champions League and La Liga at Barça and being an occasional captain of the Spanish team. This season he was pipped to the title by Madrid (despite Barca having level points and a better goal difference), reached the last 16 in Europe and still played regularly for Spain. Hardly a bad effort considering his relatively low position!

Season 2006-07 record

National Team: Spain

Apps: 6 **Goals conceded:** 5 **Cards:** 2 **0**

Club: Barcelona

Apps: 35 **Goals conceded:** 30 **Cards:** 3 **0**

Concede rate: Goal every 101 mins

Mins played: 3030 **Ave mins:** 87

Europe: Champions League last 16

Mins: 703 **Goals conceded:** 6 **Cards:** 1 **0**

■ League rating   ■ European Cups   ■ Internationals

Aug / Sep / Oct / Nov / Dec / Jan / Feb / Mar / Apr / May / June

Total points for year   ■ 197,323   ■ 57,055   ■ 16,230

15 Douglas Maicon

Age: 26 • *2nd best defender in Italian League* • **Overall World Ranking: 43**

16 Kolo Toure

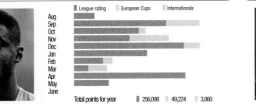

Age: 26 • *8th best defender in Premiership* • **Overall World Ranking: 46**

The young guns at Arsenal will look to Kolo Toure and Gilberto Silva to guide them now Thierry Henry has moved on. Toure has already captained the side in the Carling Cup final. Despite being just 26, he has been in a Champions League final, an African Cup final and was the most-used defender in Arsenal's 'Invincibles' season. He is a natural athlete and only Theo Walcott is faster at the club.

Season 2006-07 record

National Team: Ivory Coast

Apps: 3 **Goals conceded:** 1 **Cards:** 0 **0**

Club: Arsenal

Apps: 35 **Goals conceded:** 33 **Cards:** 6 **0**

Concede rate: Goal every 95 mins

Mins played: 3150 **Ave mins:** 90

Europe: Champions League last 16

Mins: 657 **Goals conceded:** 4 **Cards:** 0 **0**

■ League rating   ■ European Cups   ■ Internationals

Aug / Sep / Oct / Nov / Dec / Jan / Feb / Mar / Apr / May / June

Total points for year   ■ 256,098   ■ 49,224   ■ 3,060

This is the first season that Maicon has reached our top 25. He won the Italian league title at Inter Milan, with only Javier Zanetti playing more often in their defence, but he was suspended for three matches after being dragged into a melee with Valencia defender David Navarro. Maicon played for Brazil in the Copa America, taking his caps total to 26 and scoring his second goal for the samba giants in the semi-final.

Season 2006-07 record

National Team: Brazil

Apps: 10 **Goals conceded:** 5 **Cards:** 0 **0**

Club: Inter Milan

Apps: 32 **Goals conceded:** 26 **Cards:** 6 **1**

Concede rate: Goal every 100 mins

Mins played: 2597 **Ave mins:** 81

Europe: Champions League last 16

Mins: 720 **Goals conceded:** 7 **Cards:** 2 **0**

■ League rating   ■ European Cups   ■ Internationals

Aug / Sep / Oct / Nov / Dec / Jan / Feb / Mar / Apr / May / June

Total points for year   ■ 212,455   ■ 51,270   ■ 47,329

17 Gabriel Milito

Age: 26 • *5th best defender in Spanish Liga* • **Overall World Ranking: 62**

The Milito brothers are making a breakthrough. They both played for Argentina in the Copa America, and while younger brother Gabriel has made our top 25 defenders, Diego (one year older) is just outside the top 25 strikers. They played for fierce rivals Racing Club (Diego) and Independiente (Gabriel) in Buenos Aires but were united in Spain at Real Zaragoza last season before Barça signed Gabriel for £14m.

Season 2006-07 record

National Team: Argentina

Apps: 5 **Goals conceded:** 7 **Cards:** 2 **0**

Club: Real Zaragoza

Apps: 36 **Goals conceded:** 46 **Cards:** 11 **2**

Concede rate: Goal every 71 mins

Mins played: 3222 **Ave mins:** 90

Europe: Did not play

Mins: 0 **Goals conceded:** 0 **Cards:** 0 **0**

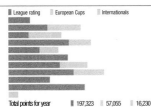

■ League rating   ■ European Cups   ■ Internationals

Aug / Sep / Oct / Nov / Dec / Jan / Feb / Mar / Apr / May / June

Total points for year   ■ 246886   ■ 0   ■ 47745

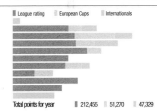

18 Tomas Ujfalusi

Age: 29 · *3rd best defender in Italian League* · **Overall World Ranking:** 64

The versatile Tomas Ujfalusi is a veteran of the Czech Republic national side and reached his 50th cap last season. For the international team he usually plays as centre-back but for Fiorentina, coach Cesare Prandelli prefers to use him on the right flank. He began his career at Sigma Olomouc in the Czech Republic and played over 100 times for Hamburg before moving to La Viola in Serie A.

Season 2006-07 record

National Team: Czeh Republic
Apps: 10 **Goals conceded:** 8 **Cards:** 0 0

Club: Fiorentina
Apps: 31 **Goals conceded:** 22 **Cards:** 7 0
Concede rate: Goal every 112 mins
Mins played: 2699 **Ave mins:** 87

Europe: Did not play
Mins: 0 **Goals conceded:** **Cards:** 0 0

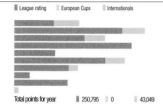

	League rating	European Cups	Internationals
Aug			
Sep			
Oct			
Nov			
Dec			
Jan			
Feb			
Mar			
Apr			
May			
June			
Total points for year	250,795	0	43,049

19 Miguel

Age: 27 · *6th best defender in Spanish Liga* · **Overall World Ranking:** 67

Luís Miguel Brito Garcia Monteiro is more commonly known as Miguel when he pulls on the shirt for Valencia or Portugal. The fullback had an impressive 2006 World Cup campaign, keeping Joe Cole quiet in the process against England. He began his career as a winger, moved to right midfield when he played for Benfica, before settling in at right-back and keeping Paulo Ferreira out of the Portugal team.

Season 2006-07 record

National Team: Portugal
Apps: 7 **Goals conceded:** 3 **Cards:** 0 0

Club: Valencia
Apps: 30 **Goals conceded:** 27 **Cards:** 5 0
Concede rate: Goal every 92 mins
Mins played: 2483 **Ave mins:** 83

Europe: Champions League quarter-finals
Mins: 810 **Goals conceded:** 10 **Cards:** 0 0

	League rating	European Cups	Internationals
Aug			
Sep			
Oct			
Nov			
Dec			
Jan			
Feb			
Mar			
Apr			
May			
June			
Total points for year	186,936	74,587	30,525

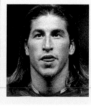

20 Sergio Ramos

Age: 26 · *7th best defender in Spanish Liga* · **Overall World Ranking:** 68

When Real Madrid paid Seville £18m for Sergio Ramos in 2005, they made him the most expensive teenager in world football after Wayne Rooney. Having made 33 appearances for Real last season, Ramos was the most used defender, pipping Fabio Cannavaro. He has now ousted Real right-back Michael Salgado from both the club and national sides and was first choice by the 2006 World Cup.

Season 2006-07 record

National Team: Spain
Apps: 10 **Goals conceded:** 4 **Cards:** 1 0

Club: Real Madrid
Apps: 32 **Goals conceded:** 38 **Cards:** 15 2
Concede rate: Goal every 76 mins
Mins played: 2863 **Ave mins:** 89

Europe: Champions League last 16
Mins: 540 **Goals conceded:** 8 **Cards:** 3 0

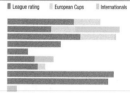

	League rating	European Cups	Internationals
Aug			
Sep			
Oct			
Nov			
Dec			
Jan			
Feb			
Mar			
Apr			
May			
June			
Total points for year	220,934	39,000	31,433

21 Alex

Age: 25 · *Best defender in Dutch League* · **Overall World Ranking:** 69

Brazilian centre-back Alex is nicknamed 'The Tank' at PSV Eindhoven. He joined the Dutch club on loan from Chelsea in 2004 and he has helped them to three consecutive Eredivisie league titles, building a case to be recognised as the best defender in that league. He made the headlines when he scored at both ends to knock Arsenal out of the Champions League in March.

Season 2006-07 record

National Team: Brazil
Apps: 5 **Goals conceded:** 2 **Cards:** 1 0

Club: PSV Eindhoven
Apps: 29 **Goals conceded:** 15 **Cards:** 3 0
Concede rate: Goal every 168 mins
Mins played: 2515 **Ave mins:** 87

Europe: Champions League last 16
Mins: 720 **Goals conceded:** 7 **Cards:** 0 0

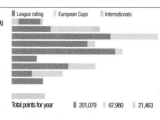

	League rating	European Cups	Internationals
July/Aug			
Sep			
Oct			
Nov			
Dec			
Jan			
Feb			
Mar			
Apr			
May			
June			
Total points for year	201,079	67,980	21,463

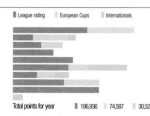

22 Pascal Chimbonda

Age: 28 ◦ *9th best defender in Premiership* ◦ **Overall World Ranking: 70**

Paul Jewell spotted the talents of Pascal Chimbonda, being relegated from the French top division with Bastia in 2005. He signed the speeding right-back and played him in Wigan's first Premiership season. At the end of it, Chimbonda angered Wigan fans by requesting a transfer and calling the club "a stepping stone". Spurs came in with a £4.5m bid and took him into European competition.

Season 2006-07 record

National Team: France
Apps: 0 **Goals conceded:** 0 **Cards:** 0 ▢

Club: Tottenham
Apps: 33 **Goals conceded:** 46 **Cards:** 5 ▢
Concede rate: Goal every 64 mins
Mins played: 2927 **Ave mins:** 89

Europe: UEFA Cup quarter-finals
Mins: 705 **Goals conceded:** 9 **Cards:** 2 ▢

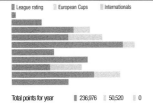

■ League rating ■ European Cups ■ Internationals

Aug Sep Oct Nov Dec Jan Feb Mar Apr May June

Total points for year ■ 236,976 ■ 50,520 ■ 0

23 Carlos Salcido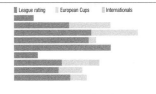

Age: 27 ◦ *2nd best defender in Dutch League* ◦ **Overall World Ranking: 73**

The breakthrough of Rafael Marques at Barcelona alerted European clubs to the talent of Mexican players and after a strong World Cup, many Mexicans came over last season. Carlos Salcido joined PSV from Chivas de Guadalajara. He played for Mexico in the Copa America and finished it on 42 caps. The flying left-back scored after a famous length of the pitch run against Argentina in 2005.

Season 2006-07 record

National Team: Mexico
Apps: 3 **Goals conceded:** 2 **Cards:** 1 ▢

Club: PSV Eindhoven
Apps: 33 **Goals conceded:** 25 **Cards:** 1 ▢
Concede rate: Goal every 119 mins
Mins played: 2970 **Ave mins:** 90

Europe: Champions League quarter-finals
Mins: 810 **Goals conceded:** 8 **Cards:** 3 ▢

■ League rating ■ European Cups ■ Internationals

Aug Sep Oct Nov Dec Jan Feb Mar Apr May June

Total points for year ■ 212,440 ■ 69,160 ■ 4,560

24 Olof Mellberg

Age: 29 ◦ *10th best defender in Premiership* ◦ **Overall World Ranking: 75**

It wasn't what Arsenal fans dreamed of, or what Villa fans expected, but the first competitive goal scored at the glittering Emirates Stadium came from Olof Mellberg. Martin O'Neill moved the Villa captaincy from Mellberg to Gareth Barry but made the Swede his key defender and was rewarded with a typically rugged and consistent season from him as he started every league game.

Season 2006-07 record

National Team: Sweden
Apps: 5 **Goals conceded:** 4 **Cards:** 0 ▢

Club: Aston Villa
Apps: 38 **Goals conceded:** 39 **Cards:** 8 ▢
Concede rate: Goal every 87 mins
Mins played: 3375 **Ave mins:** 89

Europe: Did not play
Mins: 0 **Goals conceded:** 0 **Cards:** 0 ▢

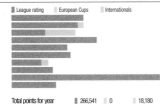

■ League rating ■ European Cups ■ Internationals

Aug Sep Oct Nov Dec Jan Feb Mar Apr May June

Total points for year ■ 266,541 ■ 0 ■ 18,180

25 Juan

Age: 28 ◦ *3rd best defender in German League* ◦ **Overall World Ranking: 80**

Season 2006-07 record

National Team: Brazil
Apps: 10 **Goals conceded:** 6 **Cards:** 0 ▢

Club: Bayer Leverkusen
Apps: 28 **Goals conceded:** 38 **Cards:** 5 ▢
Concede rate: Goal every 65 mins
Mins played: 2474 **Ave mins:** 88

Europe: UEFA Cup quarter-finals
Mins: 620 **Goals conceded:** 10 **Cards:** 0 ▢

Juan Silveira dos Santos is a name too long for the new gold and red shirt that he's wearing this season, so it's just as well this Brazilian centre-half is known as plain 'Juan'. Roma signed him from Bayer Leverkusen for £4m in the summer, after a season securing the Bundesliga side's run to fifth spot and a UEFA Cup quarter-final. He has won two Copa America trophies with Brazil.

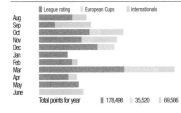

■ League rating ■ European Cups ■ Internationals

Aug Sep Oct Nov Dec Jan Feb Mar Apr May June

Total points for year ■ 178,498 ■ 35,520 ■ 69,586

---

26 Ivar Ingimarsson
Age: 29 • *11th best defender in Premiership* •
Overall World Ranking: 83
National Team: Iceland **Caps:** 8 **Con:** 15
Club: Reading **Mins:** 3420 **Con:** 47
Europe: Did not play

27 Richard Dunne
Age: 27 • *12th best defender in Premiership* •
Overall World Ranking: 84
National Team: Rep of Ireland **Caps:** 6 **Con:** 7
Club: Man City **Mins:** 3420 **Con:** 44
Europe: Did not play

28 Nicky Shorey
Age: 26 • *13th best defender in Premiership* •
Overall World Ranking: 86
National Team: England **Caps:** 1 **Con:** 1
Club: Reading **Mins:** 3330 **Con:** 46
Europe: Did not play

29 Manuel Pasqual
Age: 25 • *4th best defender in Italian League* •
Overall World Ranking: 89
National Team: Italy **Caps:** 1 **Con:** 0
Club: Fiorentina **Mins:** 3044 **Con:** 28
Europe: Did not play

30 Joris Mathijsen
Age: 27 • *4th best defender in German League* •
Overall World Ranking: 93
National Team: Holland **Caps:** 11 **Con:** 5
Club: Hamburg **Mins:** 2925 **Con:** 34
Europe: Ch Lge Group - 4th **Mins:** 540 **Con:** 15

31 Daniel Van Buyten
Age: 29 • *5th best defender in German League* •
Overall World Ranking: 94
National Team: Belgium **Caps:** 7 **Con:** 8
Club: Bayern Munich **Mins:** 2727 **Con:** 35
Europe: Ch Lge quarter-finals **Mins:** 900 **Con:** 11

32 Cris
Age: 30 • *Best defender in French League* •
Overall World Ranking: 96
National Team: Brazil **Caps:** 0 **Con:** 0
Club: Lyon **Mins:** 2880 **Con:** 23
Europe: Ch Lge last 16 **Mins:** 630 **Con:** 4

33 Marco Materazzi
Age: 33 • *5th best defender in Italian League* •
Overall World Ranking: 99
National Team: Italy **Caps:** 6 **Con:** 1
Club: Inter Milan **Mins:** 2372 **Con:** 23
Europe: Ch Lge last 16 **Mins:** 540 **Con:** 5

34 Lucas Neill
Age: 29 • *14th best defender in Premiership* •
Overall World Ranking: 101
National Team: Australia **Caps:** 3 **Con:** 1
Club: West Ham/Blackburn **Mins:** 2700 **Con:** 43
Europe: UEFA Cup Group (Blackburn) **Mins:** 270 **Con:** 1

35 David Rozehnal
Age: 27 • *2nd best defender in French League* •
Overall World Ranking: 106
National Team: Czech Republic **Caps:** 10 **Con:** 6
Club: Paris St G **Mins:** 3330 **Goals:** 39
Europe: UEFA Cup last 16 **Mins:** 270 **Con:** 1

36 Per Mertesacker
Age: 22 • *6th best defender in German League* •
Overall World Ranking: 107
National Team: Germany **Caps:** 5 **Con:** 4
Club: Werder Bremen **Mins:** 2165 **Con:** 23
Europe: UEFA Cup semis **Mins:** 720 **Con:** 3

37 Moises Hurtado
Age: 26 • *8th best defender in Spanish Liga* •
Overall World Ranking: 109
National Team: Spain **Caps:** 0 **Con:** 0
Club: Espanyol **Mins:** 2364 **Con:** 32
Europe: UEFA Cup finalist **Mins:** 697 **Con:** 6

38 Salvatore Aronica
Age: 29 • *6th best defender in Italian League* •
Overall World Ranking: 112
National Team: Italy **Caps:** 0 **Con:** 0
Club: Reggina **Mins:** 3121 **Goals:** 45
Europe: Did not play

39 Christian Panucci
Age: 34 • *7th best defender in Italian League* •
Overall World Ranking: 115
National Team: Italy **Caps:** 0 **Con:** 0
Club: Roma **Mins:** 2706 **Goals:** 27
Europe: Ch Lge quarter-finals **Mins:** 810 **Con:** 12

40 Eric Abidal
Age: 28 • *3rd best defender in French League* •
Overall World Ranking: 116
National Team: France **Caps:** 10 **Con:** 4
Club: Lyon **Mins:** 2747 **Con:** 22
Europe: Ch Lge last 16 **Mins:** 593 **Con:** 4

41 Ashley Cole
Age: 26 • *15th best defender in Premiership* •
Overall World Ranking: 118
National Team: England **Caps:** 7 **Con:** 3
Club: Chelsea **Mins:** 1847 **Con:** 15
Europe: Ch Lge Group - semis **Mins:** 817 **Con:** 7

42 Jose Carlos Araujo Nunes
Age: 30 • *9th best defender in Spanish Liga* •
Overall World Ranking: 120
National Team: Portugal **Caps:** 0 **Con:** 0
Club: Mallorca **Mins:** 3098 **Con:** 39
Europe: Did not play

43 Philippe Mexes
Age: 25 • *8th best defender in Italian League* •
Overall World Ranking: 122
National Team: France **Caps:** 1 **Con:** 0
Club: Roma **Mins:** 2411 **Con:** 26
Europe: Ch Lge quarter-finals **Mins:** 630 **Con:** 10

44 Joleon Lescott
Age: 24 • *16th best defender in Premiership* •
Overall World Ranking: 126
National Team: England **Caps:** 0 **Con:** 0
Club: Everton **Mins:** 3318 **Con:** 36
Europe: Did not play

45 Lopez Ruano Angel
Age: 26 • *10th best defender in Spanish Liga* •
Overall World Ranking: 130
National Team: Spain **Caps:** 3 **Con:** 2
Club: Celta Vigo **Mins:** 3133 **Con:** 53
Europe: UEFA Cup last 16 **Mins:** 358 **Con:** 6

46 Alvaro Arbeloa
Age: 24 • *17th best defender in Premiership* •
Overall World Ranking: 132
National Team: Spain **Caps:** 0 **Con:** 0
Club: Liverpool/Deportivo **Mins:** 2468 **Con:** 29
Europe: Ch Lge finalist **Mins:** 363 **Con:** 3

47 Francesco Modesto
Age: 25 • *9th best defender in Italian League* •
Overall World Ranking: 133
National Team: Italy **Caps:** 0 **Con:** 0
Club: Reggina **Mins:** 3013 **Con:** 46
Europe: Did not play

48 Lucio
Age: 29 • *7th best defender in German League* •
Overall World Ranking: 135
National Team: Brazil **Caps:** 6 **Con:** 4
Club: Bayern Munich **Mins:** 2272 **Con:** 30
Europe: Ch Lge quarter-finals **Mins:** 720 **Con:** 9

49 Marc Torrejon Moya
Age: 21 • *11th best defender in Spanish Liga* •
Overall World Ranking: 137
National Team: Spain **Caps:** 0 **Con:** 0
Club: Espanyol **Mins:** 2402 **Con:** 34
Europe: UEFA Cup finalist **Mins:** 750 **Con:** 5

50 Joseph Yobo
Age: 26 • *18th best defender in Premiership* •
Overall World Ranking: 140
National Team: Nigeria **Caps:** 3 **Con:** 4
Club: Everton **Mins:** 3420 **Con:** 36
Europe: Did not play

FOOTBALL CHALLENGE QUIZ 3

Do you know your football?

THINK YOU'RE A FOOTY KNOW-IT-ALL? TEST YOUR KNOWLEDGE ON THE FOUR QUIZ PAGES IN THIS ANNUAL. FILL IN YOUR ANSWERS ON PAGE 94 AND SEE HOW MANY YOU SCORED OUT OF 200!

CUP WINNERS

The teams below are celebrating a cup win, but what have they won?

1 PORTO 2003

2 LIVERPOOL 2005

3 AC MILAN 2003

4 MAN UNITED 2004

5 CHELSEA 2007

PREMIER KEEPERS WORD SEARCH

The 20 goalkeepers that are hidden in the word search below all made appearances in the Premiership last season. Can you spot them?

E	J	A	C	K	B	S	C	H	W	A	R	Z	E	R	S	O	L	Y
V	O	N	S	T	L	A	F	A	R	E	Z	E	R	E	E	N	O	A
A	N	B	C	A	R	S	O	N	J	M	A	T	Q	I	J	K	C	R
N	E	J	D	E	F	L	S	M	O	K	S	V	Z	C	H	H	S	D
D	R	U	A	I	N	A	T	K	E	L	E	F	E	Y	U	A	O	S
E	K	N	R	M	C	E	E	P	C	H	A	N	S	R	I	H	N	O
R	I	E	O	R	E	P	R	E	I	N	A	R	N	T	N	N	H	R
S	R	A	B	F	X	S	O	N	T	G	A	F	V	Y	P	E	O	E
A	K	F	H	F	R	I	E	D	E	L	L	X	I	O	D	M	W	N
R	L	S	K	N	D	T	C	Y	M	D	F	S	T	B	G	A	D	S
L	A	C	J	B	I	N	T	E	Q	G	R	E	E	N	U	N	F	O
U	N	W	E	U	T	E	Y	W	O	I	E	F	Y	I	P	N	D	N
S	D	E	G	C	X	R	M	S	G	V	I	E	H	L	C	X	P	T
I	G	A	O	T	H	T	G	I	W	E	P	Q	N	U	Z	L	Q	U
T	J	Z	H	O	W	A	R	D	H	N	U	Z	B	I	T	W	S	G
D	E	H	I	S	F	L	B	X	W	J	L	E	H	M	A	N	N	A
T	C	E	X	M	S	J	A	A	S	K	E	L	A	I	N	E	N	D
B	D	R	O	B	I	N	S	O	N	D	O	E	S	H	M	C	M	I
L	T	A	O	L	E	Y	C	I	M	E	S	A	U	B	G	J	E	X

CARSON	GREEN	KENNY	ROBINSON
CECH	HAHNEMANN	KIRKLAND	SCHWARZER
FOSTER	HOWARD	LEHMANN	SØRENSEN
FRIEDEL	JAASKELAINEN	NIEMI	VAN DER SAR
GIVEN	JAMES	REINA	WEAVER

HOW MUCH CAN YOU REMEMBER ABOUT THE 2006-07 SEASON?

1 What Real Madrid squad number was allocated to David Beckham last season?

2 With which south coast club did Chelsea defender Glen Johnson go on loan?

3 How many points did Manchester United take from Celtic in the Champions League group stage?

4 Can you name Fulham's shirt sponsor last season?

5 Which newly promoted club did Liverpool play on the opening day of last season?

6 Which London club did Manchester United play on the opening weekend of the last Premiership campaign?

7 What colour was Liverpool's third strip?

8 Who did Manchester United play on the last day?

9 Which League Two club claimed they would discipline players for "diving"?

10 Which Greek team knocked Hearts out the Champions League?

11 What colour was Manchester United's away strip in 2006-07?

12 Who did Aston Villa pay £9m to sign Ashley Young in January 2007?

GUESS THE PUNDIT

Can you work out who this Match Of The Day pundit is?

WHO CAPTAINS WHO?

Match the 2006-07 captains to their clubs...

1. NIGEL REO-COKER	A. PORTSMOUTH
2. NEIL LENNON	B. MANCHESTER CITY
3. DEJAN STEFANOVIC	C. ARSENAL
4. LUIS BOA MORTE	D. READING
5. RICHARD DUNNE	E. FULHAM
6. GRAEME MURTY	F. WEST HAM
7. THIERRY HENRY	G. COVENTRY CITY
8. STEPHEN HUGHES	H. CELTIC

MISSING WINNERS

Name three players missing from England's starting XI for the first international at the new Wembley.

PAUL ROBINSON
JAMIE CARRAGHER
LEDLEY KING
JOHN TERRY
?
_____
STEVEN GERRARD
?
_____
FRANK LAMPARD
JOE COLE
?
_____
MICHAEL OWEN

MAY THE FORC

When he's not on the pitch, Chelsea defender **WAYNE BRIDGE** has a little hobby to keep him occupied. He's an obsessive *Star Wars* fan.

WHEN WAYNE BRIDGE ANSWERS THE DOOR, there is no mistaking what the Chelsea defender's hobby is. He's a *Star Wars* fanatic. "I'm missing a bit from inside here," he says, dressed from the neck down in a Storm Trooper outfit and pointing to the helmet under his arm. "It's not sitting properly but I've got to get it right because there'll be people out there who'll notice these things."

The statement is a clear indication of the obsessive attention to detail displayed by your average *Star Wars* nut. But there is a difference here. Your average *Star Wars* nut isn't usually a world-class professional footballer playing for one of Europe's leading clubs, and boasting 25 international caps.

"Anyone want a drink?" says Wayne's girlfriend, Vanessa, who we later learn is partly responsible for this situation. "Yeah, I'll have a Jedi Juice please," answers the Chelsea and England defender, slipping further and further into character. "Even though I'm dressed as a Storm Trooper, I'm not from the Dark Side," he says. "I'm Luke Skywalker, when he dressed up as a Storm Trooper to fool the enemy. I'm a Jedi."

Opposition strikers beware, there is obviously a lot more to Wayne Bridge than meets the eye.

Is it the suit from the movie?
"It's not one from the film, no. But the guy who used to make them for the films still makes them, so Vanessa tracked him down. He was out of stock so she had to beg him to make me one."

Are they made-to-measure or are you a one-size-fits-all kind of Storm Trooper?
"They come as they are, in the one size. But they've got this stretchy lining inside and bits of Velcro, so they do adapt to different sizes."

Why did you want the Storm Trooper?
"I just love the outfit. And I've always wanted to go to a fancy dress party as a Storm Trooper – I reckon I'd look pretty good doing the running man on the dance floor in it. I'd been looking on eBay for ages but never found a decent suit that I fancied buying. But then Vanessa pulled this one out of the hat for me."

Is the guy who makes them based in the US?
"No, he's from Shepperton Design Studios. I think some of *Star Wars* was shot at Shepperton Studios actually. He even signed it inside."

They can't be cheap to buy?
"This one was a present so I don't know how much it was, but I know the ones on eBay were going for about $1500."

Where do you keep it? Does it hang in the wardrobe next to your shirts?
"Well, at the moment I'm having a new house built which will have a cinema room, so I'll be keeping it in there on a mannnequin."

E BE WITH YOU

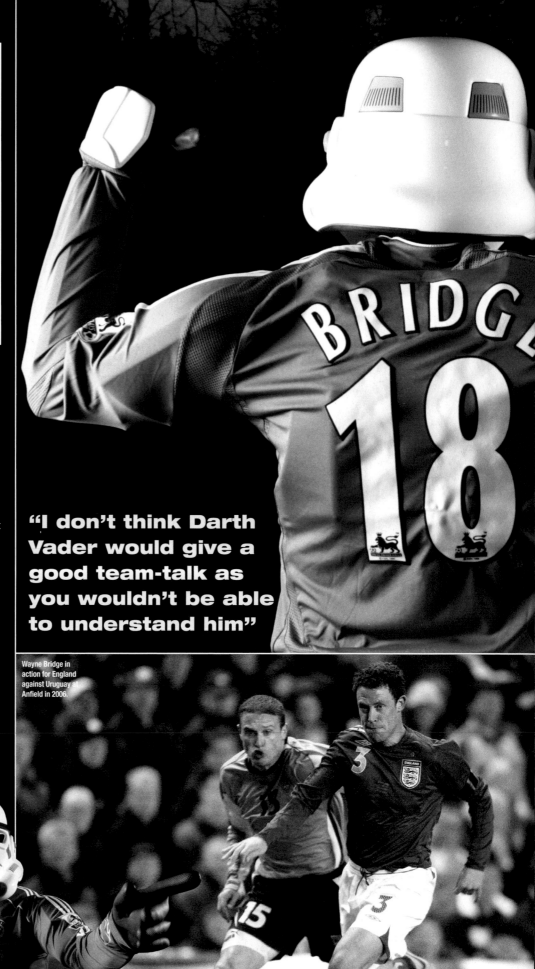

STAR WARS

Since the first *Star Wars* film (Episode IV) was released in 1977, the entire series has taken $4.3 billion at the box office.

Star Wars Episode I The Phantom Menace

Star Wars Episode II Attack of the Clones

Star Wars Episode III Revenge of the Sith

Star Wars Episode IV A New Hope (originally simply *Star Wars*)

Star Wars Episode V The Empire Strikes Back

Star Wars Episode VI Return of the Jedi

Seeing as you're doing this whole interview standing up, are we safe to assume that the average Storm Trooper isn't the most mobile *Star Wars* character?

"It's not the best on that front. I mean, you can walk around all right. I've only put it on quickly today and haven't adjusted my Velcro, which doesn't help. But overall, I wouldn't say you could go running in it. I wouldn't advise it, anyway. In fact, since I've had it and felt what it's like to wear one, I've noticed when I've watched the films again that the Storm Troopers really aren't that mobile. I was thinking of going paintballing in it but you just can't move enough. Having said that, it wouldn't hurt as much."

What happens when nature calls?

"It unclips at the front here [pointing to what can only be described as an inter-Galactic codpiece]. There's a little zip, so no problems."

Have you worn it out of the house yet?

"No, I haven't and I'm gutted, so I'm itching to find a fancy dress party if anyone's having one."

Today you've obviously put it on for our benefit, but is it something you like to slip into when chilling out at home?

"Only at bed time…" [That's a joke, we think - Ed]

It's safe to assume that you're a major *Star Wars* fan then…

"Yes, of course, and most of my mates are fans too – we have been since we were kids."

But it came out before you were even born…

"Yeah, but my mum and dad had the original film on video and I used to watch it all the time."

How often do you watch the *Star Wars* films?

"The last time was when I stumbled across one of them when it was being shown on Sky recently. I tried getting my missus to watch it but she fell asleep half way through."

"I don't think Darth Vader would give a good team-talk as you wouldn't be able to understand him"

Wayne Bridge in action for England against Uruguay at Anfield in 2006.

In his Southampton days, fending off Gazza.

WAYNE BRIDGE

Full Name: Wayne Michael Bridge

Born: August 5, 1980 in Southampton

Height: 5ft 10in

Position: Left-Back

Chelsea Squad Number: 18

		GAMES	GOALS
1997-2003	Southampton	151	2
2003-current	Chelsea	70	1
2006	Fulham (loan)	12	0

Wayne throws his arms around Chewbacca… er, Didier Drogba!

You must know it all off by heart by now…
"I know quite a few of the lines, but most of my mates are at the stage where they can quote the words before the character has even said them. My mate actually bought me a *Star Wars* trivia quiz game for Christmas so I'll have to get the lads round for a go on it. I sound so much like a geek, don't I?"

Ever been to a *Star Wars* convention?
"No, I haven't, but I've read about them – all looks a bit mad to me."

Don't fancy rocking up at one in your outfit?
"No. I just want to be the only one at the party."

Did you have all the figures as a kid?
"Yeah, the lot, Chewy, Luke, all of them. I also had a Millennium Falcon and an X-Wing Fighter. I've still got the Millennium Falcon. In fact, I've still got a Darth Vader statue that will probably go in my new cinema room."

Did you like the newer *Star Wars* films?
"I don't like them as much. They don't look the same. There was something about the time and place when the originals were made. You can't recreate magic."

If the Chelsea squad were cast in a remake of *Star Wars*, who would play Hans Solo?
"I'd say Carlo Cudicini – he's got the look, the hair with a little sweep to the side."

What about R2D2?
"It's got to be Shaun Wright-Phillips."

What about Chewbacca?
"Maybe Didier Drogba because of his hair. I'm just trying to think who the hairiest player we have is… Ricardo Carvalho is quite hairy, but then Didier's got the build of a Wookie as well."

What's the ultimate *Star Wars* item to have?
"I've got two light sabres but Storm Troopers never used light sabres so I can't have my picture taken with one because it wouldn't be right. They had these special guns. I'm trying to track one down, so if you ever want to get me anything…'

And you're missing the Storm Trooper boots.
"Yeah, we couldn't get those. They're like these little white cowboy boot things. I need to get hold of some, but until then I have to make do with a pair of white trainers with it."

Is it just Storm Troopers or would you like to dress up as any other characters?
"I'd do all of them."

So what's next, Darth Vader?
"Nah, I'd have to go back to the good side."

Is Luke your favourite character?
"Yeah, he'd have to be… although I like Yoda as well. Actually, Wrighty would make a good Yoda."

Have you spotted the scene when the Storm Trooper bangs his head on the door in the Death Star control room?
"Yeah, of course! It's a bit of a mistake, but they never took it out. Just as well they wear hard helmets really."

Was it a shock to find that Vader was Luke Skywalker's father?
"Yeah, but I got over it. I didn't cry or anything."

Would Darth Vader give a good half-time team talk?
"I don't think that he'd be that easy to understand, so no, I don't reckon that it would be that good, to be honest."

You don't think that he'd motivate you?
"We might kill a few teams off by injuring them but I don't think his tactical knowledge would be up to scratch. We'd just be kicking people to death."

What's your favourite quote from *Star Wars*?
"It would have to be: 'That was a shot in a million, kid' by Hans Solo."

Who in the Chelsea squad would make a good Jedi Knight?
"John Terry. I've seen him play darts. When he throws them they seem to go wherever he wants. It's weird."

Did you ever fancy Princess Leah?
"Nah, never had a crush on her. She was too old for me."

Anything else you want to say on the subject while we're here?
"I'm not a geek, alright!"

THE WORLD'S TOP 25

Who are the best keepers in world football? The MOTD computer picks the top 25.

OVER THE LAST 12 MONTHS WE'VE FOLLOWED 5,000 OF THE BEST PLAYERS IN world football to check on their form. Are they playing for teams that win? When they play do they make a difference to how goals are scored or conceded? Do they have an impact on the general outcome of the game? We've turned the info into a chart of the world's best strikers, midfielders, defenders and keepers.

Here is your run down on the best goalkeepers based on their form over the last 12 months. Are they players for top teams, are they winning games, are they keeping the opposition from scoring, do they command their penalty area well? We have limited ourselves to the top 25 keepers and we show where each is ranked in their division. For example, **Victor Valdes** of Barcelona is the fifth best keeper in Spain's La Liga. We also show their Overall World Ranking, how they rate in our list of all the world's top players, regardless of position.

To get among our Top Goalkeepers, they need to be a good shot stopper but they also need to organise the defence in front of them and give their defenders confidence. Are they recording clean sheets? How often do they concede a goal on average? Chelsea stopper **Petr Cech** lost three months injured and is the only keeper here with less than 2,000 league minutes. However, he still charts with the best 'Concede rate'; only letting in one goal every 190 minutes on average. He also stopped 9.67 shots on target for every goal he conceded – easily the best ratio we've recorded this season.

THE WORLD'S TOP 100 PLAYERS BY CLUB

We scanned our **Hot 100** – the best 100 players to see which clubs feature most. The three top Premier clubs did best, all with good league and Champions League form. In other top leagues the most successful clubs in Europe didn't finish in the top three. There are 39 clubs in our **Hot 100**.

	Top Clubs	No of players
1	LIVERPOOL	8
2	CHELSEA	7
=	MAN UNITED	7
4	VALENCIA	6
5	INTER MILAN	5
=	WERDER BREMEN	5
=	PSV EINDHOVEN	5
=	AC MILAN	5
9	REAL MADRID	4
=	ARSENAL	4

UNDERSTANDING THE GRAPH

To work out the world's best players, we have awarded points to each player for their performances through the season. **The Players Graph** shows the competitions where they are earning points through the year. We have used the Werder Bremen and German midfield star **Torsten Frings** to demonstrate exactly how the graph works.

Torsten Frings' Playing Record

■ League rating   ■ European Cups   ■ Internationals

Aug
Sep
Oct
Nov
Dec
Jan
Feb
Mar
Apr
May
June

Total points for year   ■ 25,6142   ■ 77,750   ■ 49,458

Points: at the bottom of the graph is a note of the points awarded to the player for his performances in each element of his season. They take into account winning, scoring, strengh of opposition, bookings and so on. Frings scored highly in all three areas.

Orange bars: the orange bars show Frings' league activity for Werder Bremen over ten months without injury. The Bundesliga finished in mid May with Bremen in contention until the end.

Yellow bars: the yellow bar shows cup games in Europe. Bremen played initially in the Champions League, finishing third in their group and transferring to the UEFA Cup where they reached the semis.

Green bars: the green bar shows games where Frings played for Germany in internationals. He played ten internationals in Germany's race to the top of Euro 2008 Qualifying Group G.

GOAL

1 ▲ Jose Reina

Age: 24 ○ Best keeper in Premiership ○ **Overall World Ranking: 11**

Jose Reina already enjoyed the reputation as a penalty saver when he joined Liverpool from Villarreal in La Liga. He's lived up to it in the last 12 months, winning an FA Cup penalty shoot-out against West Ham before earning Liverpool a semi-final win over Chelsea in the Champions League. The son of a legendary Atletico Madrid keeper, Reina set a club record of eight consecutive clean sheets in 2005.

Season 2006-07 record

National Team: Spain
Apps: 3 **Goals conceded:** 1 **Cards:** 0 0

Club: Liverpool
Apps: 35 **Goals conceded:** 23 **Cards:** 1 0
Concede rate: Goal every 137 mins
Mins played: 3150 **Ave mins:** 90

Europe: Champions League finalist
Mins: 1110 **Goals conceded:** 7 **Cards:** 1 0

	League rating	European Cups	Internationals
Aug			
Sep			
Oct			
Nov			
Dec			
Jan			
Feb			
Mar			
Apr			
May			
June			

Total points for year ▮ 23,5927 ▮ 122,980 ▮ 14,580

KEEPERS

2 | Edwin van der Sar

Age: 36 • 2nd best keeper in Premiership • **Overall World Ranking:** 12

The calm presence of Edwin van der Sar formed a vital part of United's return to Premiership winning form. He holds the record number of caps for Holland, overtaking Frank de Boer's 112 appearances in 2006 and is the current captain. He began his career winning a Champions League trophy with Ajax in 1995. The 1.97m tall goalie is one of the best keepers in the world with the ball at his feet and distributes it well.

Season 2006-07 record

National Team: Holland
Apps: 6 **Goals conceded:** 2 **Cards:** 0 0

Club: Manchester United
Apps: 32 **Goals conceded:** 25 **Cards:** 1 0
Concede rate: Goal every 115 mins
Mins played: 2880 **Ave mins:** 90

Europe: Champions League semi-finals
Mins: 1080 **Goals conceded:** 13 **Cards:** 0 0

League rating | European Cups | Internationals

Aug Sep Oct Nov Dec Jan Feb Mar Apr May June

Total points for year | 247,611 | 88,615 | 34,800

---

3 | Iker Casillas

Age: 26 • Best keeper in Spanish Liga • **Overall World Ranking:** 13

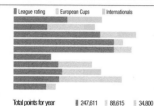

Iker Casillas is only 26, yet has notched up over 250 La Liga appearances for Real Madrid and won his third league title last summer. A youth team player at Madrid, he was promoted into the first team in 1999 and is now vice-captain of both club and country. Spain is blessed with an abundance of top keepers but Casillas is the undisputed number one and has amassed over 70 caps.

Season 2006-07 record

National Team: Spain
Apps: 8 **Goals conceded:** 7 **Cards:** 0 0

Club: Real Madrid
Apps: 38 **Goals conceded:** 40 **Cards:** 1 0
Concede rate: Goal every 86 mins
Mins played: 3420 **Ave mins:** 90

Europe: Champions League last 16
Mins: 630 **Goals conceded:** 10 **Cards:** 0 0

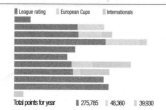

League rating | European Cups | Internationals

Aug Sep Oct Nov Dec Jan Feb Mar Apr May June

Total points for year | 275,785 | 48,360 | 39,930

---

4 | Jens Lehmann

Age: 37 • 3rd best keeper in the Premiership • **Overall World Ranking:** 19

Lehmann cuts a very moody and complaining figure in his six-yard box but he has nursed an inexperienced Arsenal defence to two strong runs in the Champions League. His career highlights include being selected, then keeping brilliantly for Germany in the 2006 World Cup and winning the title with Arsenal's undefeated 'Invincibles' in the 2003-04 season. Nine yellow cards last year show the other side to his temperament.

Season 2006-07 record

National Team: Germany
Apps: 8 **Goals conceded:** 4 **Cards:** 1 0

Club: Arsenal
Apps: 36 **Goals conceded:** 35 **Cards:** 8 0
Concede rate: Goal every 93 mins
Mins played: 3240 **Ave mins:** 90

Europe: Champions League last 16
Mins: 720 **Goals conceded:** 5 **Cards:** 0 0

League rating | European Cups | Internationals

Aug Sep Oct Nov Dec Jan Feb Mar Apr May June

Total points for year | 244,575 | 53,150 | 52,620

---

5 | Sebastien Frey

Age: 27 • Best keeper in Italian League • **Overall World Ranking:** 28

The young Cannes keeper was fast-tracked into Inter Milan in 1997, aged just 19. However, Sebastien Frey built his reputation over five seasons with rivals Parma before switching to Fiorentina in 2005. He was an ever-present last season, conceding 31 goals in 38 Serie A games to give the Florence side the top defensive stats in the Italian league. He has been called up for France but is yet to play.

Season 2006-07 record

National Team: France
Apps: 0 **Goals conceded:** 0 **Cards:** 0 0

Club: Fiorentina
Apps: 38 **Goals conceded:** 31 **Cards:** 0 0
Concede rate: Goal every 110 mins
Mins played: 3420 **Ave mins:** 90

Europe: Did not play
Mins: 0 **Goals conceded:** **Cards:** 0 0

League rating | European Cups | Internationals

Aug Sep Oct Nov Dec Jan Feb Mar Apr May June

Total points for year | 332,694 | 0 | 0

6 Heurelho Gomes

Age: 26 › *Best keeper in Dutch League* › **Overall World Ranking: 36**

Heurelho Gomes has been a regular in this chart since he arrived in Europe fresh, from winning the Brazilian league title with Cruzeiro in 2004. The 1.92m tall keeper seems to fill the net for PSV and the Dutch club has won their league title all three seasons since Gomes joined them. He is one of the main contenders, with Porto's Helton and Roma's Doni, for the Brazilian goalkeeping jersey.

Season 2006-07 record

National Team: Brazil
Apps: 4 **Goals conceded:** 2 **Cards:** 0 0

Club: PSV Eindhoven
Apps: 32 **Goals conceded:** 24 **Cards:** 0 0
Concede rate: Goal every 120 mins
Mins played: 2880 **Ave mins:** 90

Europe: Champions League quarter-finalists
Mins: 900 **Goals conceded:** 11 **Cards:** 0 0

League rating ■ European Cups ■ Internationals

Aug
Sep
Oct
Nov
Dec
Jan
Feb
Mar
Apr
May
June

Total points for year ■ 213,324 ■ 73,500 ■ 35,505

7 Roberto Abbondanzieri

Age: 34 › *2nd best keeper in Spanish Liga* › **Overall World Ranking: 45**

8 Paul Robinson

Age: 27 › *4th best keeper in Premiership* › **Overall World Ranking: 47**

Paul Robinson became a rare Premiership goalkeeping scorer when his clearance bounced over England rival Ben Foster's head and into Watford's net last March. The Spurs defence was shaky in the league but Martin Jol played his keeper in all bar five games of a 59-fixture season. He has been in good form for England of late but earned criticism when a back pass bobbled over his foot against Croatia.

Season 2006-07 record

National Team: England
Apps: 10 **Goals conceded:** 4 **Cards:** 0 0

Club: Tottenham
Apps: 38 **Goals conceded:** 54 **Cards:** 0 0
Concede rate: Goal every 63 mins
Mins played: 3240 **Ave mins:** 90

Europe: UEFA Cup quarter-finals
Mins: 630 **Goals conceded:** 8 **Cards:** 1 0

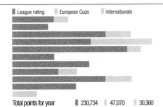

League rating ■ European Cups ■ Internationals

Aug
Sep
Oct
Nov
Dec
Jan
Feb
Mar
Apr
May
June

Total points for year ■ 230,734 ■ 47,070 ■ 30,360

Roberto Abbondanzieri was keeping top European-based goalies out of the Argentinian team, but always had his doubters until he silenced them emphatically with a move to unfashionable Getafe. In his first season, the club put together the best defensive record in La Liga, conceding only 33 goals despite finishing mid-table. An unfussy keeper, he just gets on with the job of frustrating forwards.

Season 2006-07 record

National Team: Argentina
Apps: 5 **Goals conceded:** 7 **Cards:** 0 0

Club: Getafe
Apps: 36 **Goals conceded:** 30 **Cards:** 3 0
Concede rate: Goal every 107mins
Mins played: 3216 **Ave mins:** 89

Europe: Did not play
Mins: 0 **Goals conceded:** **Cards:** 0 0

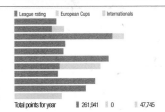

League rating ■ European Cups ■ Internationals

Aug
Sep
Oct
Nov
Dec
Jan
Feb
Mar
Apr
May
June

Total points for year ■ 261,941 ■ 0 ■ 47,745

9 Alexander Doni

Age: 27 › *2nd best keeper in Italian League* › **Overall World Ranking: 49**

Alexander Doni's worst moment of 2007 was the seven goal thrashing inflicted by Manchester United in the Champions League. However, it was the exception to a strong season in Europe and Italy, where he was second only to countryman Nelson Dida at AC Milan in the Serie A goalkeeping stats. Doni mustered a Defensive Rating of a goal conceded every 115 minutes. He has seven Brazilian caps.

Season 2006-07 record

National Team: Brazil
Apps: 3 **Goals conceded:** 2 **Cards:** 0 0

Club: Roma
Apps: 28 **Goals conceded:** 25 **Cards:** 2 0
Concede rate: Goal every 101 mins
Mins played: 2520 **Ave mins:** 90

Europe: Champions League quarter-finals
Mins: 900 **Goals conceded:** 12 **Cards:** 0 0

League rating ■ European Cups ■ Internationals

Aug
Sep
Oct
Nov
Dec
Jan
Feb
Mar
Apr
May
June

Total points for year ■ 218,073 ■ 72,510 ■ 17,280

10 Tim Wiese

Age: 25 – Best keeper in German League – Overall World Ranking: 50

Jens Lehmann and Oliver Kahn have been the bitter rivals for Germany's keeping jersey in recent years but Tim Wiese leads a new generation. The Werder Bremen keeper is ten years younger and missed only a handful of games in a season that saw Bremen compete for the Bundesliga, the Champions League and the UEFA Cup. He still has to live with a dreadful cup howler against Juventus in 2006.

Season 2006-07 record

National Team: Germany
Apps: 0 **Goals conceded:** 0 **Cards:** 0 **0**

Club: Werder Bremen
Apps: 31 **Goals conceded:** 35 **Cards:** 0 **0**
Concede rate: Goal every 80 mins
Mins played: 2790 **Ave mins:** 90

Europe: UEFA Cup semi-finals
Mins: 867 **Goals conceded:** 7 **Cards:** 1 **1**

	League rating	European Cups	Internationals
Aug			
Sep			
Oct			
Nov			
Dec			
Jan			
Feb			
Mar			
Apr			
May			
June			

Total points for year ▪ 233,807 ▪ 68,982 ▪ 0

11 Andres Palop

Age: 33 – 3rd best keeper in Spanish Liga – Overall World Ranking: 56

Seville's Andres Palop has made his name in two UEFA Cup-winning runs. In the first, he instinctively saved a Mark Viduka point-blank volley during the 2006 final. Last season he went one better and scored an injury-time equaliser against Ukraine's Shakhtar Donetsk. It kept Seville in the 2007 UEFA Cup and they went on to successfully defend their title, with Palop saving three in the final penalty shootout.

Season 2006-07 record

National Team: Spain
Apps: 0 **Goals conceded:** 0 **Cards:** 0 **0**

Club: Seville
Apps: 34 **Goals conceded:** 32 **Cards:** 3 **0**
Concede rate: Goal every 94 mins
Mins played: 3015 **Ave mins:** 89

Europe: UEFA Cup winners
Mins: 780 **Goals conceded:** 7 **Cards:** 2 **0**

	League rating	European Cups	Internationals
Aug			
Sep			
Oct			
Nov			
Dec			
Jan			
Feb			
Mar			
Apr			
May			
June			

Total points for year ▪ 240,486 ▪ 57,285 ▪ 0

12 Lopez Ricardo

Age: 35 – 4th best keeper in Spanish Liga – Overall World Ranking: 58

Ricardo was a failure at Old Trafford, where he only made one Premier League appearance in three seasons – including one on loan to Racing Santander and gave away a penalty. He left for Osasuna in La Liga in 2005 and immediately set about proving United wrong. His 31 league games he earned the Pamplona club fourth spot in 2006. That provided the platform for a fine UEFA Cup run to the semi-finals.

Season 2006-07 record

National Team: Spain
Apps: 0 **Goals conceded:** 0 **Cards:** 0 **0**

Club: Osasuna
Apps: 36 **Goals conceded:** 45 **Cards:** 4 **1**
Concede rate: Goal every 71 mins
Mins played: 3180 **Ave mins:** 88

Europe: UEFA Cup semi-finals
Mins: 720 **Goals conceded:** 4 **Cards:** 0 **0**

	League rating	European Cups	Internationals
Aug			
Sep			
Oct			
Nov			
Dec			
Jan			
Feb			
Mar			
Apr			
May			
June			

Total points for year ▪ 235,109 ▪ 61,035 ▪ 0

13 Gregory Coupet

Age: 34 – Best keeper in French League – Overall World Ranking: 59

The best French keeper couldn't break into Les Bleus for many years and his patience snapped at the 2006 World Cup. When Fabien Barthez was given the nod, Gregory Coupet was so angry he briefly walked out. The following season saw matters put right and Coupet helped Lyon to their sixth consecutive French title and he is now France's first choice, while Barthez was relegated with Nantes.

Season 2006-07 record

National Team: France
Apps: 9 **Goals conceded:** 4 **Cards:** 0 **0**

Club: Lyon
Apps: 33 **Goals conceded:** 20 **Cards:** 0 **0**
Concede rate: Goal every 149 mins
Mins played: 2970 **Ave mins:** 90

Europe: Champions League last 16
Mins: 630 **Goals conceded:** 5 **Cards:** 0 **0**

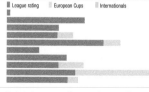

	League rating	European Cups	Internationals
Aug			
Sep			
Oct			
Nov			
Dec			
Jan			
Feb			
Mar			
Apr			
May			
June			

Total points for year ▪ 195,939 ▪ 55,560 ▪ 44,520

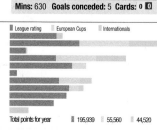

14 Brad Friedel

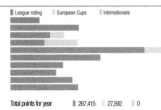

Age: 36 • *5th best keeper in Premiership* • **Overall World Ranking:** 60

Brad Friedel has become 'Mr Reliable' for Blackburn. He regularly plays every game and last season missed only 45 minutes of a 53-game UEFA and FA Cup dominated season. He is also an instinctive shot stopper, saving 5.28 shots on target for every league goal conceded and he kept out five opposition penalties. He was the only consistent element in an injury-wracked Blackburn defence.

Season 2006-07 record

National Team: USA
Apps: 0 **Goals conceded:** 0 **Cards:** 0 0

Club: Blackburn Rovers
Apps: 38 **Goals conceded:** 54 **Cards:** 0 0
Concede rate: Goal every 63mins
Mins played: 3375 **Ave mins:** 89

Europe: UEFA Cup last 32
Mins: 360 **Goals conceded:** 3 **Cards:** 0 0

	League rating	European Cups	Internationals
Aug			
Sep			
Oct			
Nov			
Dec			
Jan			
Feb			
Mar			
Apr			
May			
June			

Total points for year ▮ 267,415 ▮ 27,592 ▮ 0

15 Julio Cesar

Age: 27 • *3rd best keeper in Italian League* • **Overall World Ranking:** 61

Julio Cesar is among a host of Brazilian contenders for the role of top keeper and Dida's replacement at international level. He has already made the Inter Milan position his own, ousting long-term favourite Francesco Toldo. He began his career at Flamengo, before arriving in Europe in 2005. He has 12 caps for Brazil but didn't get selected for the two keeping places in the successful Copa America squad.

Season 2006-07 record

National Team: Brazil
Apps: 2 **Goals conceded:** 0 **Cards:** 0 0

Club: Inter Milan
Apps: 32 **Goals conceded:** 30 **Cards:** 1 0
Concede rate: Goal every 96 mins
Mins played: 2880 **Ave mins:** 90

Europe: Champions League last 16
Mins: 540 **Goals conceded:** 5 **Cards:** 0 0

	League rating	European Cups	Internationals
Aug			
Sep			
Oct			
Nov			
Dec			
Jan			
Feb			
Mar			
Apr			
May			
June			

Total points for year ▮ 245,224 ▮ 42,510 ▮ 7,020

16 Victor Valdes

Age: 25 • *5th best keeper in Spanish Liga* • **Overall World Ranking:** 63

Madrid have local boy made good Iker Casillas in goal, while Barcelona have the same in Victor Valdes behind their crop of seasoned internationals. In 2006-07, he became only the second Barça keeper, after Andoni Zubizarreta, to play every minute of La Liga season for the club. Valdes is unlucky to be part of the same generation as Casillas and has yet to earn a cap for Spain.

Season 2006-07 record

National Team: Spain
Apps: 0 **Goals conceded:** 0 **Cards:** 0 0

Club: Barcelona
Apps: 38 **Goals conceded:** 33 **Cards:** 2 0
Concede rate: Goal every 104 mins
Mins played: 3420 **Ave mins:** 90

Europe: Champions League last 16
Mins: 720 **Goals conceded:** 6 **Cards:** 0 0

	League rating	European Cups	Internationals
Aug			
Sep			
Oct			
Nov			
Dec			
Jan			
Feb			
Mar			
Apr			
May			
June			

Total points for year ▮ 236,871 ▮ 57,690 ▮ 0

17 Oliver Kahn

Age: 38 • *2nd best keeper in German League* • **Overall World Ranking:** 66

Oliver Kahn seems to go on forever. The perfectionist's training regime has seen his career stretch from local club Karlsruher in 1987 to giants Bayern Munich in 1994 and seven Bundesliga titles. His German career spanned 12 years, 86 caps and a Player Of The Tournament award for captaining Germany to the final of the 2002 World Cup, before making way for Jens Lehmann in 2006.

Season 2006-07 record

National Team: Germany
Apps: 0 **Goals conceded:** 0 **Cards:** 0 0

Club: Bayern Munich
Apps: 32 **Goals conceded:** 37 **Cards:** 4 0
Concede rate: Goal every 78 mins
Mins played: 2880 **Ave mins:** 90

Europe: Champions League quarter-finals
Mins: 810 **Goals conceded:** 9 **Cards:** 0 0

	League rating	European Cups	Internationals
Aug			
Sep			
Oct			
Nov			
Dec			
Jan			
Feb			
Mar			
Apr			
May			
June			

Total points for year ▮ 214,277 ▮ 77,895 ▮ 0

18 Dudu Aouate 🇮🇱

Age: 29 ◦ *6th best keeper in Spanish Liga* ◦ **Overall World Ranking: 76**

Dudu Aouate rises three places in our chart on the back of some defiant performances for Israel and playing consistently well for his struggling Deportivo side in Spain. He first came to notice with Hapoel Haifa, winning the Israeli league in 1999. A stint with Maccabi Haifa also saw a domestic title and he moved to Racing Santander in La Liga before switching to Deportivo last season.

Season 2006-07 record

National Team: Israel
Apps: 8 **Goals conceded:** 7 **Cards:** 0 0

Club: Deportivo La Coruna
Apps: 38 **Goals conceded:** 45 **Cards:** 3 0
Concede rate: Goal every 76 mins
Mins played: 3420 **Ave mins:** 90

Europe: Did not play
Mins: 0 **Goals conceded:** 0 **Cards:** 0 0

League rating ■ European Cups ■ Internationals
Aug
Sep
Oct
Nov
Dec
Jan
Feb
Mar
Apr
May
June

Total points for year | 256,266 | 0 | 28,450

19 Nelson Dida 🇧🇷

Age: 33 ◦ *4th best keeper in Italian League* ◦ **Overall World Ranking: 87**

Nelson Dida may have retired from International football but he still is at the peak of the club game, thwarting both Manchester United and Liverpool as AC Milan won the Champions League last season. The 1.95m tall Brazilian has a collection of 91 caps for his country and a host of silverware from his seven year association with Milan in Serie A. His worst moment was being hit by a burning flare in a Milan derby.

Season 2006-07 record

National Team: Brazil
Apps: 0 **Goals conceded:** 0 **Cards:** 0 0

Club: AC Milan
Apps: 25 **Goals conceded:** 19 **Cards:** 1 0
Concede rate: Goal every 118 mins
Mins played: 2250 **Ave mins:** 90

Europe: Champions League winner
Mins: 1007 **Goals conceded:** 8 **Cards:** 0 0

League rating ■ European Cups ■ Internationals
Aug
Sep
Oct
Nov
Dec
Jan
Feb
Mar
Apr
May
June

Total points for year | 175,223 | 106,012 | 0

20 Santiago Canizares ▬

Age: 37 ◦ *7th best keeper in Spanish Liga* ◦ **Overall World Ranking: 88**

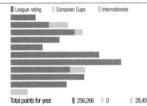

Santiago Canizares is the fifth Spanish keeper in our top 25 and it's hard to argue with his inclusion after another season where he conceded only 33 goals in 31 league games and helped Valencia into the last eight of the Champions League. He made a wonder save from Chelsea's Michael Ballack in their quarter-final but then missed a Michael Essien near-post shot that ended Valencia's run.

Season 2006-07 record

National Team: Spain
Apps: 0 **Goals conceded:** 0 **Cards:** 0 0

Club: Valencia
Apps: 32 **Goals conceded:** 36 **Cards:** 4 1
Concede rate: Goal every 77 mins
Mins played: 2781 **Ave mins:** 87

Europe: Champions League quarter-finals
Mins: 810 **Goals conceded:** 10 **Cards:** 0 0

League rating ■ European Cups ■ Internationals
Aug
Sep
Oct
Nov
Dec
Jan
Feb
Mar
Apr
May
June

Total points for year | 205,275 | 75,135 | 0

21 Tim Howard 🇺🇸

Age: 28 ◦ *6th best keeper in Premiership* ◦ **Overall World Ranking: 92**

Languishing in Manchester United's reserves didn't suit Tim Howard, so the likeable American took a loan deal to Everton. His form was so sharp that David Moyes made the deal permanent in February for a reported £3m. Howard only conceded 29 goals in 36 league games and was second to Petr Cech in our shots saved table. He stopped 8.07 shots on target for every goal conceded.

Season 2006-07 record

National Team: USA
Apps: 6 **Goals conceded:** 3 **Cards:** 0 0

Club: Everton
Apps: 36 **Goals conceded:** 29 **Cards:** 1 0
Concede rate: Goal every 112 mins
Mins played: 3240 **Ave mins:** 90

Europe: Did not play
Mins: 0 **Goals conceded:** 0 **Cards:** 0 0

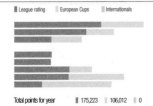

League rating ■ European Cups ■ Internationals
Aug
Sep
Oct
Nov
Dec
Jan
Feb
Mar
Apr
May
June

Total points for year | 244,394 | 0 | 28,170

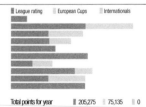

22 Jussi Jaaskelainen

Age: 32 · *7th best keepr in Premeirship* · **Overall World Ranking: 103**

Bolton have relied upon the goalkeeping skills of flying Finn Jussi Jaaskelainen since 1997, when he joined the Lancashire club for just £100,000. Since then he helped them become a fixture in the Premiership and twice helped the team win a European place. He's a good all-rounder, strong on his line, good with crosses and never better than when he's racing off his line to defy a forward.

Season 2006-07 record

National Team: Finland
Apps: 9 **Goals conceded:** 7 **Cards:** 0 **0**

Club: Bolton Wanderers
Apps: 38 **Goals conceded:** 52 **Cards:** 3 **0**
Concede rate: Goal every 66 mins
Mins played: 3420 **Ave mins:** 90

Europe: Did not play
Mins: 0 **Goals conceded:** 0 **Cards:** 0 **0**

	League rating	European Cups	Internationals
Aug			
Sep			
Oct			
Nov			
Dec			
Jan			
Feb			
Mar			
Apr			
May			
June			
Total points for year	250113	0	17620

23 Marcus Hahnemann

Age: 35 · *8th best keeper in Premiership* · **Overall World Ranking: 111**

The bald, bearded, larger than life personality of Marcus Hahnemann stood out from the team ethic at Reading. A regular spokesman for the side, he also passed 206 appearances for them during the season, having joined from Rochdale in 2001. He is behind Kasey Keller and Tim Howard in the pecking order for the United States team and has so far only played six times for his country.

Season 2006-07 record

National Team: USA
Apps: 0 **Goals conceded:** 0 **Cards:** 0 **0**

Club: Reading
Apps: 38 **Goals conceded:** 45 **Cards:** 1 **0**
Concede rate: Goal every 73 mins
Mins played: 3306 **Ave mins:** 87

Europe: Did not play
Mins: 0 **Goals conceded:** 0 **Cards:** 0 **0**

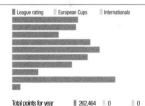

	League rating	European Cups	Internationals
Aug			
Sep			
Oct			
Nov			
Dec			
Jan			
Feb			
Mar			
Apr			
May			
June			
Total points for year	262,464	0	0

24 Petr Cech

Age: 27 · *9th best keeper in the Premiership* · **Overall World Ranking: 114**

According to Jose Mourinho, a low knee from Reading's Stephen Hunt cost Chelsea their third consecutive title. He reasons that it laid out Petr Cech and kept him from action for three months, during which time Chelsea's defence was a tad more generous than usual. Cech came back to prove the point, only conceding nine goals in 20 games and stopping 9.67 shots on target for each league goal he conceded.

Season 2006-07 record

National Team: Czech Republic
Apps: 8 **Goals conceded:** 4 **Cards:** 0 **0**

Club: Chelsea
Apps: 20 **Goals conceded:** 9 **Cards:** 1 **0**
Concede rate: Goal every 190 mins
Mins played: 1714 **Ave mins:** 86

Europe: Champions League semi-finals
Mins: 750 **Goals conceded:** 6 **Cards:** 1 **0**

	League rating	European Cups	Internationals
Aug			
Sep			
Oct			
Nov			
Dec			
Jan			
Feb			
Mar			
Apr			
May			
June			
Total points for year	154,435	73,050	34,740

25 David James

Age: 37 · *10th best keeper in Premiership* · **Overall World Ranking: 117**

David James has won over the fans of Portsmouth in just one season. Although losing his place in the England squad following mistakes in Austria and a poor half against Denmark, James is still one of the finest English shotstoppers and he earned his recall to the England squad to face Germany in August 2007. He overtook David Seaman's record of 141 Premier League clean sheets last April.

Season 2006-07 record

National Team: England
Apps: 0 **Goals conceded:** 0 **Cards:** 0 **0**

Club: Portsmouth
Apps: 38 **Goals conceded:** 42 **Cards:** 2 **0**
Concede rate: Goal every 81 mins
Mins played: 3420 **Ave mins:** 90

Europe: Did not play
Mins: 0 **Goals conceded:** 0 **Cards:** 0 **0**

	League rating	European Cups	Internationals
Aug			
Sep			
Oct			
Nov			
Dec			
Jan			
Feb			
Mar			
Apr			
May			
June			
Total points for year	261,091	0	0

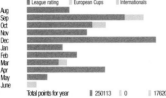
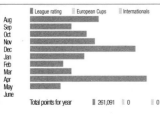
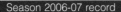
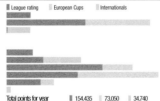

THINK YOU'RE A FOOTY KNOW-IT-ALL? TEST YOUR KNOWLEDGE ON THE FOUR QUIZ PAGES IN THIS ANNUAL. FILL IN YOUR ANSWERS ON PAGE 94 AND SEE HOW MANY YOU SCORED OUT OF 200!

NAME THE MANAGER

Can you name these current international managers and the countries they coach?

1

2

3

4

5

WHO SAID THAT?

The world of football can throw some unbelievable soundbites, but do you know who came up with these pearls of wisdom?

1. Who was Arsene Wenger talking about in 2006 when he said: "His only weakness is to believe he has no weakness"?
2. After returning from injury, which Boro player said: "My wife was having serious doubts about whether I was a footballer"?
3. Which Premiership manager said: "Pressure? What pressure? Pressure is poor people trying to feed their families"?
4. During the 2006 World Cup, which manager said: "Money isn't everything in life. I need to have sunshine, wear shorts…"
5. After beating Manchester United which manager said: "There must be a rule somewhere that says we don't go through"?
6. In November 2006 who said: "Football's a difficult business and aren't they prima donnas"?
7. Which manager said: "Please don't call me arrogant, but I'm European champion and I think I'm a special one."
8. In 2006 which manager said: "Most managers get booted out the back door… I was clapped out of the front door"?
9. Talking about the England job who said: "I've got the passion but no idea of tactics. I'd be like the black Kevin Keegan"?
10. In 2006, after his 736th game for Grimsby, who said: "I'm on first name terms with half the crowd"?
11. Talking about David Beckham, in July 2007 who said: "He's got two legs and two arms just like everybody else"?
12. In 2007, which new Premiership manager said: "Everyone needs to chill out and relax and let me do my job".

GUESS THE PUNDIT

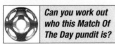 Can you work out who this Match Of The Day pundit is?

BORN WINNERS

Can you match these footballers with their place of birth?

1. JENS LEHMAN	A. PARIS, FRANCE
2. FRANK LAMPARD	B. NOTTINGHAM
3. WES BROWN	C. ROMFORD, ENGLAND
4. LOUIS SAHA	D. ESSEN, GERMANY
5. PETER CROUCH	E. MANCHESTER, ENGLAND
6. JERMAINE JENAS	F. MACCLESFIELD

GETTING SHIRTY

Can you name the players who last season wore the following shirt numbers for their clubs…

1	BOLTON WANDERERS 6
	6 _____
2	CHELSEA 7
	7 _____
3	MANCHESTER CITY 8
	8 _____
4	TOTTENHAM 25
	25 _____
5	CHELSEA 26
	26 _____
6	ARSENAL 32
	32 _____

HOW MUCH CAN YOU REMEMBER ABOUT THE 2006-07 SEASON?

1. Name the Argentinians who signed for West Ham?
2. Gary Speed became the second player to score in every Premier season. With whom did he share the honour?
3. After the World Cup who said: "I want to play for Real Madrid."
4. With which Championship team did Aston Villa's Lee Hendrie go on loan?
5. Name the first Arsenal player to score at the Emirates Stadium?
6. Brazil played two friendlies in London. Can you name their opponents?
7. Which newly promoted club did Everton play on the opening day of the season?
8. How many points did Chelsea take off Barcelona in the Champions League?
9. Who was Manchester United's shirt sponsor for the 2006-07 season?
10. What Real Madrid squad number was allocated to Ronaldo?
11. Which Israeli team did Liverpool knock out of the Champions League?
12. How many Premier teams had a third kit last season?

EURO 2

GET READY, THE EUROPEAN Championships are now just months away! Last time around Greece shocked a football mad continent with their astonishing victory over hosts Portugal, but could the same thing happen again? While a rank outsider is unlikely to win twice in a row, Euro 2008 is looking set to be every bit the global sporting occasion. From humble beginnings, in the last 20 years the tournament has become the world's second biggest sporting event, only topped by the World Cup.

For all the teams taking part, pride will be at stake. And while it's unlikely that we'll see the hosts in the final again this time, many of the world's greatest players will be on show in a festival of football that will dominate our lives for three weeks next June. Fans from all over the globe will be tuning in to watch.

Euro 2004 broke all television records for the tournament, with an average 150 million live viewers for each of the 31 matches. The final was seen by a worldwide audience of 279 million, while 7.9 billion TV viewers tuned in to watch the tournament as a whole. With even more excitement surrounding the forthcoming tournament, this will make Euro 2008 by far the largest sporting event that has ever been staged in either Austria and Switzerland and for three weeks it will be the talk of every football fan is Europe. With that being so, it's time to start going Euro 2008 mad!

HOW BIG IS THE TOURNAMENT?

Here are a few figures to show you how fantastic the European Championships are...

● In England, 12.4 million viewers saw English athlete Kelly Holmes win 1500m Olympic gold medal in Athens, while the Euro 2004 quarter-final between England and Portugal was watched by a TV audience of 21 million.

● In Germany, 13.2 million viewers watched the opening ceremony of the Olympic Games, while the Euro 2004 final was seen 24.7 million people.

● The ten highest television viewing figures in Switzerland in 2004 were all for European Championship matches.

● Euro 2004 was watched by 446 million viewers in America, 986 million viewers in Africa and as many as 1.1 billion viewers in Asia.

BERN

Stadium: Stade de Suisse, Wankdorf	Capacity: 32,000
Club: BSC Young Boys	City population: 120,000

Formerly the Wankdorf Stadium, the venue of the 'Miracle Of Bern', West Germany's famous victory over Hungary in the 1954 World Cup Final. The famous old stadium was demolished in August 2001 and was replaced in 2005 by a modern arena, featuring an artificial pitch. The ground contains one single red seat, the first to be installed – the remainder are black and yellow.

FIXTURES

JUNE 9: C1 v C2 (8.45pm)
JUNE 13: C1 v C4 (8.45pm)
JUNE 17: C1 v C3 (8.45pm)

BASEL

March 2001 saw the opening of the new St Jakob-Park (in English, St James' Park). Designed by the same architects responsible for London's Tate Modern and Beijing's Olympic Stadium, the new complex cost almost £100m to build and it houses 32 shops, plus two restaurants. The stadium has an ultra-modern infrastructure, including solar panels on the roof, which supply much of the power needed. Famous games at the old arena include the 1969, 1975 and 1984 European Cup Winners' Cup final.

Stadium: St Jakob-Park	Capacity: 42,500
Club: FC Basel	City population: 160,000

FIXTURES

JUNE 7: A1 v A2 (6pm)
JUNE 11: A1 v A4 (8.45pm)
JUNE 15: A1 v A3 (8.45pm)
JUNE 19: Quarter-final 1: WA v RB (8.45pm)
JUNE 21: Quarter-final 2: WC v RD (8.45pm)
JUNE 25: Semi-final 1: W25 v W26 (8.45pm)

SWITZERLAND

GENEVA

The home of Swiss first division side Servette, the new stadium opened in March 2003 after three years in construction. The first international was played at the ground just a month later when Switzerland took on Italy. The ground also staged the neutral clash between England and Argentina in 2005. It has also staged Rugby Union matches.

Stadium: Stade de Genève	Capacity: 30,000
Club: Servette FC	City population: 180,000

FIXTURES

JUNE 7: A3 v A4 (8.45)
JUNE 11: A2 v A3 (6pm)
JUNE 15: A4 v A2 (8.45pm)

008

Everything you could possibly need to know about Euro 2008 can be found here. So get set for the big kick-off!

© 2004 UEFA TM

EURO2008
Austria-Switzerland

INNSBRUCK

Replacing the Tivoli Stadium, Innsbruck got its new 17,400-capacity arena in 2000, but the Tivoli Neu will be extended to 30,000 in time for the 2008 finals. The stadium is part of the Olympiaworld Innsbruck complex that includes the renovated Olympic ice hall and a sports centre. Although home club FC Wacker Tirol regard themselves as the spiritual continuation of FC Tirol Innsbruck, who went bankrupt in 2002, they are not legally entitled to claim the honours won by the club's predecessor.

Stadium: Stadion Tivoli Neu **Capacity:** 30,000
Club: FC Wacker Tirol **City population:** 130,000

FIXTURES

JUNE 10: D3 v D4 (6pm)
JUNE 14: D2 v D3 (6pm)
JUNE 18: D4 v D2 (8.45pm)

SALZBURG

Situated adjacent to Salzburg airport, the stadium was opened in March 2003 with a capacity of 18,686, which will be raised to 30,000 in time for the finals. It is the only stadium in the Austrian Bundesliga to feature an artificial pitch, which was installed in 2005.

Stadium: EM Stadion Wals-Siezenheim **Capacity:** 30,000
Club: Red Bull Salzburg **City population:** 146,000

FIXTURES

JUNE 10: D1 v D2 (8.45pm)
JUNE 14: D1 v D4 (8.45pm)
JUNE 18: D1 v D3 (8.45pm)

AUSTRIA

ZURICH

VIENNA

Stadium: Ernst-Happel-Stadion **Capacity:** 50,000
Club: None **City population:** 1,500,000

The largest stadium in Austria, it was previously known as the Prater Stadium and opened in 1931. Before renovation its record attendance for an international was 92,708. It was renamed in 1992 after Ernst Happel, the great Austrian coach. It hosted the European Cup finals of 1964, '87, '90 and '95, plus Manchester City's 1970 European Cup Winners' Cup triumph. By UEFA standards it is graded as a five star stadium and it will stage the final. No club side calls it home, but both FK Austria Wien and SK Rapid Wien play their big European ties at the ground.

FIXTURES

JUNE 8: B1 v B2 (6pm)
JUNE 12: B1 v B4 (8.45pm)
JUNE 16: B1 v B3 (8.45pm)
JUNE 20: Quarter-final 3: WB v RA (8.45pm)
JUNE 22: Quarter-final 4: WD v RC (8.45pm)
JUNE 26: Semi-final 2: W27 v W28 (8.45pm)
JUNE 29: Final – W29 v W30 (8.45pm)

Stadium: Letzigrund Stadion **Capacity:** 30,000
Club: FC Zürich **City population:** 340,000

In preparation for Euro 2008 Zurich has gained a brand new stadium, built to replace the existing Letzigrund Stadium. With a running track around the football pitch, it was regarded as a respected athletics venue and witnessed the breaking of more than 20 world records. As an eco-friendly measure, the roof will be covered with vegetation and will rise just 16 metres above street level.

FIXTURES

JUNE 9: C3 v C4 (6pm)
JUNE 13: C2 v C3 (6pm)
JUNE 17: C4 v C2 (8.45pm)

KLAGENFURT

Situated near Wörthersee, the large lake near to Klagenfurt's centre, a brand new £45m football stadium replaced the 11,000-capacity Wörthersee Stadion, which was demolished in 2005. The design is similar to St Jakob Park in Basel. The 32,000 capacity will be reduced to 12,000 after Euro 2008. Its first international game is scheduled for September 2007 between Austria and Japan.

Stadium: Wörthersee Stadion **Capacity:** 30,000
Club: FC Kärnten **City population:** 1,000

FIXTURES

JUNE 8: B3 v B4 (8.45pm)
JUNE 12: B2 v B3 (6pm)
JUNE 16: B4 v B2 (8.45pm)

The Euro 2008 draw is happening on December 2, 2007. If you fill in the team names after the draw you will know the fixtures for the first stage of the tournament. Then watch the *Match Of The Day* team's coverage of the tournament, filling in the results as you go.

GROUP STAGES

GROUP A

FIXTURES		
TEAM A1		
Switzerland		
TEAM A2		
TEAM A3		
TEAM A4		

FIXTURES		
JUNE 7: MATCH 1: **A1 v A2** (6pm) BASLE	v	
JUNE 7: MATCH 2: **A3 v A4** (8.45pm) GENEVA	v	
JUNE 11: MATCH 9: **A2 v A3** (6pm) GENEVA	v	
JUNE 11: MATCH 10: **A1 v A4** (8.45pm) BASLE	v	
JUNE 15: MATCH 17: **A1 v A3** (8.45pm) BASLE	v	
JUNE 15: MATCH 18: **A4 v A2** (8.45pm) GENEVA	v	

FINAL GROUP TABLE

	P	W	D	L	F	A	Pts
1							
2							
3							
4							

GROUP B

FIXTURES		
TEAM B1		
Austria		
TEAM B2		
TEAM B3		
TEAM B4		

FIXTURES		
JUNE 8: MATCH 3: **B1 v B2** (6pm) VIENNA	v	
JUNE 8: MATCH 4: **B3 v B4** (8.45pm) KLAGENFURT	v	
JUNE 12: MATCH 11: **B2 v B3** (6pm) KLAGENFURT	v	
JUNE 12: MATCH 12: **B1 v B4** (8.45pm) VIENNA	v	
JUNE 16: MATCH 19: **B4 v B2** (8.45pm) KLAGENFURT	v	
JUNE 16: MATCH 20: **B1 v B3** (8.45pm) VIENNA	v	

FINAL GROUP TABLE

	P	W	D	L	F	A	Pts
1							
2							
3							
4							

GROUP C

FIXTURES		
TEAM C1		
TEAM C2		
TEAM C3		
TEAM C4		

FIXTURES		
JUNE 9: MATCH 5: **C3 v C4** (6pm) ZURICH	v	
JUNE 9: MATCH 6: **C1 v C2** (8.45pm) BERN	v	
JUNE 13: MATCH 13: **C2 v C3** (6pm) ZURICH	v	
JUNE 13: MATCH 14: **C1 v C4** (8.45pm) BERN	v	
JUNE 17: MATCH 21: **C1 v C3** (8.45pm) BERN	v	
JUNE 17: MATCH 22: **C4 v C2** (8.45pm) ZURICH	v	

FINAL GROUP TABLE

	P	W	D	L	F	A	Pts
1							
2							
3							
4							

GROUP D

FIXTURES		
TEAM D1		
TEAM D2		
TEAM D3		
TEAM D4		

FIXTURES		
JUNE 10: MATCH 7: **D3 v D4** (6PM) INNSBRUCK	v	
JUNE 10: MATCH 8: **D1 v D2** (8.45pm) SALZBURG	v	
JUNE 14: MATCH 15: **D2 v D3** (6pm) INNSBRUCK	v	
JUNE 14: MATCH 16: **D1 v D4** (8.45pm) SALZBURG	v	
JUNE 18: MATCH 23: **D1 v D3** (8.45pm) SALZBURG	v	
JUNE 18: MATCH 24: **D4 v D2** (8.45pm) INNSBRUCK	v	

FINAL GROUP TABLE

	P	W	D	L	F	A	Pts
1							
2							
3							
4							

QUARTER-FINALS

QUARTER-FINAL 1 JUNE 19 (8.45pm) BASLE

WINNER OF GROUP A

V

RUNNER-UP OF GROUP B

QUARTER-FINAL 2 JUNE 20 (8.45pm) VIENNA

WINNER OF GROUP B

V

V RUNNER-UP OF GROUP A

QUARTER-FINAL 3 JUNE 21 (8.45pm) BASLE

WINNER OF GROUP C

V

RUNNER-UP OF GROUP D

QUARTER-FINAL 4 JUNE 22 (8.45pm) VIENNA

WINNER OF GROUP D

V

RUNNER-UP OF GROUP C

SEMI-FINALS

SEMI-FINAL 1 JUNE 25 (8.45pm) BASLE

WINNER OF QUARTER-FINAL 1

V

WINNER OF QUARTER-FINAL 2

SEMI-FINAL 2 JUNE 26 (8.45pm) VIENNA

WINNER OF QUARTER-FINAL 3

V

WINNER OF QUARTER-FINAL 4

FINALS

FINAL JUNE 29 (8.45pm) VIENNA

WINNER OF SEMI-FINAL 1

V

WINNER OF SEMI-FINAL 2

THE HISTORY OF THE
EUROPEAN
CHAMPIONSHIP

With Euro 2008 just around the corner, here's your complete guide to the history of the European Championships.

THE EUROPEAN CHAMPIONSHIP, OR THE European Nations Cup as it was originally called, began in 1960, but the idea had originally been suggested in 1927. At that time, however, getting the World Cup off the ground was the priority. When UEFA was created in 1954 the idea was raised once again and it was soon agreed to hold the tournament every four years. But UEFA initially struggled to find enough countries willing to compete. The four British nations were among those who refused, along with West Germany, Italy and the 1958 World Cup runners-up Sweden.

In the end, 17 out of 33 countries affiliated to UEFA agreed to take part, and after a two-legged eliminator between Ireland and Czechoslovakia had whittled the number of sides down to an even 16, the qualification process could begin. The 16 nations to enter were Austria, Bulgaria, Czechoslovakia, Denmark, France, East Germany, Greece, Hungary, Norway, Poland, Portugal, Romania, Soviet Union, Spain, Turkey, and Yugoslavia. The entry fee was £50 and it was agreed that the gate receipts would be split 50-50 between FIFA and UEFA.

The initial structure of the competition was very different from the competition that we know today. Teams played home and away matches, the losing team being eliminated, and the winner proceeding to the next round. The hosts had to qualify in the same manner as the other sides. The final tournament in France consisted of just four matches – the semi-finals, the third place play-off and the final. It was contested over five days between July 6 and 10 in Paris and Marseilles and the Soviet Union were crowned the first European champions.

The competition has grown out of all recognition in the last 48 years, so take a look back at how the competition has evolved…

FRANCE 1960

WINNER **SOVIET UNION** (2-1 v Yugoslavia)

THE TOURNAMENT Only four teams contested the final stages. The hosts threw away a 4-2 lead, allowing Yugoslavia to progress to the final, while the Soviet Union proved much too strong for Czechoslovakia in the other semi-final, winning 3-0.

THE FINAL Played under floodlights at the Parc Des Princes Stadium in Paris, the final of the first European Nations Cup, as it was called at the time, was blighted by persistent drizzle, but it was still a credit to both sides. The Yugoslavs took the lead in the 43rd minute but legendary Soviet keeper Lev Yashin kept his team in the game and enabled them to snatch victory in extra-time.

TOP SCORER: **2 goals** Heutte (France), Ivanov (Soviet Union), Ponedelnik (Soviet Union), Galic (Yugoslavia), Jerkovic (Yugoslavia) FASTEST GOAL: **11 minutes** Gallic (Yugoslavia v France) TOTAL GOALS: **17**

SPAIN 1964

WINNER **SPAIN** (2-1 v Soviet Union)

THE TOURNAMENT Spain, Hungary, Soviet Union and Denmark contested the finals, staged in Madrid and Barcelona over four days in June 1964. It failed to capture the public imagination outside of Spain, although Luxembourg's shock victory over Holland in qualification had created headlines around the world.

THE FINAL Played in front of a crowd of 125,000 at the Bernabéu in Madrid, this still stand as the highest attendance for a European Championship final. The scores stood at 1-1 inside ten minutes, but the Soviets packed their defence, making it a tense game until Spain took the lead through Zaragoza centre-forward Marcelino, who scored the winner with a diving header in the 84th minute.

TOP SCORER: **2 goals** Pereda (Spain), Bene (Hungary), Novák (Hungary) FASTEST GOAL: **6 minutes** Jesus Maria Pereda (Spain v Soviet Union) TOTAL GOALS: **13**

Greece is the word!
The surprise winners
of Euro 2004!

ITALY 1968

WINNER **ITALY** (1-1, 2-0 v Yugoslavia)

THE TOURNAMENT In 1968 it became the European Football Championship and for the first time eight qualifying groups decided the four teams – England, Italy, Soviet Union and Yugoslavia – who would contest the finals. In the semi-final against Yugoslavia, Alan Mullery became the first England player to be sent-off.

THE FINAL The hosts were the favourites to win in front of a 69,000 home crowd in Rome, but Yugoslavia dominated, legendary keeper Dino Zoff keeping Italy in the game. With the scores level after extra-time, the final was settled after a replay two days later. Italy had made five changes to their team, and the transformed team didn't give Yugoslavia a chance.

TOP SCORER: 2 goals Dzajic (Yugoslavia) **FASTEST GOAL: 11 mins** Riva (Italy v Yugoslavia replay) **TOTAL GOALS: 7**

BELGIUM 1972

WINNER **WEST GERMANY** (3-0 v Soviet Union)

THE TOURNAMENT Although Belgium hosted the four-team tournament, home advantage counted for little, as their German opponents brought so many fans to Antwerp. It was the visitors who triumphed in front of a crowd of 60,000 and such was the draw of the game on live TV, only 2000 turned up to watch the other semi, between Hungary and Soviet Union.

THE FINAL The West Germans were on the offensive from the start, mounting wave after wave of attack at the Heysel Stadium. Gerd Müller ran the Soviet defence ragged and scored two of his team's three goals as West Germany lifted the trophy in front of a crowd of 43,437.

TOP SCORER: 4 goals Gerd Müller (West Germany) **FASTEST GOAL: 24 mins** Lambert (Belgium v Hungary); Müller (West Germany v Belgium) **TOTAL GOALS: 10**

YUGOSLAVIA 1976

WINNER **CZECHOSLOVAKIA** (2-2 v West Germany, 5-3 on pens)

THE TOURNAMENT Yugoslavia 76 was one of the most closely fought tournaments ever staged. Every match, both semi-finals, the final and third-place play-off went into extra-time, with Holland and Yugoslavia the unlucky semi-finalists.

THE FINAL The highly-fancied West Germans were stunned by the attacking start of the Czechs at Belgrade's Red Star Stadium and after 25 minutes they were 2-0 down. The Germans attacked relentlessly, equalising in the final minute. But in the penalty shoot-out Uli Hoeness blasted the ball over and the Czechs lifted the trophy, despite having lost 3-0 to England in qualification.

TOP SCORER: 4 goals Dieter Müller (West Germany) **FASTEST GOAL: 8 mins** Jan Svehlik (Czechoslovakia v West Germany) **TOTAL GOALS: 19**

ITALY 1980

WINNER **WEST GERMANY** (2-1 v Belgium)

THE TOURNAMENT Even the expansion of Euro 80 to an eight-team tournament could not save the competition from the negative football, poor refereeing and hooliganism. The opening fixture of the finals, between West Germany and Czechoslovakia, attracted just 11,000 fans in Rome.

THE FINAL Belgium's refusal to surrender in the final at Rome's Olympic Stadium ensured that a dull competition was brought to an exciting climax, but with just a minute remaining, Hrubesch met Rummenigge's corner to win it for the West Germans.

TOP SCORER: 3 goals Klaus Allofs (West Germany) **FASTEST GOAL: 6 mins** Antonin Panenka (Czechoslovakia v Greece)**TOTAL GOALS: 27**

FRANCE 1984

WINNER **FRANCE** (2-0 v Spain)

THE TOURNAMENT Euro 84 produced some of the finest football that the competition had ever seen, despite the absence of Holland, England and World Cup holders Italy, who all failed to qualify. France and West Germany were favourites, but the Germans were knocked out of the competition at the group stage by a last-minute goal from Spain.

THE FINAL In front of a home crowd of 47,368 at Parc Des Princes Stadium in Paris, France lifted the trophy, but they were helped by a mistake from the Spanish keeper, who let in a Platini free-kick. As Spain threw players forward in search of an equaliser, Bellone broke clear to chip the keeper for France's second.

TOP SCORER: 9 goals Platini (France) **FASTEST GOAL: 3 mins** Platini (France v Belgium) **TOTAL GOALS: 41**

???????????????

WEST GERMANY 1988

WINNER **HOLLAND** (2-0 v Soviet Union)

THE TOURNAMENT The best championship since 1976, but this time all the leading nations except defending champions France made it to the finals. England might have wished they had stayed at home though, eventually returning without a point from three games.

THE FINAL Twelve minutes before half-time Ruud Gullit headed Holland in front, but the final will always be remembered for Marco Van Basten's wonder goal ten minutes into the second-half, making him the tournament's top scorer and ensuring his team lifted the trophy in front of a crowd of 72,308 at Munich's Olympic Stadium. Despite appearing in two World Cup finals, it was Holland's first major competition triumph.

TOP SCORER: 5 goals Van Basten (Holland) **FASTEST GOAL: 3 mins** Aleinikov (England v Soviet Union) **TOTAL GOALS: 34**

SWEDEN 1992

WINNER **DENMARK** (2-0 v Germany)

THE TOURNAMENT An extraordinary competition staged as Europe was in flux. The players of failed qualifiers Denmark were recalled from their summer holidays to replace a Yugoslav team disqualified in line with United Nations sanctions. The former Soviet Union competed as the Commonwealth Of Independent States (CIS), while East and West Germany were represented by a single unified country.

THE FINAL Germany started well in the final in Gothenburg, but the Danes soaked up the early pressure and took the lead in the 18th minute, when Jensen rifled the ball into the net. Germany tried to reassert themselves but were twice denied by keeper Peter Schmeichel. With 12 minutes left Denmark sealed a famous win when Kim Vilfort made it 2-0.

TOP SCORERS: 3 goals Bergkamp (Holland), Brolin (Sweden), Larsen (Denmark), Riedle (Germany) **FASTEST GOAL: 2 mins** Rijkaard (Holland v Germany) **TOTAL GOALS: 32**

Didier Deschamps lifts the trophy for France in 2000.

ENGLAND 1996

WINNER **GERMANY** (2-1 v Czech Republic)

THE TOURNAMENT With the number of teams doubled to 16, this was the first championship in its current format and it delivered three weeks of fantastic goals, enthusiastic support and penalty shoot-outs. England progressed to the semi-finals, via thrilling victories over Scotland and Holland, and it took a rollercoaster encounter with Germany, and a penalty shoot-out, to finally dispatch the hosts.

THE FINAL The enthusiastic spirit of Euro 96 continued into the final at Wembley. Germany were favourites but fell behind to a 59th minute penalty. Substitute Oliver Bierhoff equalised only four minutes after coming on, before scoring the first ever golden goal in a major final with just four minutes of extra-time on the clock.

TOP SCORERS: 5 goals Shearer (England) **FASTEST GOAL: 3 mins** Shearer (England v Germany); Stoichkov (Bulgaria v Romania) **TOTAL GOALS: 64**

BELGIUM/HOLLAND 2000

WINNER **FRANCE** (2-1 v Italy)

THE TOURNAMENT Many would have preferred to see the attacking play of Holland against France make it to the final at De Kuip Stadium in Rotterdam rather than the defensive Italians, but nevertheless the climax to Euro 2000 was a fascinating affair.

THE FINAL Having gone a goal down in the 54th minute to Delvecchio, France threw on subs Wiltord and Trezeguet after 75 minutes. Wiltord scored the injury time goal that sent the game into extra-time and Trezeguet notching the golden goal winner.

TOP SCORERS: 5 goals Kluivert (Holland), Milosevic (Yugoslavia) **FASTEST GOAL: 3 mins** Scholes (England v Portugal) **TOTAL GOALS: 85 goals**

PORTUGAL 2004

WINNER **GREECE** (1-0 v Portugal)

THE TOURNAMENT Euro 2004 was a tournament like no other, with a rank outsider making it all the way to the final and snatching the biggest prize in European football. During the course of the tournament Greece dispatched the highly rated France and the Czech Republic and they also beat hosts Portugal twice, in their first game and in the final.

THE FINAL When Greece lifted the famous trophy in front of a home crowd of 62,865 in Lisbon, they had pulled off one of world football's biggest upsets. An Angelos Charisteas header on 57 minutes was enough to put Portugal to the sword, making the Werder Bremen striker a modern-day God in his homeland. Greece had ended the tournament as they had started it, humbling hosts Portugal into submission.

TOP SCORER: 5 goals Baros (Czech Republic) **FASTEST GOAL: 68 seconds** Kirichenko (Russia v Greece) **TOTAL GOALS 77**

CLUB GUIDE

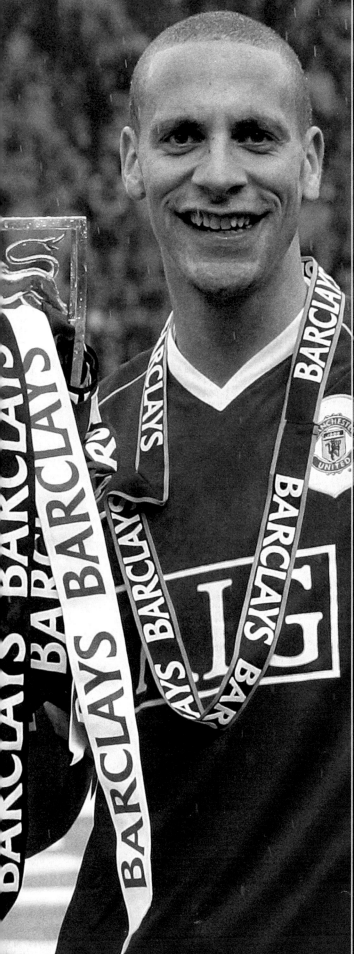

Everything you needed to know about the Premier League season, team by team, club by club!

SATURDAY NIGHT IN FRONT OF THE TELLY WATCHING Match Of The Day will be so much easier now you have the Match Of The Day Annual 2008 to keep you informed. You'll be able to keep it with you while you watch the show and look up the players to see what kind of form they've been in for club and country throughout the last season.

For every club in last season's Premiership we list last season's squads, with each player's record. We also give you all of last season's results and goalscorers so you can see how each team is doing compared to last year. All in all, you have everything you need to know about last season's campaign, right at your fingertips.

For each striker and midfielder we show their attacking strengths, and for each defender and goalkeeper we highlight how many goals their team has conceded while the player was on the pitch. This way you get a clear picture of just how much each player contributed to his team's performance.

Through the last year we've studied the contributions made by every major player to his team's performance, and it has helped us to come up with a series of rankings for every player in the Premiership, regardless of where they played last year. You can see where they are ranked within their respective leagues, you can see where they are ranked in the world by position, and you can see where they are ranked in the world regardless of position. Sounds like stat heaven – you'll soon be giving Motty a run for his money!

PREMIERSHIP CLUB GUIDE CONTENTS

>>>>> *NOW TURN OVER* >>>>>

ARSENAL

ARSENAL FACTS

MANAGER	CAPTAIN
ARSENE WENGER	THIERRY HENRY

CLUB

Stadium: Emirates Stadium

Capacity: 60,432

Average Attendance 2006-07: 60,045

Pitch Size: 105m x 68m

Website: www.arsenal.com

STRIP

Home: Red shirts, white shorts

Away: White shirts, Maroon shorts

SPONSORS

Shirt: Fly Emirates

Kit Partner: Nike

CHEAPEST TICKET PRICES

Adult: £32

Junior: £13

RECORDS

Record Home Attendance: 73,707 v RC Lens (European Cup, Wembley Nov. 25 1998

Record Victory: 12-0 v Loughborough Town (league) March 12 1900; v Ashford United (FA Cup) October 14 1893

Record Defeat: 0-6 Derby County (FA Cup) January 28 1899

Most League Goals: Thierry Henry 174

Most League Apps: David O'Leary 558

Most Capped Player: Patrick Vieira, 79 (France)

HONOURS

Premiership: 1998, 2002, 2004

Division One: 1931, 1933, 1934, 1935, 1938, 1948, 1953, 1971, 1989, 1991

FA Cup: 1930, 1936, 1950, 1971, 1979, 1993, 1998, 2002, 2003, 2005

League Cup: 1987, 1993

UEFA Cup: 1970 (as Fairs Cup)

European Cup Winners Cup: 1994

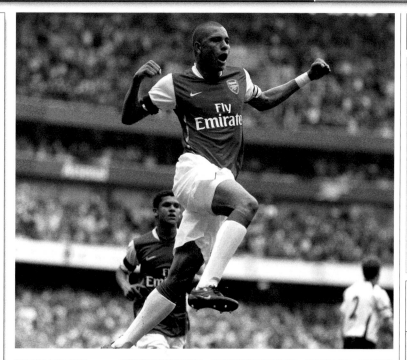

SQUAD RECORD 2006-07

	CLUB				INTERNATIONAL			POSITIONAL RANKING		OVERALL RANKING
	Mins	Goals	Mins per goal	% played	Country	Games	Goals	Domestic	World	All positions
GOALKEEPERS		CONCEDED					CONCEDED			
JENS LEHMANN	3240	35	93	95%	Germany	8	4	3	4	19
DEFENDERS		CONCEDED					CONCEDED			
HABIB KOLO TOURE	3150	33	95	92%	Ivory Coast	3	0	8	16	46
WILLIAM GALLAS	1880	18	104	55%	France	9	2	24	64	169
GAEL CLICHY	2350	27	87	69%	France	0	0	35	107	289
EMMANUEL EBOUE	2059	24	86	60%	Ivory Coast	2	1	42	140	391
JOHAN DJOUROU	1539	12	128	45%	Switzerland	0	0	63	297	792
JUSTIN HOYTE	1503	13	116	44%	England	0	0	72	357	982
PHILIPPE SENDEROS	809	11	74	24%	Switzerland	4	9	121	577	1568
MIDFIELDERS		SCORED					SCORED			
GILBERTO SILVA	2933	10	293	86%	Brazil	11	0	5	8	20
CESC FABREGAS	3182	2	1591	93%	Spain	8	0	6	9	21
ALEXANDER HLEB	2355	2	1178	69%	Belarus	0	0	28	65	208
TOMAS ROSICKY	1828	3	609	53%	Czech Rep.	8	0	31	74	232
FREDRIK LJUNGBERG	1198	0	0	35%	Sweden	5	0	79	366	1017
MATHIEU FLAMINI	966	3	322	28%	France	0	0	114	539	1528
FORWARDS		SCORED					SCORED			
EMMANUEL ADEBAYOR	1986	8	248	58%	Togo	1	0	15	57	374
ROBIN VAN PERSIE	1457	11	132	43%	Holland	5	5	27	100	583
THIERRY HENRY	1474	10	147	43%	France	7	3	21	72	422
JULIO BAPTISTA	1138	3	379	33%	Brazil	4	0	100	494	1385

KEY: Club stats are all for the 2006-07 season. Mins = Minutes played in the league for club; Goals conceded = goals let in when the player is on the pitch; Goals scored = scored by the player; Mins per goal = number of minutes on average between each goal conceded or scored; % played = the percentage of the league season the player played; Domestic = player ranking by position in domestic league; World = player ranking by position in World; Overall Position = player ranking in world across all positions.

THE STARS OF LAST SEASON

TEAM OF THE SEASON

- G — Lehmann
- D — Eboue
- D — Gallas
- D — Toure
- D — Clichy
- M — Hleb
- M — Fabregas
- M — Gilberto
- M — Rosicky
- F — Henry
- F — Van Persie

G STAR GOALKEEPER

JENS LEHMANN: He left some of his World Cup form in Germany and was not among the league's top 15 shot-stoppers.

Average goals per game conceded by club	0.92
Goals per game conceded when player on pitch	0.97
Points per game club won when player on pitch	1.78
Minutes played	3420	Clean sheets	10

D STAR DEFENDER

KOLO TOURE: With Campbell departed Toure lead the defensive line for the Gunners, he was their rock at the back last year.

Goals per game conceded when player on pitch	0.94
Points per game club won when player on pitch	1.77
Goals scored by player	3
Minutes played	3150	Clean sheets	11

M STAR MIDFIELDER

TOMAS ROSICKY: Wenger's top signing in 2006 is pure class but left his scoring boots in the Czech Republic.

Goals per game conceded when player on pitch	0.84
Goals per game club scored when player on pitch	1.73
Goals scored by player	3
Minutes played	1828	Assists	2

F STAR FORWARD

ROBIN VAN PERSIE: He was injured scoring a goal against United but with the best 2006-07 Strike Rate in the league when he played.

Average goals per game scored by club	1.66
Goals per game scored when player on pitch	2.25
% of club goals scored by player	17.5
Minutes played	1457	Assists	5

2006-07 RESULTS ROUND-UP

☐ Premiership ☐ League Cup ☐ FA Cup ☐ UEFA Cup ☐ Champions League

Din Zagreb	A	3-0
Fabregas 63, 79, van Persie 64		
Aston Villa	H	1-1
Gilberto 84		
Din Zagreb	H	2-1
Ljungberg 77, Flamini 90		
Man City	A	0-1
Middlesbrough	H	1-1
Henry 67 pen		
Hamburg	A	2-1
Gilberto 12 pen, Rosicky 53		
Man Utd	A	1-0
Adebayor 85		
Sheff Utd	H	3-0
Gallas 65, Jagielka 69 og, Henry 80		
Porto	H	2-0
Henry 38, Hleb 48		

Charlton	A	2-1
van Persie 32, 49		
Watford	H	3-0
Stewart 33 og, Henry 43, Adebayor 67		
CSKA Moscow	A	0-1
Reading	A	4-0
Henry 1, 70 pen, Hleb 39, van Persie 50		
West Brom	A	2-0
Aliadiere 33 pen, 49		
Everton	H	1-1
van Persie 71		
CSKA Moscow	H	0-0
West Ham	A	0-1

Newcastle	H	1-1
Henry 70		
Hamburg	H	3-1
van Persie 52, Eboue 83, Baptista 88		
Bolton	A	1-3
Gilberto 45		
Fulham	A	1-2
van Persie 36		
Tottenham	H	3-0
Adebayor 20, Gilberto 42 pen, 72 pen		
Porto	A	0-0
Chelsea	A	1-1
Flamini 78		
Wigan	A	1-0
Adebayor 88		
Portsmouth	H	2-2
Adebayor 58, Gilberto 60		

Blackburn	H	6-2
Gilberto Silva 10, Hleb 23, Adebayor 27 pen, van Persie 85, 88, Flamini 90		
Watford	A	2-1
Gilberto Silva 19, van Persie 83		
Sheff Utd	A	0-1
Charlton	H	4-0
Henry 30 pen, Hoyte 45, van Persie 75 pen, 90		
Liverpool	A	3-1
Rosicky 37, 45, Henry 84		
Liverpool	A	6-3
Aliadiere 27, Baptista 40, 45, 60, 84, Song 45		
Blackburn	A	2-0
Toure 37, Henry 71		
Man Utd	H	2-1
van Persie 83, Henry 90		

Tottenham	A	2-2
Baptista 64, 77		
Bolton	H	1-1
Toure 78		
Tottenham	H	3-1
Adebayor 77, Aliadiere 105, Chimbonda 113 og		
Middlesbrough	A	1-1
Henry 77		
Wigan	H	2-1
Hall 81 og, Rosicky 84		
Bolton	A	3-1
Adebayor 13, 120, Ljungberg 108		
Blackburn	H	0-0
PSV	A	0-1
Chelsea	N	1-2
Walcott 12		

Blackburn	A	0-1
Reading	H	2-1
Gilberto Silva 51 pen, Baptista 62		
PSV	H	1-1
Alex 58 og		
Aston Villa	A	1-0
Diaby 10		
Everton	A	0-1

Liverpool	A	1-4
Gallas 73		
West Ham	H	0-1
Newcastle	A	0-0
Bolton	H	2-1
Rosicky 31, Fabregas 46		
Man City	H	3-1
Rosicky 12, Fabregas 73, Baptista 80		
Tottenham	A	2-2
Toure 64, Adebayor 78		
Fulham	H	3-1
Baptista 4, Adebayor 84, Gilberto Silva 87 pen		
Chelsea	H	1-1
Gilberto Silva 43 pen		
Portsmouth	A	0-0

ASTON VILLA

VILLA FACTS

MANAGER	CAPTAIN
MARTIN O'NEILL	GARETH BARRY

CLUB

Stadium: Villa Park

Capacity: 42,573

Average Attendance 2006-07: 36,214

Pitch Size: 105m x 66 metres

Website: www.avfc.co.uk

STRIP

Home: Claret shirts with blue sleeves, white shorts

Away: White shirts, light blue shorts

SPONSORS

Shirt: 32Red.com

Kit Partner: Hummel

CHEAPEST TICKET PRICES

Adult: £15.00

Junior: £7.00

RECORDS

Record Home Attendance: 78,588 v Derby County (FA Cup) March 2, 1946

Record Victory: 13-0 v Wednesday Old Athletic (FA Cup) October 30, 1886

Record Defeat: 1-8 v Blackburn (FA Cup)

Most League Goals: Harry Hampton (215)

Most League Apps: Charlie Aikin (561)

Most Capped Player: Steve Staunton 64 (Republic of Ireland)

HONOURS

Division One: 1894, 1896, 1897, 1899, 1900, 1910, 1981

Division Two: 1938, 1960

Division Three: 1972

FA Cup: 1887, 1895, 1897, 1905, 1913, 1920, 1957

League Cup: 1961, 1975, 1977, 1994, 1996

European Cup: 1982

SQUAD RECORD 2006-07

	CLUB				INTERNATIONAL			POSITIONAL RANKING		OVERALL RANKING
	Mins	Goals	Mins per goal	% played	Country	Games	Goals	Domestic	World	All positions
GOALKEEPERS		CONCEDED					CONCEDED			
THOMAS SORENSEN	2544	24	106	74%	Denmark	9	4	11	29	146
DEFENDERS		CONCEDED					CONCEDED			
OLOF MELLBERG	3375	39	87	99%	Sweden	5	4	10	24	75
WILFRED BOUMA	1973	24	82	58%	Holland	4	1	47	157	446
PHILLIP BARDSLEY	1569	14	112	46%	England	0	0	73	361	992
LIAM RIDGEWELL	1766	23	77	52%	England	0	0	79	380	1035
GARY CAHILL	1745	26	67	51%	England	0	0	89	431	1173
AARON HUGHES	1292	18	72	38%	N Ireland	8	7	107	506	1377
MARTIN LAURSEN	1054	8	132	31%	Denmark	1	0	98	453	1244
MIDFIELDERS		SCORED					SCORED			
GARETH BARRY	3119	8	390	91%	England	1	0	15	33	97
STEVEN DAVIS	1652	0	0	48%	N Ireland	7	0	85	413	1145
STILIAN PETROV	2904	4	726	85%	Bulgaria	5	0	37	95	307
GAVIN MCCANN	2421	1	2421	71%	England	0	0	50	147	440
CRAIG GARDNER	971	2	486	28%	England	0	0	109	524	1477
FORWARDS		SCORED					SCORED			
GABRIEL AGBONLAHOR	3325	9	369	97%	England	0	0	8	28	198
JOHN ALIEU CAREW	1384	4	346	40%	Norway	6	3	30	114	683
JUAN PABLO ANGEL	1493	4	373	44%	Columbia	0	0	46	230	1220
LUKE MOORE	642	4	161	19%	England	0	0	65	361	1739
ASHLEY YOUNG	2778	5	556	81%	England	0	0	32	129	754

KEY: Club stats are all for the 2006-07 season. Mins = Minutes played in the league for club; Goals conceded = goals let in when the player is on the pitch; Goals scored = scored by the player; Mins per goal = number of minutes on average between each goal conceded or scored; % played = the percentage of the league season the player played; Domestic = player ranking by position in domestic league; World = player ranking by position in World; Overall Position = player ranking in world across all positions.

THE STARS OF LAST SEASON

TEAM OF THE SEASON

G Sorensen

D Bardsley | D Ridgewell | D Mellberg | D Bouma

M Davis | M McCann | M Petrov | M Barry

F Carew | F Agbonlahor

G STAR GOALKEEPER

THOMAS SORENSEN: The Danish star had the fifth best defensive record among keepers in the Premiership.

Average goals per game conceded by club	1.08
Goals per game conceded when player on pitch	0.85
Points per game club won when player on pitch	1.61
Minutes played 2544	Clean sheets 12

D STAR DEFENDER

OLOF MELLBERG: Scored the first goal of O'Neill's reign and, along with Distin, is the league's most under-rated centre-half.

Goals per game conceded when player on pitch	1.04
Points per game club won when player on pitch	1.35
Goals scored by player	1
Minutes played 3375	Clean sheets 13

M STAR MIDFIELDER

GARETH BARRY: O'Neill's choice as captain is increasingly dominant in midfield. He is also the league's joint top penalty scorer.

Goals per game conceded when player on pitch	1.10
Goals per game club scored when player on pitch	1.15
Goals scored by player	8
Minutes played 3119	Assists 4

F STAR FORWARD

GABRIEL AGBONLAHOR: He didn't get 500 minutes from O'Leary but now ranks as one of England's top attacking prospects.

Average goals per game scored by club	1.13
Goals per game scored when player on pitch	1.14
% of club goals scored by player	20.9
Minutes played 3325	Assists 6

2006-07 RESULTS ROUND-UP

■ Premiership ■ League Cup ■ FA Cup ■ UEFA Cup ■ Champions League

Arsenal	A	1-1
Mellberg 53		
Reading	H	2-1
Angel 33 pen, Barry 62		
Newcastle	H	2-0
L.Moore 5, Angel 38		
West Ham	A	1-1
Ridgewell 4		

Watford	A	0-0
Scunthorpe	A	2-1
Angel 42, 64		
Charlton	H	2-0
Agbonlahor 35, L.Moore 62		
Chelsea	A	1-1
Agbonlahor 45		

Tottenham	H	1-1
Barry 81		
Fulham	H	1-1
Barry 26 pen		
Leicester	A	3-2
Angel 5, Barry 45 pen, Agbonlahor 119		
Liverpool	A	1-3
Agbonlahor 56		
Blackburn	H	2-0
Barry 39 pen, Angel 50		
Chelsea	A	0-4
Everton	A	1-0
Sutton 42		
Wigan	A	0-0
Middlesbrough	H	1-1
Barry 45 pen		

Man City	H	1-3
McCann 66		
Portsmouth	A	2-2
Barry 37 pen, Angel 82		
Sheff Utd	A	2-2
Petrov 2, Baros 65		
Bolton	H	0-1
Man Utd	H	0-3
Tottenham	A	1-2
Barry 81		
Charlton	A	1-2
Barry 39 pen		
Chelsea	H	0-0
Man Utd	A	1-2
Baros 74		
Man Utd	A	1-3
Agbonlahor 52		

Watford	H	2-0
Mahon 86 og, Agbonlahor 90		
Newcastle	A	1-3
Young 25		
West Ham	H	1-0
Carew 36		

Reading	A	0-2
Fulham	A	1-1
Carew 21		
Arsenal	H	0-1
Liverpool	H	0-0
Everton	H	1-1
Agbonlahor 83		
Blackburn	A	2-1
Berger 34, Agbonlahor 73		
Wigan	H	1-1
Agbonlahor 50		
Middlesbrough	A	3-1
Gardner 45, L.Moore 70, Petrov 77		
Portsmouth	H	0-0
Man City	A	2-0
Carew 24, Maloney 75		

Sheff Utd	H	3-0
Agbonlahor 25, Young 42, Berger 59		
Bolton	A	2-2
Gardner 37, L.Moore 81		

BLACKBURN ROVERS

BLACKURN FACTS

MANAGER	CAPTAIN
MARK HUGHES	RYAN NELSON

CLUB

Stadium: Ewood Park

Capacity: 31,367

Average Attendance 2006-07: 21,566

Pitch Size: 105m x 68.6m

Website: www.rovers .co.uk

STRIP

Home: Blue and white shirts, white shorts

Away: Red and black shirts, black shorts

SPONSORS

Shirt: Bet 24 (£400,000 per year)

Kit Partner: Lonsdale

CHEAPEST TICKET PRICES

Adult: £20.00

Junior: £7.00

RECORDS

Record Home Attendance: 62,522 v Bolton (FA Cup) Mar 2 1929

Record Victory: 11-0 v Rossendale (FA Cup) October 13, 1884

Record Defeat: 0-8 v Arsenal (league) February 25, 1933

Most League Goals: Simon Garner (168)

Most League Apps: Derek Fazackerley (596)

Most Capped Player: Henning Berg, 52 (Norway)

HONOURS

Premiership: 1995

Division One: 1912, 1914

Division Two: 1939

Division Three: 1975

FA Cup: 1884, 1885, 1886, 1890, 1891, 1928

League Cup: 2002

SQUAD RECORD 2006-07

	CLUB				INTERNATIONAL			POSITIONAL RANKING		OVERALL RANKING
	Mins	Goals	Mins per goal	% played	Country	Games	Goals	Domestic	World	All positions
GOALKEEPERS		CONCEDED					CONCEDED			
BRAD FRIEDEL	3375	54	63	99%	United States	0	0	5	14	60
DEFENDERS		CONCEDED					CONCEDED			
BRETT EMERTON	2929	43	68	86%	Australia	4	5	20	57	151
ANDRE OOIJER	1712	26	66	50%	Holland	6	3	50	170	478
ZURAB KHIZANISHVILI	1567	20	78	46%	Georgia	4	5	82	386	1044
STEPHEN WARNOCK	1220	21	58	36%	England	0	0	93	443	1216
CHRISTOPHER SAMBA	1236	21	59	36%	Congo	0	0	100	468	1282
RYAN NELSEN	1080	19	57	32%	New Zealand	1	2	106	499	1357
STEPHANE HENCHOZ	826	11	75	24%	Switzerland	0	0	133	616	1701
MIDFIELDERS		SCORED					SCORED			
MORTEN GAMST PEDERSEN	3104	6	517	91%	Norway	7	2	12	27	81
DAVID BENTLEY	3069	4	767	90%	England	0	0	13	28	82
KERIMOGLU TUGAY	2202	1	2202	64%	Turkey	0	0	49	144	437
ROBBIE SAVAGE	1839	0	0	54%	Wales	0	0	51	157	453
AARON MOKOENA	1686	0	0	49%	South Africa	3	0	75	350	966
DAVID DUNN	1357	1	1357	40%	England	0	0	124	592	1666
FORWARDS		SCORED					SCORED			
BENNI MCCARTHY	3049	18	169	89%	South Africa	0	0	4	9	71
SHABANI NONDA	1555	7	222	45%	D.R. Congo	2	0	40	155	879
JASON ROBERTS	1031	4	258	30%	Grenada	0	0	51	284	1443
MATTHEW DERBYSHIRE	784	5	157	23%	England	0	0	60	339	1684

KEY: Club stats are all for the 2006-07 season. Mins = Minutes played in the league for club; Goals conceded = goals let in when the player is on the pitch; Goals scored = scored by the player; Mins per goal = number of minutes on average between each goal conceded or scored; % played = the percentage of the league season the player played; Domestic = player ranking by position in domestic league; World = player ranking by position in World; Overall Position = player ranking in world across all positions.

THE STARS OF LAST SEASON

TEAM OF THE SEASON

G Friedel

D Neill — **D** Khizanishvili — **D** Ooijer — **D** Samba

M Bentley — **M** Mokoena — **M** Savage — **M** Pedersen

F McCarthy — **F** Derbyshire

G STAR GOALKEEPER

BRAD FRIEDEL: The likable American put in his usual heavy workload behind a changing defence beset by injuries.

Average goals per game conceded by club	1.42
Goals per game conceded when player on pitch	1.44
Points per game club won when player on pitch	1.32
Minutes played	3375	Clean sheets	12

D STAR DEFENDER

ZURAB KHIZANISHVILI: The powerful Georgian began last season strongly, performing well alongside Ooijer.

Goals per game conceded when player on pitch	1.15
Points per game club won when player on pitch	1.35
Goals scored by player	0
Minutes played	1567	Clean sheets	4

M STAR MIDFIELDER

DAVID BENTLEY: He hit seven goals in all competitions and had 11 assists, showing the kind of form that led to an England call-up.

Goals per game conceded when player on pitch	1.27
Goals per game club scored when player on pitch	1.48
Goals scored by player	7
Minutes played	3069	Assists	11

F STAR FORWARD

BENNI MCCARTHY: The South African proved an inspired signing from Porto and only Didier Drogba hit more league goals.

Average goals per game scored by club	1.37
Goals per game scored when player on pitch	1.30
% of club goals scored by player	34.6
Minutes played	3049	Assists	2

2006-07 RESULTS ROUND-UP

■ Premiership ■ League Cup ■ FA Cup ■ UEFA Cup ■ Champions League

Portsmouth	A	0-3
Everton	H	1-1
McCarthy 50		
Chelsea	H	0-2
Sheff Utd	A	0-0

Salzburg	A	2-2
Savage 32, McCarthy 39		
Man City	H	4-2
Sinclair 16 og, Pedersen 43, McCarthy 66, Gallagher 88		
Middlesbrough	A	1-0
Nonda 27		
Salzburg	H	2-0
McCarthy 32, Bentley 56		
Wigan	H	2-1
Bentley 45, McCarthy 81		
Liverpool	A	1-1
McCarthy 17		
Wisla Krakow	A	2-1
Savage 56, Bentley 89		
Bolton	H	0-1
Chelsea	H	0-2

West Ham	A	1-2
Bentley 90		
Basel	H	3-0
Tugay 75, Jeffers 89 pen, McCarthy 90		
Aston Villa	A	0-2
Man Utd	H	0-1
Tottenham	H	1-1
Tugay 22		
Feyenoord	A	0-0
Fulham	H	2-0
Nonda 6, McCarthy 24		
Charlton	A	0-1
Newcastle	H	1-3
Pedersen 47		
Nancy	H	1-0
Neill 90		

Reading	A	2-1
McCarthy 64, Bentley 84		
Arsenal	A	2-6
Nonda 3 pen, 69		
Liverpool	H	1-0
McCarthy 49		
Middlesbrough	H	2-1
Nonda 9, McCarthy 74		
Wigan	A	3-0
Heskey 37 og, Derbyshire 58, McCarthy 76 pen		
Everton	A	4-1
Derbyshire 5, Pedersen 21, Gallagher 38, McCarthy 90		
Arsenal	H	0-2
Man City	A	3-0
Pedersen 44, 62, Derbyshire 90		

Watford	A	1-2
McCarthy 45		
Luton	A	4-0
Derbyshire 10, 56, McCarthy 36, Pedersen 74		
Chelsea	A	0-3
Sheff Utd	H	2-1
Pedersen 22, 90		

Everton	A	0-1
B Leverkusen	A	2-3
Bentley 39, Nonda 86		
Arsenal	A	0-0
B Leverkusen	H	0-0
Portsmouth	H	3-0
Nonda 1, 25, Warnock 50		
Arsenal	H	1-0
McCarthy 87		
Bolton	A	2-1
McCarthy 58 pen, 68 pen		
Man City	H	2-0
Mokoena 28, Derbyshire 90		
West Ham	H	1-2
Samba 47		
Man Utd	A	1-4
Derbyshire 29		

Aston Villa	H	1-2
McCarthy 24 pen		
Chelsea	N	1-2
Roberts 64		
Watford	H	3-1
Samba 7, Roberts 10, McCarthy 32		
Fulham	A	1-1
McCarthy 61		
Charlton	H	4-1
Roberts 60, 80, Hreidarsson 77 og, Derbyshire 83		
Newcastle	A	2-0
McCarthy 14, Roberts 73		
Tottenham	H	1-1
McCarthy 33		
Reading	H	3-3
McCarthy 21, Bentley 56, Derbyshire 67		

BOLTON FACTS

MANAGER	CAPTAIN
SAMMY LEE	KEVIN NOLAN

CLUB

Stadium: Reebok Stadium

Capacity: 27,879

Average Attendance 2006-07: 23,606

Pitch Size: 105m x 68m

Website: www.bwfc.co.uk

STRIP

Home: All white with red stripe around shoulder

Away: All black with blue shoulder flash

SPONSORS

Shirt: Reebok (£500,000 per year)

Kit Partner: Reebok

CHEAPEST TICKET PRICES

Adult: £31.00

Junior: £16.00

RECORDS

Record Home Attendance: 69,912 v Manchester City (FA Cup) February 18, 1933

Record Victory: 13-0 v Sheffield United (FA Cup) February 1, 1890

Record Defeat: 1-9 v Preston (FA Cup) December 10 1887

Most League Goals: Nat Lofthouse (255)

Most League Apps: Eddie Hopkinson (519)

Most Capped Player: Mark Fish, 34 (South Africa)

HONOURS

Division One: 1997

Division Two: 1909, 1978

Division Three: 1973

FA Cup: 1923, 1926, 1929, 1958

SQUAD RECORD 2006-07

	CLUB				INTERNATIONAL			POSITIONAL RANKING		OVERALL RANKING
	Mins	Goals	Mins per goal	% played	Country	Games	Goals	Domestic	World	All positions
GOALKEEPERS			CONCEDED				CONCEDED			
JUSSI JAASKELAINEN	3420	52	66	100%	Finland	9	7	7	22	103
DEFENDERS			CONCEDED				CONCEDED			
ABDOULAYE MEITE	3127	43	73	91%	Ivory Coast	4	1	33	90	242
NICKY HUNT	2627	35	75	77%	England	0	0	49	167	472
HENRIK PEDERSEN	926	16	58	27%	Denmark	0	0	120	576	1566
RICARDO GARDNER	1234	26	47	36%	Jamaica	0	0	126	597	1623
TAL BEN HAIM	2685	39	69	79%	Israel	6	6	51	171	479
ABDOULAYE FAYE	2520	40	63	74%	Senegal	4	4	71	349	956
MIDFIELDERS			SCORED				SCORED			
GARY SPEED	3257	8	407	95%	Wales	0	0	21	52	165
IVAN CAMPO	2837	4	709	83%	Spain	0	0	42	116	360
KEVIN NOLAN	2687	3	896	79%	England	0	0	43	123	378
ANDRANIK TEYMOURIAN	832	2	416	24%	Iran	0	0	136	647	1810
DAVID THOMPSON	732	0	0	21%	England	0	0	138	668	1880
STELIOS GIANNAKOPOULOS	934	0	0	27%	Greece	0	0	140	693	1973
IDAN TAL	522	0	0	15%	Israel	0	0	149	747	2123
FORWARDS			SCORED				SCORED			
NICOLAS ANELKA	3010	11	274	88%	France	7	3	9	29	203
EL HADJI DIOUF	2665	5	533	78%	Senegal	2	0	18	64	394
KEVIN DAVIES	2521	8	315	74%	England	0	0	20	67	411
RICARDO VAZ TE	855	0	0	25%	Portugal	0	0	70	373	1786

KEY: Club stats are all for the 2006-07 season. Mins = Minutes played in the league for club; Goals conceded = goals let in when the player is on the pitch; Goals scored = scored by the player; Mins per goal = number of minutes on average between each goal conceded or scored; % played = the percentage of the league season the player played; Domestic = player ranking by position in domestic league; World = player ranking by position in World; Overall Position = player ranking in world across all positions.

2006-07 RESULTS ROUND-UP

■ Premiership ■ League Cup ■ FA Cup ■ UEFA Cup ■ Champions League

Tottenham	H 2-0		
Davies 9, Campo 13			
Fulham	A 1-1		
Diouf 74 pen			
Charlton	A 0-2		
Watford	H 1-0		
Speed 90 pen			
Middlesbrough	H 0-0		
Walsall	A 3-1		
Nolan 68, Campo 88, Anelka 90			
Portsmouth	A 1-0		
Nolan 22			
Liverpool	H 2-0		
Speed 30, Campo 51			
Newcastle	A 2-1		
Diouf 55, 56			

Blackburn	A 1-0	
Campo 62		
Charlton	A 0-1	
Man Utd	H 0-4	

Wigan	H 0-1
Sheff Utd	A 2-2
Diouf 34, Davies 59	
Everton	A 0-1
Arsenal	H 3-1
Faye 9, Anelka 45, 76	
Chelsea	H 0-1
Reading	A 0-1
West Ham	H 4-0
Davies 17, 52, Diouf 77, Anelka 78	
Aston Villa	A 1-0
Speed 75 pen	
Man City	A 2-0
Anelka 8, 25	
Newcastle	H 2-1
Ramage 32 og, Anelka 57	

Portsmouth	H 3-2
Faye 30, Campo 40, Anelka 62	
Liverpool	A 0-3
Doncaster	A 4-0
Davies 8, Teimourian 22, 49, Tal 33	
Man City	H 0-0
Middlesbrough	A 1-5
Nolan 25	
Arsenal	A 1-1
Nolan 50	
Charlton	H 1-1
Pedersen 6	
Watford	A 1-0
Fulham	H 2-1
Speed 22 pen, Nolan 50	

Arsenal	H 1-3
Meite 90	
Tottenham	A 1-4
Speed 37 pen	

Blackburn	H 1-2
Anelka 87	
Man Utd	A 1-4
Speed 87 pen	

Sheff Utd	H 1-0
Davies 80	
Wigan	A 3-1
Anelka 44, Teimourian 68, 73	
Everton	H 1-1
Davies 18	
Arsenal	A 1-2
Anelka 11	
Reading	H 1-3
Shorey 64 og	
Chelsea	A 2-2
Michalik 19, Davies 54	
West Ham	A 1-3
Speed 67	
Aston Villa	H 2-2
Speed 32, Davies 58	

CHARLTON ATHLETIC

CHARLTON FACTS

MANAGER	CAPTAIN
ALAN PARDEW	DARREN BENT

CLUB

Stadium: The Valley

Capacity: 27,111

Average Attendance 2006-07: 26,184

Pitch Size: 102.5m x 66.7m

Website: www.fafc.co.uk

STRIP

Home: Red shirts, white trim, white shorts

Away: Navy and light blue striped shirts, navy shorts

SPONSORS

Shirt: Llanera (£750,000 per year)

Kit Partner: Joma

CHEAPEST TICKET PRICES

Adult: £20.00

Junior: £15.00

RECORDS

Record Home Attendance: 75,031 v Aston Villa (FA Cup) February 12, 1938

Record Victory: 8-1 v Middlesbrough (league) September 12, 1953

Record Defeat: 1-11 v Aston Villa (league) Nov 14, 1959

Most League Goals: Stuart Leary (153)

Most League Apps: Sam Bartrum (583)

Most Capped Player: Joh Robinson 30 (Wales)

HONOURS

Division One: 2000

Division Three (South): 1929, 1935

FA Cup: 1947

SQUAD RECORD 2006-07

	CLUB				INTERNATIONAL			POSITIONAL RANKING		OVERALL RANKING
	Mins	Goals	Mins per goal	% played	Country	Games	Goals	Domestic	World	All positions
GOALKEEPERS		CONCEDED					CONCEDED			
SCOTT CARSON	3240	55	59	95%	England	0	0	19	91	905
DEFENDERS		CONCEDED					CONCEDED			
TALAL EL KARKOURI	3240	56	58	95%	Morocco	0	0	74	362	994
BEN THATCHER	1867	27	69	55%	Wales	3	4	78	379	1033
HERMANN HREIDARSSON	2590	46	56	76%	Iceland	5	7	113	548	1496
LUKE YOUNG	2587	42	62	76%	England	0	0	86	401	1078
MADJID BOUGHERRA	2723	46	59	80%	Algeria	0	0	108	515	1405
SOULEYMANE DIAWARA	1919	30	64	56%	Senegal	0	0	118	569	1546
JONATHAN FORTUNE	1884	31	61	55%	England	0	0	139	649	1844
MIDFIELDERS		SCORED					SCORED			
MATT HOLLAND	2443	1	2443	71%	Rep of Ireland	0	0	101	495	1386
ALEXANDRE SONG	1040	0	0	30%	Cameroon	0	0	103	513	1453
DENNIS ROMMEDAHL	1749	0	0	51%	Denmark	7	4	111	532	1505
JEROME THOMAS	1360	3	453	40%	England	0	0	113	537	1520
DARREN AMBROSE	1746	3	582	51%	England	0	0	117	549	1560
AMDY FAYE	2081	1	2081	61%	Senegal	0	0	126	608	1699
ANDREW REID	1201	2	601	35%	Rep of Ireland	2	0	132	636	1773
ZHI ZHENG	842	1	842	25%	China	0	0	74	386	1819
MIDFIELDERS		SCORED					SCORED			
DARREN BENT	2863	13	220	84%	England	1	0	43	192	1068
MARCUS BENT	1484	1	1484	43%	England	0	0	88	452	2035

KEY: Club stats are all for the 2006-07 season. Mins = Minutes played in the league for club; Goals conceded = goals let in when the player is on the pitch; Goals scored = scored by the player; Mins per goal = number of minutes on average between each goal conceded or scored; % played = the percentage of the league season the player played; Domestic = player ranking by position in domestic league; World = player ranking by position in World; Overall Position = player ranking in world across all positions.

THE STARS OF LAST SEASON

TEAM OF THE SEASON

G — Carson

D — Young, Diawara, El Karkouri, Hreidarsson

M — Rommedahl, Faye, Holland, Thomas

F — M. Bent, D. Bent

G STAR GOALKEEPER

SCOTT CARSON: A season in the spotlight of relegation action did the on-loan Liverpool youngster no harm.

Average goals per game conceded by club	1.58
Goals per game conceded when player on pitch	1.53
Points per game club won when player on pitch	0.92
Minutes played 3240	Clean sheets 11

D STAR DEFENDER

LUKE YOUNG: He went backwards in the England fullback pecking order but was still Charlton's top defender.

Goals per game conceded when player on pitch	1.46
Points per game club won when player on pitch	0.93
Goals scored by player	1
Minutes played 2587	Clean sheets 10

M STAR MIDFIELDER

JEROME THOMAS: Two spells of injury cost his club dear as the young winger was their best performer.

Goals per game conceded when player on pitch	0.87
Goals per game club scored when player on pitch	1.20
Goals scored by player	3
Minutes played 1360	Assists 2

F STAR FORWARD

DARREN BENT: He proved that he could still hit goals in a side struggling for form and was rewarded with a big money transfer to Spurs.

Average goals per game scored by club	0.89
Goals per game scored when player on pitch	0.95
% of club goals scored by player	38.2
Minutes played 2863	Assists 2

2006-07 RESULTS ROUND-UP

■ Premiership ■ League Cup ■ FA Cup ■ UEFA Cup ■ Champions League

West Ham	A	1-3
D.Bent 15 pen		
Man Utd	H	0-3
Bolton	H	2-0
D.Bent 65 pen, 85		
Chelsea	A	1-2
Hasselbaink 54		
Portsmouth	H	0-1
Carlisle	H	1-0
D.Bent 57		
Aston Villa	A	0-2
Arsenal	H	1-2
D.Bent 21		
Fulham	A	1-2
D.Bent 78		
Watford	H	0-0

Bolton	H	1-0
M.Bent 17		
Newcastle	A	0-0
Man City	H	1-0
D.Bent 28		
Chesterfield	A	4-3*
Hasselbaink 40, 93, D.Bent 73		
(*on penalties)		
Wigan	A	2-3
De Zeeuw 52 og, M.Bent 90		
Reading	A	0-2
Everton	H	1-1
Reid 68		
Sheff Utd	A	1-1
Reid 17		
Blackburn	H	1-0
El Karkouri 90		

Tottenham	A	1-5
Dawson 43 og		
Liverpool	H	0-3
Wycombe	H	0-1
Middlesbrough	A	0-2

Fulham	H	2-2
Ambrose 19, D.Bent 45		
Aston Villa	H	2-1
D.Bent 57, Hughes 90		
Arsenal	A	0-4
Nottm Forest	A	0-2
Middlesbrough	H	1-3
Hasselbaink 27		
Portsmouth	A	1-0
Faye 79		
Bolton	A	1-1
El Karkouri 12		
Chelsea	H	0-1
Man Utd	A	0-2
West Ham	H	4-0
Ambrose 24, Thomas 34, 80, D.Bent 41		

Watford	A	2-2
Young 67, Ambrose 89		
Newcastle	H	2-0
Z.Zheng 53, Thomas 88 pen		
Wigan	H	1-0
D.Bent 86 pen		
Man City	A	0-0

Reading	H	0-0
Everton	A	1-2
D.Bent 89		
Sheff Utd	H	1-1
El Karkouri 59		

Blackburn	A	1-4
D.Bent 71		
Tottenham	H	0-20
Liverpool	A	2-2
Holland 2, D.Bent 72		

CHELSEA

CHELSEA FACTS

MANAGER	CAPTAIN
JOSE MOURINHO	JOHN TERRY

CLUB

Stadium: Stamford Bridge

Capacity: 42,522

Average Attendance 2006-07: 41,541

Pitch Size: 103m x 67.6m

Website: www.chelseafc.com

STRIP

Home: All blue with white shoulder flash

Away: Yellow shirts with black stripe, black shorts

SPONSORS

Shirt: Samsung Mobile (£10m per year)

Kit Partner: Adidas

CHEAPEST TICKET PRICES

Adult: £20.00

Junior: £10.00

RECORDS

Record Home Attendance: 82,905 v Arsenal (league) October 12 1935

Record Victory: 13-0 v Jeunesse Haufcharge (ECWC) September 29 1971

Record Defeat: 1-8 v Wolves (league) September 26, 1923

Most League Goals: Bobby Tambling (164)

Most League Apps: Ron Harris (655)

Most Capped Player: Marcel Desailly, 67 (France)

HONOURS

Premiership: 1955, 2005, 2006

FA Cup: 1970, 1997, 2000, 2007

League Cup: 1965, 1998, 2005, 2007

UEFA Cup: 1970

European Cup Winners Cup: 1971, 1998

SQUAD RECORD 2006-07

	CLUB				INTERNATIONAL			POSITIONAL RANKING		OVERALL RANKING
	Mins	Goals	Mins per goal	% played	Country	Games	Goals	Domestic	World	All positions
GOALKEEPERS		CONCEDED					CONCEDED			
PETR CECH	1714	9	190	50%	Czech Rep.	8	4	9	24	114
HENRIQUE HILARIO	990	12	83	29%	Portugal	0	0	22	111	1348
DEFENDERS		CONCEDED					CONCEDED			
RICARDO CARVALHO	2638	19	139	77%	Portugal	7	4	3	3	15
JOHN TERRY	2413	14	172	71%	England	10	3	5	9	26
ASHLEY COLE	1847	15	123	54%	England	7	3	15	41	118
PAULO FERREIRA	1710	12	143	50%	Portugal	6	2	52	175	489
WAYNE BRIDGE	1548	10	155	45%	England	2	0	62	284	762
GEREMI NJITAP	1156	9	128	34%	Nigeria	0	0	110	524	1423
MIDFIELDERS		SCORED					SCORED			
FRANK LAMPARD	3243	11	295	95%	England	10	1	1	1	1
MICHAEL ESSIEN	2970	2	1485	87%	Ghana	3	1	4	7	17
CLAUDE MAKELELE	2268	1	2268	66%	France	8	0	10	24	72
MICHAEL BALLACK	2016	4	504	59%	Germany	7	4	16	34	100
ARJEN ROBBEN	1343	2	672	39%	Holland	6	1	46	140	431
JOHN OBI MIKEL	957	0	0	28%	Nigeria	0	0	78	365	1015
SHAUN WRIGHT-PHILLIPS	1270	2	635	37%	England	4	0	89	431	1186
FORWARDS		SCORED					SCORED			
DIDIER DROGBA	2944	20	147	86%	Ivory Coast	5	2	1	2	8
ANDRIY SHEVCHENKO	1797	4	449	53%	Ukraine	3	2	10	30	209
SALOMON KALOU	1944	7	278	57%	Ivory Coast	0	0	29	108	633

KEY: Club stats are all for the 2006-07 season. Mins = Minutes played in the league for club; Goals conceded = goals let in when the player is on the pitch; Goals scored = scored by the player; Mins per goal = number of minutes on average between each goal conceded or scored; % played = the percentage of the league season the player played; Domestic = player ranking by position in domestic league; World = player ranking by position in World; Overall Position = player ranking in world across all positions.

THE STARS OF LAST SEASON

TEAM OF THE SEASON

- **G** Cech
- **D** Ferreira
- **D** Carvalho
- **D** Terry
- **D** Bridge
- **M** Essien
- **M** Lampard
- **M** Makelele
- **M** Robben
- **F** Kalou
- **F** Drogba

G STAR GOALKEEPER

PETR CECH: Chelsea's form during his spell out with a head injury proved that he is the world's best keeper.

Average goals per game conceded by club	0.63
Goals per game conceded when player on pitch	0.47
Points per game club won when player on pitch	2.32
Minutes played	1714	Clean sheets	12

D STAR DEFENDER

JOHN TERRY: He began last season scoring on his debut as England skipper and ended it with two cups.

Goals per game conceded when player on pitch	0.52
Points per game club won when player on pitch	2.19
Goals scored by player	1
Minutes played	2413	Clean sheets	16

M STAR MIDFIELDER

FRANK LAMPARD: Booed in an England shirt but for midfield goals and consistency he's still the man.

Goals per game conceded when player on pitch	0.64
Goals per game club scored when player on pitch	1.73
Goals scored by player	11
Minutes played	3243	Assists	12

F STAR FORWARD

DIDIER DROGBA: In the form that made him the top striker in the French league in 2005, he was immense last season.

Average goals per game scored by club	1.68
Goals per game scored when player on pitch	1.73
% of club goals scored by player	31.3
Minutes played	2944	Assists	9

2006-07 RESULTS ROUND-UP

■ Premiership ■ League Cup ■ FA Cup ■ UEFA Cup ■ Champions League

Man City H 3-0	**Reading** A 1-0	**West Ham** H 1-0	**Wigan** A 3-2
Terry 11, Lampard 26, Drogba 78	Ingimarsson 45 og	Geremi 22	Lampard 13, Kalou 31, Robben 90
Middlesbrough A 1-2	**Barcelona** H 1-0	**W Bremen** A 0-1	**Reading** H 2-2
Shevchenko 15	Drogba 46		Drogba 38, 72
Blackburn A 2-0	**Portsmouth** H 2-1	**Man Utd** A 1-1	**Fulham** H 2-2
Lampard 49 pen, Drogba 80	Shevchenko 55, Ballack 57	Carvalho 69	Rosenior 35 og, Drogba 62
Charlton H 2-1	**Blackburn** A 2-0	**Bolton** A 1-0	**Aston Villa** A 0-0
Drogba 6, Carvalho 63	J.Cole 53, Kalou 81	Ballack 45	
W Bremen H 2-0	**Sheff Utd** A 2-0	**Levski Sofia** H 2-0	**Macclesfield** H 6-1
Essien 24, Ballack 68 pen	Lampard 43, Ballack 49	Shevchenko 27, Wright-Phillips 83	Lampard 16, 41, 51 pen, Wright-Phillips 68, Mikel 82, Carvalho 86
Liverpool H 1-0	**Barcelona** A 2-2	**Arsenal** H 1-1	**Wycombe** A 1-1
Drogba 42	Lampard 52, Drogba 90	Essien 84	Bridge 36
Fulham A 2-0	**Tottenham** A 1-2	**Newcastle** H 1-0	**Wigan** H 4-0
Lampard 73 pen, 80	Makelele 15	Drogba 74	Lampard 13, Robben 30, Kirkland 70 og, Drogba 90
Levski Sofia A 3-1	**Aston Villa** H 4-0	**Everton** A 3-2	**Liverpool** A 0-2
Drogba 39, 52, 68	Lampard 32, Shevchenko 65, Essien 82, Drogba 84	Howard 49 og, Lampard 81, Drogba 87	
Aston Villa H 1-1	**Watford** H 4-0	**Newcastle** A 1-0	**Wycombe** H 4-0
Drogba 3	Drogba 27, 36, 69, Shevchenko 52	Drogba 78	Shevchenko 22, 43, Lampard 69, 90

Nottm Forest H 3-0	**Tottenham** H 3-3	**West Ham** A 4-1
Shevchenko 9, Drogba 18, Mikel 45	Lampard 22, 71, Kalou 86	Wright-Phillips 31, 36, Kalou 52, Drogba 62
Blackburn H 3-0	**Man City** A 1-0	**Newcastle** A 0-0
Drogba 6, Lampard 67, Kalou 90	Lampard 28 pen	
Charlton A 1-0	**Sheff Utd** H 3-0	**Liverpool** H 1-0
Lampard 18	Shevchenko 4, Kalou 17, Ballack 58	J.Cole 29
Middlesbrough H 3-0	**Tottenham** A 2-1	**Bolton** H 2-2
Drogba 45, 83, Xavier 66 og	Shevchenko 55, Wright-Phillips 61	Kalou 22, Jaaskelainen 34 og
Norwich H 4-0	**Watford** H 1-0	**Liverpool** A 1-4*
Wright-Phillips 39, Drogba 51, Essien 90, Shevchenko 90	Kalou 90	(*on penalties)
Porto A 1-1	**Valencia** H 1-1	**Arsenal** A 1-1
Shevchenko 15	Drogba 53	Essien 70
Arsenal N 2-1	**Tottenham** H 1-0	**Man Utd** H 0-0
Drogba 20, 84	Carvalho 52	
Portsmouth A 2-0	**Valencia** A 2-1	**Everton** H 1-1
Drogba 33, Kalou 82	Shevchenko 52, Essien 90	Drogba 57
Porto H 2-1	**Blackburn** N 2-1	**Man Utd** N 1-0
Lampard 16, Ballack 109	Lampard 16, Ballack 109	Drogba 116
	Robben 48, Ballack 79	

EVERTON FACTS

MANAGER	CAPTAIN
DAVID MOYES	PHIL NEVILLE

CLUB

Stadium: Goodison Park

Capacity: 40, 565

Average Attendance 2006-07: 36,738

Pitch Size: 102.5m x 71m

Website: www.evertonfc.com

STRIP

Home: Blue shirts, white shorts

Away: White shirts, black shorts

SPONSORS

Shirt: Chang Beer (£1m)

Kit Partner: Umbro

CHEAPEST TICKET PRICES

Adult: £28.00

Junior: £17.00

RECORDS

Record Home Attendance: 78,229 v Liverpool (league) September 18 1948

Record Victory: 11-2 v Derby County (FA Cup) January 18 1890

Record Defeat: 4-10 v Tottenham (league) October 11, 1958

Most League Goals: William 'Dixie' Dean 349

Most League Apps: Neville Southall (578)

Most Capped Player: Neville Southall, 92 (Wales)

HONOURS

Division One: 1891, 1915, 1928, 1932, 1939, 1963, 1970, 1985, 1987

Division Two: 1931

FA Cup: 1906, 1933, 1966, 1984, 1995

European Cup Winners Cup: 1985

SQUAD RECORD 2006-07

	CLUB				INTERNATIONAL			POSITIONAL RANKING		OVERALL RANKING
	Mins	Goals	Mins per goal	% played	Country	Games	Goals	Domestic	World	All positions
GOALKEEPERS			CONCEDED				CONCEDED			
TIM HOWARD	3240	29	112	95%	United States	6	3	6	21	92
DEFENDERS			CONCEDED				CONCEDED			
JOLEON LESCOTT	3318	36	92	97%	England	0	0	16	44	126
JOSEPH YOBO	3420	36	95	100%	Nigeria	1	4	17	50	140
PHIL NEVILLE	3111	34	92	91%	England	4	1	21	61	163
ALAN STUBBS	1997	23	87	58%	England	0	0	65	304	810
GARY NAYSMITH	990	10	99	29%	Scotland	6	4	119	574	1556
TONY HIBBERT	1014	15	68	30%	England	0	0	123	583	1587
DAVID WEIR	1412	13	109	41%	Scotland	8	6	54	182	507
MIDFIELDERS			SCORED				SCORED			
LEE CARSLEY	3375	1	3375	99%	Rep of Ireland	5	0	17	35	102
MIKEL ARTETA	3134	9	348	92%	Spain	0	0	18	41	134
LEON OSMAN	2808	3	936	82%	England	0	0	33	87	273
TIM CAHILL	1405	5	281	41%	Australia	3	0	93	461	1287
MANUEL FERNANDES	742	2	371	22%	Portugal	0	0	128	613	1715
FORWARDS			SCORED				SCORED			
ANDREW JOHNSON	2711	11	246	79%	England	5	0	12	43	271
JAMES BEATTIE	1465	2	733	43%	England	0	0	54	302	1517
JAMES VAUGHAN	652	4	163	19%	England	0	0	64	356	1729
JAMES MCFADDEN	794	2	397	23%	Scotland	4	1	76	398	1855
VICTOR ANICHEBE	626	3	209	18%	Nigeria	0	0	82	430	1957

KEY: Club stats are all for the 2006-07 season. Mins = Minutes played in the league for club; Goals conceded = goals let in when the player is on the pitch; Goals scored = scored by the player; Mins per goal = number of minutes on average between each goal conceded or scored; % played = the percentage of the league season the player played; Domestic = player ranking by position in domestic league; World = player ranking by position in World; Overall Position = player ranking in world across all positions.

THE STARS OF LAST SEASON

TEAM OF THE SEASON

G Howard

D P Neville D Yobo D Stubbs D Lescott

M Arteta M Cahill M Carsley M Osman

F Johnson F Vaughan

G STAR GOALKEEPER

TIM HOWARD: The goalkeeping revelation of the 2006-07 season, the United reserve was second only to Cech in shot-stopping.

Average goals per game conceded by club	0.95
Goals per game conceded when player on pitch	0.81
Points per game club won when player on pitch	1.61
Minutes played	3240	Clean sheets	14

D STAR DEFENDER

JOSEPH YOBO: He played every minute of Everton's league season, showing the form that has made him Nigeria's captain.

Goals per game conceded when player on pitch	0.37
Points per game club won when player on pitch	1.53
Goals scored by player	2
Minutes played	3420	Clean sheets	14

M STAR MIDFIELDER

MIKEL ARTETA: The former Rangers star looked back to his best, clinical with the dead ball and making the midfield tick.

Goals per game conceded when player on pitch	0.89
Goals per game club scored when player on pitch	1.36
Goals scored by player	9
Minutes played	3134	Assists	9

F STAR FORWARD

ANDREW JOHNSON: Added a much-needed cutting edge without really getting among the goals as his Strike Rate shows.

Average goals per game scored by club	1.37
Goals per game scored when player on pitch	1.36
% of club goals scored by player	21.2
Minutes played	2711	Assists	6

2006-07 RESULTS ROUND-UP

■ Premiership ■ League Cup ■ FA Cup ■ UEFA Cup ■ Champions League

Watford H 2-1	Middlesbrough A 1-2	Luton H 4-0	Fulham A 0-1
Johnson 15, Arteta 82 pen	*Cahill 77*	*Cahill 23, Keane 34 og, McFadden 53, Anichebe 83*	
Blackburn A 1-1	Sheff Utd H 2-0		Arsenal H 0-1
Cahill 84	*Arteta 13, Beattie 33 pen*	Arsenal A 1-1	Aston Villa H 0-1
Tottenham A 2-0		*Cahill 11*	Bolton H 1-0
Davenport 53 og, Johnson 66			*Arteta 60*
Liverpool H 3-0			Charlton A 1-1
Cahill 24, Johnson 36, 90			*Hreidarsson 52 og*
Wigan H 2-2			Man Utd A 0-3
Johnson 49, Beattie 66 pen			West Ham H 2-0
Peterborough A 2-1			*Osman 51, Vaughan 90*
Stirling 24 og, Cahill 87			Portsmouth A 0-2
Newcastle A 1-1			Chelsea H 2-3
Cahill 40			*Arteta 38 pen, Yobo 64*
Man City H 1-1			Reading A 2-0
Johnson 44			*Johnson 14, McFadden 47*

Middlesbrough H 0-0	Watford A 3-0
Newcastle H 3-0	*Fernandes 23, Johnson 25 pen, Osman 90*
Anichebe 9, 58, P.Neville 62	Sheff Utd A 1-1
Man City A 1-2	*Arteta 75 pen*
Osman 84	Arsenal H 1-0
Blackburn H 1-4	*Johnson 90*
Johnson 68 pen	Aston Villa A 1-1
Reading H 1-1	*Lescott 14*
Johnson 81	Fulham H 4-1
Wigan A 2-0	*Carsley 25, Stubbs 34, Vaughan 45, Anichebe 80*
Arteta 65 pen, 90	Bolton A 1-1
Liverpool A 0-0	*Vaughan 33*
Blackburn A 1-0	Charlton H 2-1
Johnson 10	*Lescott 81, McFadden 90*
Tottenham H 1-2	West Ham A 0-1
Arteta 42	

Man Utd H 2-4
Stubbs 12, Fernandes 50
Portsmouth H 3-0
Arteta 59 pen, Yobo 62, Naysmith 90
Chelsea A 1-1
Vaughan 50

FULHAM

FULHAM FACTS

MANAGER	CAPTAIN
LAWRIE SANCHEZ	MICHAEL BROWN

CLUB

Stadium: Craven Cottage

Capacity: 24,600

Average Attendance 2006-07: 22,279

Pitch Size: 100.5m x 68.5m

Website: www.fulhamfc.com

STRIP

Home: White shirts black shorts

Away: Grey and black stripe shirts with red and black sleeves, white shorts

SPONSORS

Shirt: Pipex (£900,000 per year)

Kit Partner: Puma

CHEAPEST TICKET PRICES

Adult: £22.00

Junior: £5.00

RECORDS

Record Home Attendance: 49,335 v Millwall (league) October 8, 1938

Record Victory: 10-1 v Ipswich (league) December 26, 1963

Record Defeat: 0-10 v Liverpool (League Cup) September 23, 1986

Most League Goals: Gordon Davies (159)

Most League Apps: Johnny Haynes (594)

Most Capped Player: Johnny Haynes 56 (England)

HONOURS

Division One: 2001

Division Two: 1949, 1999

Division Three (South): 1932

SQUAD RECORD 2006-07

	CLUB				INTERNATIONAL			POSITIONAL RANKING		OVERALL RANKING
	Mins	Goals	Mins per goal	% played	Country	Games	Goals	Domestic	World	All positions
GOALKEEPERS		CONCEDED					CONCEDED			
ANTTI NIEMI	2760	45	61	81%	Finland	0	0	15	59	359
JAN LASTUVKA	660	15	44	19%	Czech Rep	0	0	30	165	2056
DEFENDERS		CONCEDED					CONCEDED			
LIAM ROSENIOR	3397	58	59	99%	England	0	0	28	77	204
CARLOS BOCANEGRA	2332	38	61	68%	United States	5	3	48	159	454
FRANCK QUEUDRUE	2515	37	68	74%	France	0	0	53	179	499
ZATYIAH KNIGHT	2033	37	55	59%	England	0	0	69	343	939
MORITZ VOLZ	2020	42	48	59%	Germany	0	0	75	363	996
IAN PEARCE	1838	31	59	54%	England	0	0	85	396	1067
PHILIPPE CHRISTANVAL	1696	35	48	50%	France	0	0	87	404	1082
MIDFIELDERS		SCORED					SCORED			
MICHAEL BROWN	2930	0	0	86%	England	0	0	38	103	324
SIMON DAVIES	2343	2	1172	69%	Wales	11	0	67	312	882
PAPA BOUBA DIOP	1704	0	0	50%	Senegal	2	0	86	419	1158
WAYNE ROUTLEDGE	1419	0	0	41%	England	0	0	95	468	1311
CLAUS JENSEN	912	2	456	27%	Denmark	5	0	123	591	1662
FORWARDS		SCORED					SCORED			
BRIAN MCBRIDE	2897	9	322	85%	United States	0	0	14	49	311
TOMASZ RADZINSKI	2236	2	1118	65%	Canada	1	0	33	133	771
HEIDAR HELGUSON	1466	3	489	43%	Iceland	1	0	50	275	1418
COLLINS JOHN	916	1	916	27%	Holland	0	0	73	381	1811

KEY: Club stats are all for the 2006-07 season. Mins = Minutes played in the league for club; Goals conceded = goals let in when the player is on the pitch; Goals scored = scored by the player; Mins per goal = number of minutes on average between each goal conceded or scored; % played = the percentage of the league season the player played; Domestic = player ranking by position in domestic league; World = player ranking by position in World; Overall Position = player ranking in world across all positions.

THE STARS OF LAST SEASON

TEAM OF THE SEASON

- G Niemi
- D Rosenior
- D Knight
- D Bocanegra
- D Queudrue
- M Davies
- M Diop
- M Brown
- M Routledge
- F Montella
- F McBride

G STAR GOALKEEPER

ANTTI NIEMI: The brave and usually brilliant Finn was not in his best form behind a stuttering defence.

Average goals per game conceded by club	1.58
Goals per game conceded when player on pitch	1.47
Points per game club won when player on pitch	1.10
Minutes played	2760
Clean sheets	6

D STAR DEFENDER

FRANCK QUEUDRUE: The signing from Middlesbrough was hit by injuries but still showed his strength and versatility.

Goals per game conceded when player on pitch	0.50
Points per game club won when player on pitch	1.53
Goals scored by player	1
Minutes played	2515
Clean sheets	6

M STAR MIDFIELDER

WAYNE ROUTLEDGE: A loan capture from Spurs who sparkled on the wing but didn't add goals or assists.

Goals per game conceded when player on pitch	1.41
Goals per game club scored when player on pitch	1.34
Goals scored by player	0
Minutes played	1419
Assists	1

F STAR FORWARD

BRIAN MCBRIDE: One of the biggest aerial threats in world football and a tireless target man for his team.

Average goals per game scored by club	1.00
Goals per game scored when player on pitch	1.06
% of club goals scored by player	23.7
Minutes played	2897
Assists	2

2006-07 RESULTS ROUND-UP

■ Premiership ■ League Cup ■ FA Cup □ UEFA Cup □ Champions League

Man Utd	A	1-5
Ferdinand 40 og		
Bolton	H	1-1
Bullard 90 pen		
Sheff Utd	H	1-0
Bullard 40		
Newcastle	A	2-1
McBride 82, Bocanegra 89		
Tottenham	A	0-0
Wycombe	H	1-2
Helguson 47		
Chelsea	H	0-2
Watford	A	3-3
McBride 71, Helguson 83, Francis 87 og		
Charlton	H	2-1
McBride 65, C.Jensen 68		

Aston Villa	A	1-1
Volz 45		
Wigan	H	0-1
Everton	H	1-0
C.Jensen 66		
Portsmouth	A	1-1
Knight 57		
Man City	A	1-3
John 62		
Reading	H	0-1
Arsenal	H	2-1
McBride 6, Radzinski 19		
Blackburn	A	0-2
Liverpool	A	0-4
Middlesbrough	H	2-1
Helguson 12 pen, McBride 35		

West Ham	H	0-0
Charlton	A	2-2
McBride 13, Queudrue 90		
Chelsea	A	2-2
Volz 16, Bocanegra 84		

Watford	H	0-0
Leicester	A	2-2
McBride 69, Volz 83		
West Ham	A	3-3
Radzinski 16, McBride 59, Christanval 90		
Leicester	H	4-3
McBride 35, Montella 51, 60, Routledge 90		
Tottenham	H	1-1
Montella 84 pen		
Stoke	H	3-0
Montella 11, McBride 38, Radzinski 54		
Sheff Utd	A	0-2
Newcastle	A	2-1
Helguson 49, McBride 73		

Bolton	A	1-2
Knight 66		
Tottenham	H	0-4
Man Utd	H	1-2
McBride 17		
Aston Villa	H	1-1
Bocanegra 23		
Wigan	A	0-0
Portsmouth	H	1-1
Pearce 90		
Everton	A	1-4
Bocanegra 22		
Man City	H	1-3
Bocanegra 76		
Reading	A	0-1

Blackburn	H	1-1
Montella 10		
Arsenal	A	1-3
S.Davies 78		

Liverpool	H	1-0
Dempsey 69		
Middlesbrough	A	1-3
S.Davies 42		

LIVERPOOL

LIVERPOOL FACTS

MANAGER	CAPTAIN
RAFA BENITEZ	**STEVEN GERRARD**

CLUB

Stadium: Anfield

Capacity: 45,362

Average Attendance 2006-07: 43,561

Pitch Size: 105.5m x 68.5m

Website: www.liverpoolfc.tv

STRIP

Home: All red with white shoulder flash

Away: White shirts with red flash, black shorts

SPONSORS

Shirt: Carlsberg (£m per year)

Kit Partner: Adidas

CHEAPEST TICKET PRICES

Adult: £30.00

Junior: £16.00

RECORDS

Record Home Attendance: 61,905 v Wolves (FA Cup) February 2, 1952

Record Victory: 11-0 v Stromgodset (European Cup Winners Cup) September 17, 1974

Record Defeat: 1-9 v Birmingham City (league) December 11, 1954

Most League Goals: Roger Hunt (245)

Most League Apps: Ian Callaghan (640)

Most Capped Player: Ian Rush, 67 (Wales)

HONOURS

Division One: 1901, 1906, 1922, 1923, 1947, 1964, 1966, 1973, 1976, 1977, 1979, 1980, 1982, 1983, 1984, 1986, 1988, 1990

Division Two: 1894, 1896, 1905, 1962

FA Cup: 1965, 1974, 1986, 1989, 1992, 2001, 2006

League Cup: 1981, 1982, 1983, 1984, 1995, 2001, 2003

European Cup: 1977, 1978, 1981, 1984, 2005

UEFA Cup: 1973, 1976, 2001

SQUAD RECORD 2006-07

	CLUB				INTERNATIONAL			POSITIONAL RANKING		OVERALL RANKING
	Mins	Goals	Mins per goal	% played	Country	Games	Goals	Domestic	World	All positions
GOALKEEPERS			CONCEDED				CONCEDED			
JOSE REINA	3150	23	137	92%	Spain	0	1	1	1	11
DEFENDERS			CONCEDED				CONCEDED			
JAMIE CARRAGHER	2978	22	135	87%	England	0	3	1	1	5
STEVE FINNAN	2889	22	131	84%	Rep of Ireland	0	11	4	8	25
DANIEL AGGER	2167	11	197	63%	Denmark	0	4	6	11	31
ALVARO ARBELOA	2468	29	85	72%	Spain	0	0	41	136	371
SAMI HYYPIA	2031	20	102	59%	Finland	1	7	45	148	414
FABIO AURELIO	1016	8	127	30%	Brazil	0	0	102	472	1286
MIDFIELDERS			SCORED				SCORED			
STEVEN GERRARD	3076	7	439	90%	England	10	3	2	3	3
XABI ALONSO	2662	4	666	78%	Spain	8	0	8	14	38
JOHN ARNE RIISE	2582	1	2582	75%	Norway	8	1	14	29	85
JERMAINE PENNANT	1974	1	1974	58%	England	0	0	30	72	229
MOMO SISSOKO	1222	0	0	36%	Mali	0	0	83	409	1135
JAVIER MASCHERANO	851	0	0	25%	Argentina	3	0	90	440	1210
MARK GONZALEZ	1214	2	607	35%	Chile	0	0	97	476	1331
BOUDEWIJN ZENDEN	811	0	0	24%	Holland	0	0	87	427	1179
FORWARDS			SCORED				SCORED			
DIRK KUYT	2577	12	215	75%	Holland	9	1	5	10	77
PETER CROUCH	1511	9	168	44%	England	8	6	7	25	187
CRAIG BELLAMY	1908	7	273	56%	Wales	11	4	23	78	477

KEY: Club stats are all for the 2006-07 season. Mins = Minutes played in the league for club; Goals conceded = goals let in when the player is on the pitch; Goals scored = scored by the player; Mins per goal = number of minutes on average between each goal conceded or scored; % played = the percentage of the league season the player played; Domestic = player ranking by position in domestic league; World = player ranking by position in World; Overall Position = player ranking in world across all positions.

THE STARS OF LAST SEASON

TEAM OF THE SEASON

G Reina

D Finnan | **D** Carragher | **D** Hyypia | **D** Agger

M Pennant | **M** Gerrard | **M** Alonso | **M** Riise

F Crouch | **F** Kuyt

G STAR GOALKEEPER

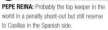

PEPE REINA: Probably the top keeper in the world in a penalty shoot-out but still reserve to Casillas in the Spanish side.

Average goals per game conceded by club	0.71
Goals per game conceded when player on pitch	0.66
Points per game club won when player on pitch	1.83
Minutes played	3150	Clean sheets	19

D STAR DEFENDER

DANIEL AGGER: The young Dane is proving a smart buy with one of the top Defensive Ratings in the Premiership.

Goals per game conceded when player on pitch	0.58
Points per game club won when player on pitch	1.96
Goals scored by player	2
Minutes played	2167	Clean sheets	15

M STAR MIDFIELDER

STEVEN GERRARD: On the right wing, in the centre or behind the striker… as long as he's on the pitch he'll perform.

Goals per game conceded when player on pitch	0.68
Goals per game club scored when player on pitch	1.53
Goals scored by player	7
Minutes played	3076	Assists	6

F STAR FORWARD

PETER CROUCH: Poorly used in the league by Benitez, but he still had a better Strike Rate than Benni McCarthy.

Average goals per game scored by club	1.50
Goals per game scored when player on pitch	1.88
% of club goals scored by player	15.8
Minutes played	1511	Assists	8

2006-07 RESULTS ROUND-UP

■ Premiership ■ League Cup ■ FA Cup ■ UEFA Cup ■ Champions League

Maccabi Haifa	H	2-1
Bellamy 33, M.Gonzalez 88		
Sheff Utd	A	1-1
Fowler 70 pen		
Maccabi Haifa	A	1-1
Crouch 54		
West Ham	H	2-1
Agger 42, Crouch 45		
Everton	A	0-3
PSV	A	0-0
Chelsea	A	0-1
Newcastle	H	2-0
Kuijt 29, Xabi Alonso 79		
Tottenham	H	3-0
Gonzalez 63, Kuijt 73, Riise 89		
Galatasaray	H	3-2
Crouch 8, 52, Luis Garcia 14		

Bolton	A	0-2
Blackburn	H	1-1
Bellamy 64		
Bordeaux	A	1-0
Crouch 58		
Man Utd	A	0-2
Reading	H	4-3
Fowler 44, Riise 45, Paletta 50, Crouch 77		

Aston Villa	H	3-1
Kuijt 31, Crouch 38, Luis Garcia 44		
Bordeaux	H	3-0
Luis Garcia 23, 76, Gerrard 71		
Reading	H	2-0
Kuijt 14, 73		
Birmingham	H	1-0
Agger 45		
Arsenal	A	0-3
Middlesbrough	A	0-0
PSV	H	2-0
Gerrard 65, Crouch 88		
Man City	H	1-0
Gerrard 67		
Portsmouth	H	0-0
Wigan	A	4-0
Bellamy 9, 26, Kuijt 40, McCulloch 45 og		

Galatasaray	A	2-3
Fowler 22, 90		
Fulham	H	4-0
Gerrard 54, Carragher 61, Luis Garcia 66, Gonzalez 90		
Charlton	A	3-0
Xabi Alonso 3 pen, Bellamy 82, Gerrard 88		
Watford	H	2-0
Bellamy 47, Xabi Alonso 88		
Blackburn	A	0-1
Tottenham	A	1-0
Luis Garcia 45		
Bolton	H	3-0
Crouch 61, Gerrard 63, Kuijt 83		
Arsenal	H	1-3
Kuijt 71		

Arsenal	H	3-6
Fowler 32, Gerrard 68, Hyypia 80		
Watford	A	3-0
Bellamy 34, Crouch 39, 48		
Chelsea	H	2-0
Kuijt 4, Pennant 18		
West Ham	A	2-1
Kuijt 46, Crouch 53		

Everton	H	0-0
Newcastle	A	1-2
Bellamy 6		
Barcelona	A	2-1
Bellamy 43, Riise 74		
Sheff Utd	H	4-0
Fowler 20 pen, 25 pen, Hyypia 70, Gerrard 73		
Man Utd	H	0-1
Barcelona	H	0-1
Aston Villa	H	4-1
Crouch 4, 35, 81, Agger 60		
PSV	A	3-0
Gerrard 27, Riise 49, Crouch 63		
Reading	A	2-1
Arbeloa 15, Kuijt 86		

PSV	H	1-0
Crouch 68		
Man City	A	0-0
Middlesbrough	H	2-0
Gerrard 58, 65 pen		
Wigan	H	2-0
Kuijt 30, 68		
Chelsea	A	0-1
Portsmouth	A	1-2
Hyypia 59		
Chelsea	H	4-1*
*Agger 22 (*on penalties)*		
Fulham	A	0-1
Charlton	H	2-2
Xabi Alonso 62, Kewell 90 pen		
AC Milan	A	1-2
Kuijt 89		

MANCHESTER CITY

MAN CITY FACTS

MANAGER	CAPTAIN
STUART PEARCE	RICHARD DUNNE

CLUB

Stadium: City of Manchester Stadium

Capacity: 47,500

Average Attendance 2006-07: 39,997

Pitch Size: 106.5m x 71m

Website: www.mcfc.co.uk

STRIP

Home: Pale blue shirts with white stripe, white shorts

Away: Purple shirts with white stripe, purple shorts

SPONSORS

Shirt: Thomas Cook (£1m per year)

Kit Partner: Reebok

CHEAPEST TICKET PRICES

Adult: £20.00

Junior: £5.00

RECORDS

Record Home Attendance: 84,569 v Stoke (FA Cup) March 3, 1934

Record Victory: 10-1 v Huddersfield (league) November 7, 1987; v Swindon (FA Cup) January 29, 1930

Record Defeat: 1-9 v Everton (league) September 3, 1906

Most League Goals: Tommy Johnson (158)

Most League Apps: Alan Oakes (565)

Most Capped Player: Colin Bell, 48 (England)

HONOURS

Division One: 1937, 1968, 2002*

Division Two: 1899, 1903, 1910, 1928, 1947, 1996

FA Cup: 1904, 1934, 1956, 1969

League Cup: 1970, 1976

European Cup Winners Cup: 1970

THE STARS OF LAST SEASON

TEAM OF THE SEASON

G Weaver

D Richards | D Distin | D Dunne | D Onuoha

M Trabelsi | M Ireland | M Barton | M Sinclair

F Vassell | F Samaras

G STAR GOALKEEPER

NICKY WEAVER: Initially kept out by Swedish international Isaksson and ended the season with better stats.

Average goals per game conceded by club	1.16
Goals per game conceded when player on pitch	1.17
Points per game club won when player on pitch	1.26
Minutes played	2149	Clean sheets	9

D STAR DEFENDER

SYLVAIN DISTIN: One of the most consistent centre halves in the league, he will be hard for Sven to replace.

Goals per game conceded when player on pitch	1.05
Points per game club won when player on pitch	1.17
Goals scored by player	2
Minutes played	3254	Clean sheets	14

M STAR MIDFIELDER

JOEY BARTON: Hot-headed but inspiring going forward, he departed the club as City's top goalscorer.

Goals per game conceded when player on pitch	1.13
Goals per game club scored when player on pitch	0.76
Goals scored by player	6
Minutes played	2966	Assists	5

F STAR FORWARD

GEORGIOS SAMARAS: A Greek international, for his club he only showed his eye for goal in patches.

Average goals per game scored by club	0.76
Goals per game scored when player on pitch	0.96
% of club goals scored by player	13.8
Minutes played	1706	Assists	5

SQUAD RECORD 2006-07

	CLUB				INTERNATIONAL			POSITIONAL RANKING		OVERALL RANKING
	Mins	Goals	Mins per goal	% played	Country	Games	Goals	Domestic	World	All positions
GOALKEEPERS		CONCEDED				CONCEDED				
NICKY WEAVER	2149	28	77	63%	England	0	0	18	85	697
ANDREAS ISAKSSON	1181	16	74	35%	Sweden	3	3	23	120	1455
DEFENDERS		CONCEDED				CONCEDED				
RICHARD DUNNE	3420	44	78	100%	Rep of Ireland	6	7	12	27	84
SYLVAIN DISTIN	3254	38	86	95%	France	0	0	18	52	142
MICAH RICHARDS	2342	31	76	68%	England	4	1	46	156	441
NEDUM ONUOHA	1324	13	102	39%	England	0	0	97	451	1234
MICHAEL BALL	1075	12	90	31%	England	0	0	112	547	1492
STEPHEN JORDAN	1041	18	58	30%	England	0	0	125	596	1621
MIDFIELDERS		SCORED				SCORED				
HATEM TRABELSI	1367	1	1367	40%	Tunisia	0	0	99	492	1380
JOEY BARTON	2966	6	494	87%	England	0	0	23	56	177
DAMARCUS BEASLEY	1027	3	342	30%	United States	5	3	104	515	1459
TREVOR SINCLAIR	1296	0	0	38%	England	0	0	105	516	1461
STEPHEN IRELAND	1338	1	1338	39%	Rep of Ireland	4	3	110	525	1478
MICHAEL JOHNSON	900	0	0	26%	England	0	0	116	548	1559
FORWARDS		SCORED				SCORED				
DARIUS VASSELL	2558	3	853	75%	England	0	0	24	83	495
GEORGIOS SAMARAS	1706	4	427	50%	Greece	4	0	44	210	1122
BERNARDO CORRADI	1582	3	527	46%	Italy	0	0	48	251	1306
EMILE MPENZA	826	3	275	24%	Belgium	5	0	57	318	1598

KEY: Club stats are all for the 2006-07 season. Mins = Minutes played in the league for club; Goals conceded = goals let in when the player is on the pitch; Goals scored = scored by the player; Mins per goal = number of minutes on average between each goal conceded or scored; % played = the percentage of the league season the player played; Domestic = player ranking by position in domestic league; World = player ranking by position in World; Overall Position = player ranking in world across all positions.

2006-07 RESULTS ROUND-UP

■ Premiership ■ League Cup ■ FA Cup ■ UEFA Cup ■ Champions League

Chelsea	A	0-3
Portsmouth	H	0-0
Arsenal	H	1-0
Barton 41 pen		

Reading	A	0-1
Blackburn	A	2-4
Barton 39, Ooijer 44 og		
Chesterfield	A	1-2
Samaras 40		

West Ham	H	2-0
Samaras 50, 63		
Everton	A	1-1
Richards 90		
Sheff Utd	H	0-0
Wigan	A	0-4
Middlesbrough	H	1-0
Dunne 23		
Charlton	A	0-1
Newcastle	H	0-0
Fulham	H	3-1
Corradi 12, 32, Barton 45		
Liverpool	H	0-0
Aston Villa	A	3-1
Vassell 18, Barton 32, Distin 75		
Watford	H	0-0

Man Utd	A	1-3
Trabelsi 72		
Tottenham	H	1-2
Barton 64		
Bolton	H	0-2
Sheff Utd	A	1-0
Ireland 78		
West Ham	A	1-0
Beasley 83		
Everton	H	2-1
Samaras 50, 72 pen		
Sheff Wed	A	1-1
Samaras 78 pen		
Bolton	A	0-0
Sheff Wed	H	2-1
Ireland 44, Vassell 56		

Blackburn	H	0-3
Southampton	H	3-1
Vassell 26, Barton 45, Beasley 70		
Reading	H	0-2
Portsmouth	A	1-2
Corradi 62		

Preston	A	3-1
Ball 35, Hill 84 og, Ireland 90		
Wigan	H	0-1
Blackburn	A	0-2
Chelsea	H	0-1

Middlesbrough	A	2-0
Distin 61, Mpenza 74		
Newcastle	A	1-0
Mpenza 80		
Charlton	H	0-0
Fulham	A	3-1
Barton 21, Beasley 36, Vassell 59		
Liverpool	A	1-3
Beasley 41		
Watford	A	1-1
Vassell 53		
Aston Villa	H	0-2
Man Utd	H	0-1
Tottenham	A	1-2
Mpenza 40		

MANCHESTER UNITED

MAN UTD FACTS

MANAGER

SIR ALEX FERGUSON

CAPTAIN
GARY NEVILLE

CLUB

Stadium: Old Trafford

Capacity: 76,212

Average Attendance 2006-07: 75,825

Pitch Size: 106m x 69.5m

Website: www.manutd.com

STRIP

Home: Red shirts, white shorts

Away: White shirts, gold trim, black shorts

SPONSORS

Shirt: AIG (£14m per year)

Kit Partner: Nike

CHEAPEST TICKET PRICES

Adult: £25.00

Junior: £10.00

RECORDS

Record Home Attendance: 76,098 v Blackburn Mar 31, 2007

Record Victory: 10-0 RSC Anderlecht (European Cup) September 26, 1956

Record Defeat: 0-7 v Blackburn (league) December 27, 1930; v Wolves (league) December 26, 1931

Most League Goals: Bobby Charlton 199

Most League Apps: Bobby Charlton 606

Most Capped Player: Bobby Charlton, 106, England

HONOURS

Premiership: 1993, 1994, 1996, 1997, 1999, 2000, 2001, 2003, 2007

Division One: 1908, 1911, 1952, 1956, 1957, 1965, 1967

Division Two: 1975

FA Cup: 1909, 1948, 1963, 1997, 1983, 1985, 1990, 1994, 1996, 1999, 2004

League Cup: 1992, 2006

European Cup: 1968, 1999

European Cup Winners Cup: 1991

SQUAD RECORD 2006-07

	CLUB				INTERNATIONAL			POSITIONAL RANKING		OVERALL RANKING
	Mins	Goals	Mins per goal	% played	Country	Games	Goals	Domestic	World	All positions
GOALKEEPERS		CONCEDED					CONCEDED			
EDWIN VAN DER SAR	2880	25	115	84%	Holland	6	2	2	2	12
TOMASZ KUSZCZAK	540	2	270	16%	Poland	0	0	29	164	2044
DEFENDERS		CONCEDED					CONCEDED			
RIO FERDINAND	2925	23	127	86%	England	7	4	2	2	14
NEMANJA VIDIC	2139	15	143	63%	Serbia	5	4	19	53	143
GARY NEVILLE	1976	13	152	58%	England	4	3	26	72	190
JOHN O'SHEA	1737	16	109	51%	Rep of Ireland	8	11	34	97	262
PATRICE EVRA	1852	13	142	54%	France	1	0	39	123	339
GABRIEL IVAN HEINZE	1506	17	89	44%	Argentina	3	2	43	141	395
WES BROWN	1604	16	100	47%	England	3	1	55	200	541
MIDFIELDERS		SCORED					SCORED			
CRISTIANO RONALDO	2783	17	164	81%	Portugal	7	5	3	4	4
PAUL SCHOLES	2594	6	432	76%	England	0	0	7	13	37
MICHAEL CARRICK	2505	3	835	73%	England	6	0	9	16	42
RYAN GIGGS	2303	4	576	67%	Wales	8	1	11	25	74
DARREN FLETCHER	1430	3	477	42%	Scotland	6	1	60	258	747
JI-SUNG PARK	774	5	155	23%	South Korea	3	0	115	547	1558
FORWARDS		SCORED					SCORED			
WAYNE ROONEY	2926	14	209	86%	England	5	1	2	4	10
LOUIS SAHA	1628	8	204	48%	France	6	2	19	66	401
OLE GUNNAR SOLSKJAER	925	7	132	27%	Norway	3	2	49	265	1375

KEY: Club stats are all for the 2006-07 season. Mins = Minutes played in the league for club; Goals conceded = goals let in when the player is on the pitch; Goals scored = scored by the player; Mins per goal = number of minutes on average between each goal conceded or scored; % played = the percentage of the league season the player played; Domestic = player ranking by position in domestic league; World = player ranking by position in World; Overall Position = player ranking in world across all positions.

TEAM OF THE SEASON

- **G** Van Der Sar
- **D** Neville
- **D** Ferdinand
- **D** Vidic
- **D** Evra
- **M** Ronaldo
- **M** Carrick
- **M** Scholes
- **M** Giggs
- **F** Rooney
- **F** Saha

G STAR GOALKEEPER

EDWIN VAN DER SAR: He earned a broken nose to show for his bravery, while he helps to settle United's defence.

Average goals per game conceded by club	0.71
Goals per game conceded when player on pitch	0.78
Points per game club won when player on pitch	2.38
Minutes played	2880	Clean sheets	12

D STAR DEFENDER

GARY NEVILLE: The club captain had never been faster flying down the right wing – until injury stopped him.

Goals per game conceded when player on pitch	0.59
Points per game club won when player on pitch	2.29
Goals scored by player	0
Minutes played	1976	Clean sheets	14

M STAR MIDFIELDER

CRISTIANO RONALDO: Claimed the league record for midfield goals and he ended the season top of the assists chart – phenomenal!

Goals per game conceded when player on pitch	0.65
Goals per game club scored when player on pitch	2.31
Goals scored by player	17
Minutes played	2783	Assists	15

F STAR FORWARD

WAYNE ROONEY: A Strike Rate above 200 minutes isn't world class but he also added 13 assists to his tally.

Average goals per game scored by club	2.18
Goals per game scored when player on pitch	2.25
% of club goals scored by player	16.9
Minutes played	2926	Assists	13

2006-07 RESULTS ROUND-UP

■ Premiership ■ League Cup ■ FA Cup ■ UEFA Cup ■ Champions League

Fulham	H	5-1
Saha 7, Pearce 15 og, Rooney 16, 64, Ronaldo 19		
Charlton	A	3-0
Fletcher 48, Saha 80, Solskjaer 90		
Watford	A	2-1
Silvestre 12, Giggs 52		
Tottenham	H	1-0
Giggs 9		
Celtic	H	3-2
Saha 30 pen, 40, Solskjaer 47		
Arsenal	A	0-1
Reading	A	1-1
Ronaldo 73		
Benfica	A	1-0
Saha 60		
Newcastle	H	2-0
Solskjaer 40, 48		

Wigan	A	3-1
Vidic 62, Saha 66, Solskjaer 90		
Copenhagen	H	3-0
Scholes 39, O'Shea 46, Richardson 83		
Liverpool	H	2-0
Scholes 39, Ferdinand 66		
Crewe	A	2-1
Solskjaer 26, Lee 119		
Bolton	A	4-0
Rooney 10, 16, 89, Ronaldo 82		
Copenhagen	A	0-1
Portsmouth	H	3-0
Saha 3 pen, Ronaldo 10, Vidic 66		
Southend	A	0-1
Blackburn	A	1-0
Saha 64		
Sheff Utd	A	2-1
Rooney 30, 75		

Celtic	A	0-1
Chelsea	H	1-1
Saha 29		
Everton	H	3-0
Ronaldo 39, Evra 63, O'Shea 89		
Middlesbrough	A	2-1
Saha 19 pen, Fletcher 68		
Benfica	H	3-1
Vidic 45, Giggs 61, Saha 75		
Man City	H	3-1
Rooney 5, Saha 45, Ronaldo 84		
West Ham	A	0-1
Aston Villa	H	3-0
Ronaldo 58, 85, Scholes 64		
Wigan	H	3-1
Ronaldo 47, 51, Solskjaer 59		
Reading	H	3-2
Solskjaer 33, Ronaldo 59, 77		

Newcastle	A	2-2
Scholes 40, 46		
Aston Villa	H	2-1
Larsson 55, Solskjaer 90		
Aston Villa	H	3-1
Park 11, Carrick 13, Ronaldo 35		
Arsenal	A	1-2
Rooney 53		
Portsmouth	H	2-1
Rooney 77, 83		
Watford	H	4-0
Ronaldo 20 pen, Doyley 61 og, Larsson 70, Rooney 71		
Tottenham	A	4-0
Ronaldo 45 pen, Vidic 48, Scholes 54, Giggs 77		
Charlton	H	2-0
Park 24, Fletcher 82		

Reading	H	1-1
Carrick 45		
Lille	A	1-0
Giggs 83		
Fulham	A	2-1
Giggs 29, Ronaldo 88		
Reading	A	3-2
Heinze 2, Saha 4, Solskjaer 6		
Liverpool	A	1-0
O'Shea 90		

Lille	H	1-0
Larsson 71		
Middlesbrough	A	2-2
Rooney 23, Ronaldo 68 pen		
Bolton	H	4-1
Park 14, 25, Rooney 17, 74		
Middlesbrough	H	1-0
Ronaldo 76 pen		
Blackburn	H	4-1
Scholes 61, Carrick 73, Park 83, Solskjaer 90		
Roma	A	1-2
Rooney 60		
Portsmouth	A	1-2
O'Shea 90		
Roma	H	7-1
Carrick 11, 60, Smith 17, Rooney 19, Ronaldo 44, 49, Evra 81		

Watford	A	4-1
Rooney 7, 66, Ronaldo 28, Richardson 82		
Sheff Utd	H	2-0
Carrick 4, Rooney 50		
Middlesbrough	H	1-1
Richardson 3		
AC Milan	H	3-2
Ronaldo 5, Rooney 59, 90		
Everton	A	4-2
O'Shea 61, P.Neville 67 og, Rooney 79, Eagles 90		
AC Milan	A	0-3
Man City	A	1-0
Ronaldo 33 pen		
Chelsea	A	0-0
West Ham	H	0-1
Chelsea	A	0-1

MIDDLESBOROUGH

BORO FACTS

MANAGER	CAPTAIN
GARETH SOUTHGATE	GEORGE BOATENG

CLUB

Stadium: The Riverside Stadium

Capacity: 35,120

Average Attendance 2006-07: 27,729

Pitch Size: 105 by 68.5 metres

Website: www.mfc.co.uk

STRIP

Home: All red with white shirt cuffs

Away: White shirt with gold trim, gold shorts

SPONSORS

Shirt: 888.com (£500,000)

Kit Partner: Errea

CHEAPEST TICKET PRICES

Adult: £24.00

Junior: £15.00

RECORDS

Record Home Attendance: 53,536 v Newcastle (league) December 27, 1949

Record Victory: 9-0 v Brighton (league) August 23, 1958

Record Defeat: 0-9 v Blackburn (league) November 6, 1954

Most League Goals: George Camsell (325)

Most League Apps: Ted Williamson (563)

Most Capped Player: Wilf Mannion, 26 (England)

HONOURS

Division One: 1995

Division Two: 1927, 1929, 1974

League Cup: 2004

SQUAD RECORD 2006-07

	CLUB				INTERNATIONAL			POSITIONAL RANKING		OVERALL RANKING
	Mins	Goals	Mins per goal	% played	Country	Games	Goals	Domestic	World	All positions
GOALKEEPERS		CONCEDED					CONCEDED			
MARK SCHWARZER	3240	48	68	95%	Australia	3	1	12	32	182
BRAD JONES	1504	21	72	44%	Australia	0	0	20	95	1016
DEFENDERS		CONCEDED					CONCEDED			
EMANUEL POGATETZ	3002	41	73	88%	Austria	0	0	25	67	172
JONATHAN WOODGATE	2597	30	87	76%	England	1	1	29	79	207
ANDREW TAYLOR	2966	40	74	87%	England	0	0	31	87	234
ANDREW DAVIES	1900	25	76	56%	England	0	0	70	346	945
ABEL XAVIER	1257	21	60	37%	Portugal	0	0	104	494	1339
ROBERT HUTH	794	11	72	23%	Germany	0	0	136	632	1780
CHRIS RIGGOTT	488	13	38	14%	England	0	0	151	783	2266
STUART PARNABY	860	16	54	25%	England	0	0	144	701	2003
MIDFIELDERS		SCORED					SCORED			
STEWART DOWNING	3037	2	1519	89%	England	9	0	25	58	180
GEORGE BOATENG	3017	1	3017	88%	Holland	0	0	27	64	206
LEE CATTERMOLE	1960	1	1960	57%	England	0	0	56	235	682
JULIO ARCA	1539	2	770	45%	Argentina	0	0	70	319	897
FABIO ROCHEMBACK	1536	2	768	45%	Brazil	0	0	96	470	1314
JAMES MORRISON	1523	2	762	45%	England	0	0	98	482	1353
FORWARDS		SCORED					SCORED			
MARK VIDUKA	2081	14	149	61%	Australia	1	0	22	76	463
AYEGBENI YAKUBU	3164	12	264	93%	Nigeria	1	0	11	42	259

KEY: Club stats are all for the 2006-07 season. Mins = Minutes played in the league for club; Goals conceded = goals let in when the player is on the pitch; Goals scored = scored by the player; Mins per goal = number of minutes on average between each goal conceded or scored; % played = the percentage of the league season the player played; Domestic = player ranking by position in domestic league; World = player ranking by position in World; Overall Position = player ranking in world across all positions.

THE STARS OF LAST SEASON

TEAM OF THE SEASON

- G — Schwarzer
- D — Xavier
- D — Woodgate
- D — Pogatetz
- D — Taylor
- M — Rochemback
- M — Boateng
- M — Arca
- M — Downing
- F — Viduka
- F — Yakubu

G STAR GOALKEEPER

MARK SCHWARZER: One of his more together seasons as Gareth Southgate got the best out of the big Aussie.

Average goals per game conceded by club	1.29
Goals per game conceded when player on pitch	1.33
Points per game club won when player on pitch	1.22
Minutes played	3240	Clean sheets	8

D STAR DEFENDER

JONATHAN WOODGATE: The best defender in the team when at Leeds, Newcastle, Madrid (when not injured) and now at Boro.

Goals per game conceded when player on pitch	1.04
Points per game club won when player on pitch	1.21
Goals scored by player	0
Minutes played	2597	Clean sheets	9

M STAR MIDFIELDER

STUART DOWNING: Arca was in fine form but it is Stuart Downing who gets the nod for his 13 assists.

Goals per game conceded when player on pitch	1.41
Goals per game club scored when player on pitch	1.29
Goals scored by player	2
Minutes played	3037	Assists	13

F STAR FORWARD

MARK VIDUKA: Made the most of his time on the pitch and finished strongly with a sub 50-minute Strike Rate.

Average goals per game scored by club	1.16
Goals per game scored when player on pitch	1.67
% of club goals scored by player	31.8
Minutes played	2081	Assists	5

2006-07 RESULTS ROUND-UP

■ Premiership   ■ League Cup   ■ FA Cup   ■ UEFA Cup   ■ Champions League

Reading	A	2-3
Downing 11, Yakubu 21

| Chelsea | H | 2-1 |
Pogatetz 80, Viduka 90

| Portsmouth | H | 0-4 |

| Arsenal | A | 1-1 |
Morrison 22

| Bolton | A | 0-0 |

| Notts County | H | 0-1 |

| Blackburn | H | 0-1 |

| Sheff Utd | A | 1-2 |
Yakubu 49

| Everton | H | 2-1 |
Yakubu 27 pen, Viduka 71

| Newcastle | H | 1-0 |
Yakubu 84

| Man City | A | 0-1 |

| Watford | A | 0-2 |

| West Ham | H | 1-0 |
Maccarone 74

| Liverpool | H | 0-0 |

Aston Villa	A	1-1
Christie 43

| Man Utd | H | 1-2 |
Morrison 66

| Tottenham | A | 1-2 |
Huth 79

| Wigan | H | 1-1 |
Yakubu 67

| Fulham | A | 1-2 |
Viduka 74

| Charlton | H | 2-0 |
Yakubu 29, Arca 52

| Everton | A | 0-0 |

| Blackburn | A | 1-2 |
Yakubu 61 pen

| Sheff Utd | H | 3-1 |
Yakubu 36, Yakubu 69, 76 pen

Hull City	A	1-1
Viduka 73

| Charlton | A | 3-1 |
Cattermole 45, Arca 63, Yakubu 68

| Hull City | H | 4-3 |
Hines 32, Viduka 49, 64, Yakubu 57 pen

Bolton	H	5-1
Speed 6 og, Xavier 10, Viduka 23, 84, Downing 43

| Bristol City | A | 2-2 |
Yakubu 4, Christie 23

| Portsmouth | A | 0-0 |

| Arsenal | H | 1-1 |
Yakubu 63 pen

| Chelsea | A | 0-3 |

| Bristol City | H | 5-4* |
*Viduka 69, Yakubu 102 (*on penalties)*

| West Brom | H | 2-2 |
Arca 29, Yakubu 43 pen

| Reading | H | 2-1 |
Viduka 7, Yakubu 69

| West Brom | A | 5-4* |
*Viduka 63 (*on penalties)*

Newcastle	A	0-0

| Man Utd | H | 2-2 |
Cattermole 45, Boateng 47

| Man City | H | 0-2 |

| Man Utd | A | 0-1 |

| West Ham | A | 0-0 |

| Watford | H | 4-1 |
Viduka 5, 75, Boateng 27, Rochemback 79

| Aston Villa | H | 1-3 |
Rochemback 13

| Liverpool | A | 0-2 |

| Man Utd | A | 1-1 |
Viduka 45

Wigan	A	1-0
Viduka 29

| Fulham | H | 3-1 |
Viduka 34, 47, Wheater 45

Tottenham	H	2-3
Viduka 66, Pogatetz 89

NEWCASTLE FACTS

MANAGER	CAPTAIN
GLENN ROEDER	SCOTT PARKER

CLUB

Stadium: St James' Park

Capacity: 52,387

Average Attendance 2006-07: 50,686

Pitch Size: 105m by 67m

Website: ww.nufc.co.uk

STRIP

Home: Black and white stripe shirts, black shorts

Away: All pale blue with black trim

SPONSORS

Shirt: Northern Rock (£5m per year)

Kit Partner: Adidas

CHEAPEST TICKET PRICES

Adult: £27.00

Junior: £10.00

RECORDS

Record Home Attendance: 68,386 v Chelsea (league) September 3, 1930

Record Victory: 13-0 v Newport County (league) October 5, 1946

Record Defeat: 0-9 v Burton Wanderers (league) April 15, 1895

Most League Goals: Jackie Milburn (178)

Most League Apps: Jim Lawrence (432)

Most Capped Player: Alf McMichael, 40 (Northen Ireland)

HONOURS

Division One: 1905, 1907, 1909, 1927, 1993 (old Second Division)

Division Two 1965

FA Cup 1910, 1924, 1932, 1951, 1952, 1955

UEFA Cup: 1969 (as Fairs Cup)

SQUAD RECORD 2006-07

	CLUB				INTERNATIONAL			POSITIONAL RANKING		OVERALL RANKING
	Mins	Goals	Mins per goal	% played	Country	Games	Goals	Domestic	World	All positions
GOALKEEPERS			CONCEDED				CONCEDED			
SHAY GIVEN	1880	27	70	55%	Rep of Ireland	4	1	16	64	408
STEVE HARPER	1445	18	80	42%	England	0	0	21	110	1335
DEFENDERS			CONCEDED				CONCEDED			
STEVEN TAYLOR	2385	31	77	70%	England	0	0	27	74	197
PETER RAMAGE	1706	26	66	50%	England	0	0	59	257	692
STEPHEN CARR	2055	27	76	60%	Rep of Ireland	2	5	67	332	914
CELESTINE BABAYARO	1035	13	80	30%	Nigeria	0	0	115	559	1524
CRAIG MOORE	1404	18	78	41%	Australia	1	0	103	480	1304
TITUS BRAMBLE	1493	17	88	44%	England	0	0	80	381	1037
MIDFIELDERS			SCORED				SCORED			
JAMES MILNER	2680	3	893	78%	England	0	0	26	63	199
NICKY BUTT	2290	1	2290	67%	England	0	0	35	91	286
SCOTT PARKER	2420	3	807	71%	England	1	0	48	142	433
NOLBERTO SOLANO	2142	2	1071	63%	Peru	4	0	44	125	382
EMRE BELOZOGLU	1819	2	910	53%	Turkey	1	0	55	232	677
KIERON DYER	1683	5	337	49%	England	4	0	59	245	709
DAMIEN DUFF	1725	1	1725	50%	Rep of Ireland	7	0	73	346	958
CHARLES N'ZOGBIA	1130	0	0	33%	France	0	0	94	463	1289
MIDFIELDERS			SCORED				SCORED			
OBAFEMI MARTINS	2863	11	260	84%	Nigeria	3	2	6	19	131
ANTOINE SIBIERSKI	1453	3	484	42%	France	0	0	41	175	978

KEY: Club stats are all for the 2006-07 season. Mins = Minutes played in the league for club; Goals conceded = goals let in when the player is on the pitch; Goals scored = scored by the player; Mins per goal = number of minutes on average between each goal conceded or scored; % played = the percentage of the league season the player played; Domestic = player ranking by position in domestic league; World = player ranking by position in World; Overall Position = player ranking in world across all positions.

THE STARS OF LAST SEASON

TEAM OF THE SEASON

- **G** Given
- **D** Carr — **D** Taylor — **D** Bramble — **D** Babayaro
- **M** Solano — **M** Dyer — **M** Parker — **M** Duff
- **F** Sibierski — **F** Martins

G STAR GOALKEEPER

SHAY GIVEN: Injuries meant rival Harper saw plenty of action and both were in good form but Given was the club's top point earner.

Average goals per game conceded by club	1.24
Goals per game conceded when player on pitch	1.29
Points per game club won when player on pitch	1.55
Minutes played 1880	Clean sheets 4

D STAR DEFENDER

TITUS BRAMBLE: Often given a hard time by the fans but the Magpie's defence was tightest when Titus was in it.

Goals per game conceded when player on pitch	1.81
Points per game club won when player on pitch	1.21
Goals scored by player	0
Minutes played 1493	Clean sheets 4

M STAR MIDFIELDER

KIERON DYER: Returned to the side in the second half of the season, adding enough spice to the attack to earn an England recall.

Goals per game conceded when player on pitch	1.13
Goals per game club scored when player on pitch	1.18
Goals scored by player	5
Minutes played 1683	Assists 3

F STAR FORWARD

OBAFEMI MARTINS: He hit 17 goals in all competitions but a league Strike Rate of a goal every 260 minutes isn't Owen class.

Average goals per game scored by club	1.00
Goals per game scored when player on pitch	1.11
% of club goals scored by player	28.9
Minutes played 2863	Assists 5

2006-07 RESULTS ROUND-UP

■ Premiership ■ League Cup ■ FA Cup ■ UEFA Cup ■ Champions League

FK Ventspils	A	1-0
Bramble 70		
Wigan	H	2-1
Parker 38, Ameobi 62		

FK Ventspils	H	0-0
Sibierski 10		
Aston Villa	A	0-2
Fulham	H	1-2
Parker 54		

Levadia Tallinn	A	1-0
West Ham	A	2-0
Duff 49, Martins 74		
Liverpool	A	0-2
Everton	H	1-1
Ameobi 14		
Levadia Tallinn	H	2-1
Martins 47, 50		
Man Utd	A	0-2
Bolton	H	1-2
Ameobi 17 pen		
Fenerbahce	H	1-0
Sibierski 79		
Middlesbrough	A	0-1
Portsmouth	H	3-0
Rossi 48, Solano 53, 90		

Charlton	H	0-0
Palermo	A	1-0
Luque 37		
Sheff Utd	H	0-1
Watford	A	5-4*
*Sibierski 3, Parker 116 (*on penalties)*		
Man City	A	0-0
Arsenal	A	1-1
Dyer 30		
Celta Vigo	H	2-1
Sibierski 37, Taylor 86		
Portsmouth	H	1-0
Sibierski 69		
intr Frankfurt	A	0-0
Reading	H	3-2
Sibierski 23, Martins 57 pen, Emre Belozoglu 84		

Blackburn	A	3-1
Martins 31, 90, Taylor 35		
Chelsea	A	0-1
Watford	H	2-1
Martins 49, 85		
Chelsea	H	0-1
Tottenham	H	3-1
Dyer 3, Martins 7, Parker 34		
Bolton	A	1-2
Dyer 8		
Everton	A	0-3
Man Utd	H	2-2
Milner 33, Edgar 73		
Birmingham	A	2-2
Taylor 40, Dyer 54		
Tottenham	A	3-2
Huntington 16, Martins 72, Butt 74		

Birmingham	H	1-5
Milner 56		
West Ham	H	2-2
Milner 45, Solano 53 pen		
Aston Villa	H	3-1
Milner 5, Dyer 7, Sibierski 90		
Fulham	A	1-2
Martins 90		
Liverpool	H	2-1
Martins 26, Solano 70 pen		
Z-Waregem	A	3-1
Dindeleux 47 og, Martins 59 pen, Sibierski 76		
Z-Waregem	H	1-0
Martins 68		
Wigan	A	0-1
Middlesbrough	H	0-0

AZ Alkmaar	H	4-2
Steinsson 7 og, Dyer 22, Martins 23, 37		
AZ Alkmaar	A	0-2
Charlton	A	0-2
Man City	H	0-1
Sheff Utd	A	2-1
Martins 17, Taylor 80		
Arsenal	H	0-0
Portsmouth	A	1-2
Emre Belozoglu 69 pen		
Chelsea	H	0-0
Reading	A	0-1
Blackburn	H	0-2
Watford	A	1-1
Dyer 29		

PORTSMOUTH

Premiership position 06-07 **9th**
FA Cup **Round 4**
Carling Cup **Round 3**

PORTSMOUTH FACTS

MANAGER	CAPTAIN
HARRY REDKNAPP	DEJAN STEFANOVIC

CLUB
Stadium: Fratton Park
Capacity: 20,288
Average Attendance 2006-07: 19,878
Pitch Size: 105m by 67m
Website: www.pompeyfc.co.uk

STRIP
Home: Blue shirts with white trim, white shorts
Away: White shirts with blue, blue shorts

SPONSORS
Shirt: OKI Printing Solutions (£350,000)
Kit Partner: JAKO

CHEAPEST TICKET PRICES
Adult: £26.00
Junior: £12.00

RECORDS
Record Home Attendance: 51,585 v Derby County (FA Cup) February 26, 1949
Record Victory: 9-1 v Notts County (league) April 9, 1927
Record Defeat: 0-10 v Leicester City (league) October 20, 1928
Most League Goals: Peter Harris (194)
Most League Apps: Jimmy Dickinson (764)
Most Capped Player: Jimmy Dickinson, 48 (England)

HONOURS
Division One: 1949, 1950, 2003*
Division Three: 1962, 1983
Division Three (South): 1924
FA Cup: 1939

SQUAD RECORD 2006-07

	CLUB				INTERNATIONAL			POSITIONAL RANKING		OVERALL RANKING
	Mins	Goals	Mins per goal	% played	Country	Games	Goals	Domestic	World	All positions
GOALKEEPERS		CONCEDED					CONCEDED			
DAVID JAMES	3420	42	81	100%	England	0	0	10	25	117
DEFENDERS		CONCEDED					CONCEDED			
LINVOY PRIMUS	3142	37	85	92%	England	0	0	23	63	167
SOL CAMPBELL	2880	30	96	84%	England	0	0	32	89	238
DEJAN STEFANOVIC	1703	17	100	50%	Serbia	0	0	68	336	925
GLEN JOHNSON	2258	25	90	66%	England	0	0	61	279	751
NOE PAMAROT	1807	31	58	53%	France	0	0	88	421	1152
DJIMI TRAORE	1598	31	52	47%	France	0	0	95	446	1226
ETAME MAYER LAUREN	797	8	100	23%	Cameroon	0	0	130	604	1650
MIDFIELDERS		SCORED					SCORED			
GARY O'NEIL	3088	1	3088	90%	England	0	0	29	71	227
MATTHEW TAYLOR	2687	8	336	79%	England	0	0	40	107	329
SEAN DAVIS	2491	0	0	73%	England	0	0	52	164	491
PEDRO MENDES	2075	2	1038	61%	Portugal	0	0	68	315	890
NIKO KRANJCAR	1289	2	645	38%	Croatia	9	0	91	446	1225
RICHARD HUGHES	1055	0	0	31%	Scotland	0	0	108	523	1476
ARNOLD MVUEMBA	282	1	282	8%	France	0	0	167	869	2467
FORWARDS		SCORED					SCORED			
NWANKWO KANU	2709	10	271	79%	Nigeria	3	1	16	59	383
BENJANI MWARUWARI	2030	6	338	59%	Zimbabwe	2	0	36	141	796
LOMANA LUALUA	957	2	479	28%	DR Congo	2	0	68	369	1762

KEY: Club stats are all for the 2006-07 season. Mins = Minutes played in the league for club; Goals conceded = goals let in when the player is on the pitch; Goals scored = scored by the player; Mins per goal = number of minutes on average between each goal conceded or scored; % played = the percentage of the league season the player played; Domestic = player ranking by position in domestic league; World = player ranking by position in World; Overall Position = player ranking in world across all positions.

THE STARS OF LAST SEASON

TEAM OF THE SEASON

G — James

D — Johnson | D — Primus | D — Campbell | D — Stefanovic

M — O'Neil | M — Davis | M — Mendes | M — Taylor

F — Mwaruwari | F — Kanu

G STAR GOALKEEPER

DAVID JAMES: Became the Premiership's top collector of clean sheets, overtaking Seaman's record of 141 in a return to form.

Average goals per game conceded by club	1.11
Goals per game conceded when player on pitch	1.11
Points per game club won when player on pitch	1.42
Minutes played **3420**	Clean sheets **12**

D STAR DEFENDER
SOL CAMPBELL: Formed a strong understanding with Primus and former England colleague James to offer solidity.

Goals per game conceded when player on pitch	0.94
Points per game club won when player on pitch	1.47
Goals scored by player	1
Minutes played **2880**	Clean sheets **11**

M STAR MIDFIELDER
PEDRO MENDES: Already a favourite with the Fratton crowd, Mendes won more fans by his lenient response to Thatcher's elbow.

Goals per game conceded when player on pitch	1.08
Goals per game club scored when player on pitch	1.18
Goals scored by player	2
Minutes played **2075**	Assists **5**

F STAR FORWARD
NWANKWO KANU: Four goals in the first three games promised much but that Strike Rate slipped despite his silky skills.

Average goals per game scored by club	1.18
Goals per game scored when player on pitch	1.23
% of club goals scored by player	22.2
Minutes played **2709**	Assists **3**

2006-07 RESULTS ROUND-UP

■ Premiership ■ League Cup ■ FA Cup ■ UEFA Cup ■ Champions League

Blackburn	H	3-0
Todorov 26, Kanu 62, 84

Man City	A	0-0

Middlesbrough	A	4-0
Kanu 7, 57, Mwaruwari 50, Todorov 90

Wigan	H	1-0
Mwaruwari 49

Charlton	A	1-0
LuaLua 74

Mansfield	A	2-1
Manuel Fernandes 5, Taylor 33

Bolton	H	0-1

Tottenham	A	1-2
Kanu 40

West Ham	H	2-0
Kanu 24, Cole 82

Chelsea	A	1-2
Mwaruwari 69

Newcastle	A	0-3

Reading	H	3-1
Gunnarsson 10 og, Kanu 52, Mendes 66

Man Utd	A	0-3

Fulham	H	1-1
Cole 74

Watford	H	2-1
Kanu 44, LuaLua 89 pen

Newcastle	A	0-1

Liverpool	A	0-0

Aston Villa	H	2-2
Taylor 52, 80 pen

Everton	H	2-0
Taylor 14, Kanu 26

Arsenal	A	2-2
Pamarot 45, Taylor 47

Sheff Utd	H	3-1
Kozluk 48 og, Campbell 54, Pamarot 68

West Ham	A	2-1
Primus 16, 38

Bolton	A	2-3
Taylor 2, Cole 90

Tottenham	H	1-1
Mwaruwari 29

Wigan	H	2-1
Cole 64, Kanu 90

Sheff Utd	A	1-1
O'Neil 81

Charlton	H	0-1

Man Utd	A	1-2
Kanu 87

Middlesbrough	H	0-0

Wigan	A	0-1

Man City	H	2-1
Mendes 5, Kanu 81

Blackburn	A	0-3

Chelsea	H	0-2

Reading	A	0-0

Fulham	A	1-1
Kranjcar 4

Man Utd	H	2-1
Taylor 30, Ferdinand 89 og

Watford	A	2-4
Taylor 16, Mvuemba 81

Newcastle	H	2-1
Mwaruwari 7, Taylor 59

Aston Villa	A	0-0

Liverpool	H	2-1
Mwaruwari 27, Kranjcar 32

Everton	A	0-3

Arsenal	H	0-0

READING

READING FACTS

MANAGER	CAPTAIN
STEVE COPPELL	GRAEME MURTY

CLUB

Stadium: Madejski Stadium

Capacity: 24,200

Average Attendance 2006-07: 23,829

Pitch Size: 102m by 70m

Website: www.readingfc.co.uk

STRIP

Home: White shirt with blue hoops, blue shorts

Away: Black shirt with pale green hoops, black shorts

SPONSORS

Shirt: Kyocera (£300,000 per year)

Kit Partner: Puma

CHEAPEST TICKET PRICES

Adult: £28.00

Junior: £7.00

RECORDS

Record Home Attendance: 24,122 v Aston Villa (league) February 10, 2007

Record Victory: 11-0 v Chesham Generals (FA Cup) November 17, 1901

Record Defeat: 0-18 v Preston North End (FA Cup) January 27, 1894

Most League Goals: Ronny Blackman (158)

Most League Apps: Martin Hicks (500)

Most Capped Player: Jimmy Quinn, 17 (Northern Ireland)

HONOURS

Championship: 2006

Division Two: 1994

Division Three: 1926, 1986

Division Four: 1979

THE STARS OF LAST SEASON

TEAM OF THE SEASON

G Hahnemann

D Murty — D Ingimarsson — D Sonko — D Shorey

M Little — M Harper — M Sidwell — M Hunt

F Lita — F Doyle

G STAR GOALKEEPER

MARCUS HAHNEMANN: The American looked at home in the Premiership and finished sixth in our shot-stoppers chart.

Average goals per game conceded by club	1.24
Goals per game conceded when player on pitch	1.23
Points per game club won when player on pitch	1.50
Minutes played	3306	Clean sheets	13

D STAR DEFENDER

IVAR INGIMARSSON: Played every minute of the season as other defenders chopped and changed around him.

Goals per game conceded when player on pitch	1.24
Points per game club won when player on pitch	1.45
Goals scored by player	2
Minutes played	3420	Clean sheets	13

M STAR MIDFIELDER

JAMES HARPER: Another who repaid Coppell's faith in spades and the hardest worked player in an under-rated midfield.

Goals per game conceded when player on pitch	1.27
Goals per game club scored when player on pitch	1.38
Goals scored by player	3
Minutes played	3199	Assists	3

F STAR FORWARD

KEVIN DOYLE: A bargain buy from Cork for £78,000, who makes finishing seem easy and won an international call-up.

Average goals per game scored by club	1.37
Goals per game scored when player on pitch	1.48
% of club goals scored by player	25.0
Minutes played	2469	Assists	3

SQUAD RECORD 2006-07

	CLUB				INTERNATIONAL			POSITIONAL RANKING		OVERALL RANKING
	Mins	Goals	Mins per goal	% played	Country	Games	Goals	Domestic	World	All positions
GOALKEEPERS		CONCEDED				CONCEDED				
MARCUS HAHNEMANN	3306	45	73	97%	United States	0	0	8	23	111
DEFENDERS		CONCEDED				CONCEDED				
IVAR INGIMARSSON	3420	47	73	100%	Iceland	8	15	11	26	83
NICKY SHOREY	3330	46	72	97%	England	1	1	13	28	86
GRAEME MURTY	1981	25	79	58%	Scotland	0	0	56	228	614
IBRAHIMA SONKO	1926	30	64	56%	Senegal	0	0	57	246	652
ULISES DE LA CRUZ	748	8	94	22%	Ecuador	4	10	117	568	1542
ANDRE BIKEY	832	8	104	24%	Cameroon	0	0	131	611	1681
MIDFIELDERS		SCORED				SCORED				
JAMES HARPER	3199	3	1066	94%	England	0	0	20	48	155
STEVEN SIDWELL	3092	4	773	90%	England	0	0	19	42	136
STEPHEN HUNT	2426	4	607	71%	Rep of Ireland	4	0	45	129	392
GLEN LITTLE	1591	0	0	47%	England	0	0	84	412	1144
BRYNJAR GUNNARSSON	1167	3	389	34%	Iceland	0	0	102	496	1388
JOHN OSTER	852	1	852	25%	Wales	0	0	130	617	1721
FORWARDS		SCORED				SCORED				
KEVIN DOYLE	2469	13	190	72%	Rep of Ireland	4	2	13	45	282
LEROY LITA	2005	7	286	59%	England	0	0	34	135	780
KI-HYEON SEOL	1818	4	455	53%	South Korea	2	0	39	153	864
DAVID KITSON	804	2	402	24%	England	0	0	59	335	1665
SHANE LONG	814	2	407	24%	Rep of Ireland	3	0	61	350	1710

KEY: Club stats are all for the 2006-07 season. Mins = Minutes played in the league for club; Goals conceded = goals let in when the player is on the pitch; Goals scored = scored by the player; Mins per goal = number of minutes on average between each goal conceded or scored; % played = the percentage of the league season the player played; Domestic = player ranking by position in domestic league; World = player ranking by position in World; Overall Position = player ranking in world across all positions.

2006-07 RESULTS ROUND-UP

■ Premiership ■ League Cup ■ FA Cup ■ UEFA Cup ■ Champions League

Middlesbrough	H	3-2
Kitson 43, Sidwell 44, Lita 55		
Aston Villa	A	1-2
Doyle 4		
Wigan	A	0-1
Man City	H	1-0
Ingimarsson 22		
Sheff Utd	A	2-1
Doyle 1, Seol 25		
Darlington	H	4-2*
*Lita 31, 35, Mate 86 (*on penalties)*		
Man Utd	H	1-1
Doyle 48 pen		
West Ham	A	1-0
Seol 2		
Chelsea	H	0-1

Arsenal	H	0-4
Liverpool	A	3-4
Bikey 75, Lita 81, Long 85		
Portsmouth	A	1-3
Doyle 84		
Liverpool	A	0-2
Tottenham	H	3-1
Shorey 38, Sidwell 45, Doyle 79		
Charlton	H	2-0
Seol 18, Doyle 72		
Fulham	A	1-0
Doyle 17 pen		
Bolton	H	1-0
Doyle 33		
Newcastle	A	2-3
Harper 37, 42		

Watford	A	0-0
Blackburn	H	1-2
Harper 41		
Everton	H	0-2

Chelsea	A	2-2
Lita 67, Essien 85 og		
Man Utd	A	2-3
Sonko 38, Lita 90		
West Ham	H	6-0
Gunnarsson 12, Hunt 15, Ferdinand 30 og, Doyle 36, 78, Lita 53		
Burnley	H	3-2
Lita 28, Long 37, Sodje 55		
Everton	A	1-1
Lescott 27 og		
Sheff Utd	H	3-1
Long 44, De La Cruz 50, Hunt 70		
Birmingham	A	3-2
Kitson 3, Lita 41, 82		
Wigan	H	3-2
Ingimarsson 31, Long 51, Lita 88		

Man City	A	2-0
Lita 79, 89		
Aston Villa	H	2-0
Sidwell 16, 90		
Man Utd	A	1-1
Gunnarsson 67		

Middlesbrough	A	1-2
Oster 87		
Man Utd	H	2-3
Kitson 23, Lita 84		
Arsenal	A	1-2
Fabregas 87 og		

Portsmouth	H	0-0
Tottenham	A	0-1
Liverpool	H	1-2
Gunnarsson 47		
Charlton	A	0-0
Fulham	H	1-0
Hunt 15		
Bolton	A	3-1
Doyle 84 pen, 89, Hunt 90		
Newcastle	H	1-0
Kitson 51		
Watford	H	0-2
Blackburn	A	3-3
Seol 36, Doyle 58, Gunnarsson 77		

SHEFFIELD UNITED

SHEFF UTD FACTS

MANAGER	CAPTAIN
NEIL WARNOCK	CHRIS MORGAN

CLUB

Stadium: Bramall Lane

Capacity: 32,609

Average Attendance 2006-07: 30,512

Pitch Size: 102m x 66m

Website: www.sufc.co.uk

STRIP

Home: Red and white striped shirts, black shorts

Away: Green shirts, black shorts

SPONSORS

Shirt: Capital One (£350,000 per year)

Kit Partner: Le Coq Sportif

CHEAPEST TICKET PRICES

Adult: £15.00

Junior: £10.00

RECORDS

Record Home Attendance: 68,287 v Leeds United (FA Cup) February 15, 1936

Record Victory: 10-0 v Port Vale (league) December 10, 1892; Burnley (league) January 19, 1929

Record Defeat: 0-13 v Bolton Wanderers (FA Cup) February 1 1890

Most League Goals: Harry Johnson (201)

Most League Apps: Joe Shaw (632)

Most Capped Player: Billy Gillespie, 25 (Northern Ireland)

HONOURS

Division One: 1898

Division Two: 1953

Division Four: 1982

FA Cup: 1899, 1902, 1915, 1925

SQUAD RECORD 2006-07

	CLUB				INTERNATIONAL			POSITIONAL RANKING		OVERALL RANKING
	Mins	Goals	Mins per goal	% played	Country	Games	Goals	Domestic	World	All positions
GOALKEEPERS		CONCEDED					CONCEDED			
PATRICK KENNY	3031	46	66	89%	Rep of Ireland	2	9	25	131	1633
DEFENDERS		CONCEDED					CONCEDED			
DEREK GEARY	2217	36	62	65%	Rep of Ireland	0	0	22	62	166
CHRIS MORGAN	2033	32	64	59%	England	0	0	109	520	1413
CHRIS ARMSTRONG	2214	37	60	65%	England	0	0	143	694	1978
ROBERT KOZLUK	1489	25	60	44%	England	0	0	91	436	1187
LEIGH BROMBY	1139	19	60	33%	England	0	0	116	562	1529
CLAUDE DAVIS	1494	24	62	44%	Jamaica	0	0	146	738	2140
MIDFIELDERS		SCORED					SCORED			
KEITH GILLESPIE	2376	2	1188	69%	N Ireland	7	0	173	923	2638
PHILIP JAGIELKA	3420	4	855	100%	England	0	0	107	520	1470
NICK MONTGOMERY	1988	0	0	58%	England	0	0	178	960	2769
MIKELE LEIGERTWOOD	1410	0	0	41%	England	0	0	179	963	2775
MICHAEL TONGE	2012	2	1006	59%	England	0	0	106	518	1465
STEPHEN QUINN	1200	2	600	35%	Rep of Ireland	0	0	186	1012	2942
COLIN KAZIM-RICHARDS	1506	1	1506	44%	England	0	0	152	779	2198
FORWARDS		SCORED					SCORED			
JONATHAN STEAD	2497	9	277	73%	England	0	0	42	185	1032
CHRISTIAN NADE	926	3	309	27%	France	0	0	105	630	2689
ROBERT HULSE	2450	8	306	72%	England	0	0	53	301	1506
DANNY WEBBER	1156	3	385	34%	England	0	0	72	376	1796

KEY: Club stats are all for the 2006-07 season. Mins = Minutes played in the league for club; Goals conceded = goals let in when the player is on the pitch; Goals scored = scored by the player; Mins per goal = number of minutes on average between each goal conceded or scored; % played = the percentage of the league season the player played; Domestic = player ranking by position in domestic league; World = player ranking by position in World; Overall Position = player ranking in world across all positions.

THE STARS OF LAST SEASON

TEAM OF THE SEASON

- G: Kenny
- D: Kozluk, Armstrong, Morgan, Geary
- M: Kazim-Richards, Jagielka, Montgomery, Tonge
- F: Stead, Hulse

G STAR GOALKEEPER

PADDY KENNY: Lost an eyebrow in a fight and raised a few with some of his on-field antics but a fine shot-stopper.

Average goals per game conceded by club	1.45
Goals per game conceded when player on pitch	1.37
Points per game club won when player on pitch	1.83
Minutes played	3031	Clean sheets	8

D STAR DEFENDER

DEREK GEARY: The small fullback who's full of running and Warnock's most consistent defensive choice.

Goals per game conceded when player on pitch	1.46
Points per game club won when player on pitch	1.25
Goals scored by player	0
Minutes played	2217	Clean sheets	6

M STAR MIDFIELDER

COLIN KAZIM-RICHARDS: Scored a rare goal from distance against Bolton and added spice to the attack.

Goals per game conceded when player on pitch	1.50
Goals per game club scored when player on pitch	1.02
Goals scored by player	1
Minutes played	1506	Assists	3

F STAR FORWARD

JONATHAN STEAD: Signed to take over Danny Webber's place in the side and ended up leading the attack.

Average goals per game scored by club	0.84
Goals per game scored when player on pitch	1.20
% of club goals scored by player	15.6
Minutes played	1059	Assists	0

2006-07 RESULTS ROUND-UP

■ Premiership ■ League Cup ■ FA Cup ■ UEFA Cup ■ Champions League

Liverpool	H	1-1
Hulse 46		
Tottenham	A	0-2
Fulham	A	0-1
Blackburn	H	0-0
Reading	H	1-2
Hulse 61		
Bury	H	1-0
Nade 16		
Arsenal	A	0-3
Middlesbrough	H	2-1
Hulse 35, Jagielka 90		
Man City	A	0-0
Everton	A	0-2

Birmingham	H	2-4
Akinbiyi 21, Montgomery 85		
Chelsea	H	0-2
Newcastle	A	1-0
Webber 68		
Bolton	H	2-2
Hulse 70, Kazim-Richards 73		
Man Utd	H	1-2
Gillespie 13		
West Ham	A	0-1
Watford	A	1-0
Webber 88		
Charlton	H	2-1
Morgan 64, Gillespie 88		
Aston Villa	H	2-2
S.Quinn 50, Webber 64		
Wigan	A	1-0
Hulse 45		

Portsmouth	A	1-3
Hulse 4		
Man City	H	0-1
Arsenal	H	1-0
Nade 41		
Middlesbrough	A	1-3
Jagielka 45 pen		
Swansea	H	0-3
Portsmouth	H	1-1
S.Quinn 22		
Reading	A	1-3
Nade 77		
Fulham	H	2-0
Stead 23, Tonge 28		

Blackburn	A	1-2
Stead 25		
Tottenham	H	2-1
Hulse 27, Jagielka 62 pen		
Liverpool	A	0-4
Everton	H	1-1
Hulse 52		
Chelsea	A	0-3
Bolton	A	0-1
Newcastle	H	1-2
Nade 74		
West Ham	H	3-0
Tonge 39, Jagielka 68, Stead 78		
Man Utd	A	0-2

Charlton	A	1-1
Stead 69		
Watford	H	1-0
Powell 44 og		
Aston Villa	A	0-3
Wigan	H	1-2
Stead 38		

SPURS FACTS

MANAGER	CAPTAIN
MARTIN JOL	LEDLEY KING

CLUB
Stadium: White Hart Lane
Capacity: 36,326
Average Attendance 2006-07: 35,739
Pitch Size: 105m x 66.8m
Website: www.tottenhamhotspur.com

STRIP
Home: All white
Away: All dark blue

SPONSORS
Shirt: Mansion (£8.5m per year)
Kit Partner: Puma

CHEAPEST TICKET PRICES
Adult: £27.00
Junior: £14.00

RECORDS
Record Home Attendance: 75,038 v Sunderland (FA Cup) March 5, 1938
Record Victory: 13-2 v Crewe Alexander (FA Cup) February 3, 1960
Record Defeat: 0-8 v Cologne (InterToto) July 22, 1995
Most League Goals: Jimmy Greaves (202)
Most League Apps: Steve Perryman (655)
Most Capped Player: Pat Jennings, 74 (Northern Ireland)

HONOURS
League Champions: 1951, 1961
Division Two: 1920, 1950
FA Cup: 1901, 1921, 1961, 1962, 1967, 1981, 1982, 1991
League Cup: 1971, 1973, 1999
UEFA Cup: 1972, 1984
European Cup Winners Cup: 1963

WINNERS 1999

SQUAD RECORD 2006-07

	CLUB				INTERNATIONAL			POSITIONAL RANKING		OVERALL RANKING
	Mins	Goals	Mins per goal	% played	Country	Games	Goals	Domestic	World	All positions
GOALKEEPERS										
	CONCEDED					CONCEDED				
PAUL ROBINSON	3420	54	63	100%	England	10	4	4	8	47
DEFENDERS										
	CONCEDED					CONCEDED				
MICHAEL DAWSON	3282	52	63	96%	England	0	0	7	13	39
PASCAL CHIMBONDA	2927	46	64	86%	France	0	0	9	22	70
LEDLEY KING	1880	27	70	55%	England	3	1	37	116	306
YOUNG-PYO LEE	1764	29	61	52%	South Korea	2	2	60	259	702
RICARDO ROCHA	765	12	64	22%	Portugal	3	2	64	298	799
BENOIT ASSOU-EKOTTO	1395	20	70	41%	Cameroon	0	0	84	394	1065
MIDFIELDERS										
	SCORED					SCORED				
DIDIER ZOKORA	2302	0	0	67%	Ivory Coast	4	0	22	54	173
AARON LENNON	1974	3	658	58%	England	5	0	34	90	280
JERMAINE JENAS	2160	6	360	63%	England	2	0	36	93	300
STEED MALBRANQUE	1589	2	795	46%	France	0	0	63	286	822
TOM HUDDLESTONE	1510	1	1510	44%	England	0	0	65	300	855
TEEMU TAINIO	1491	2	746	44%	Finland	5	0	71	321	899
HOSSAM GHALY	1394	1	1394	41%	Egypt	3	0	82	392	1094
FORWARDS										
	SCORED					SCORED				
DIMITAR BERBATOV	2716	12	226	79%	Bulgaria	8	2	3	6	34
ROBBIE KEANE	1655	11	150	48%	Rep of Ireland	5	3	17	60	385
JERMAIN DEFOE	1933	10	193	57%	England	8	2	25	84	497
HOSSAM MIDO	653	1	653	19%	Egypt	0	0	85	445	2010

KEY: Club stats are all for the 2006-07 season. Mins = Minutes played in the league for club; Goals conceded = goals let in when the player is on the pitch; Goals scored = scored by the player; Mins per goal = number of minutes on average between each goal conceded or scored; % played = the percentage of the league season the player played; Domestic = player ranking by position in domestic league; World = player ranking by position in World; Overall Position = player ranking in world across all positions.

THE STARS OF LAST SEASON

TEAM OF THE SEASON

G Robinson
D Chimbonda — D Dawson — D King — D Lee
M Lennon — M Zokora — M Jenas — M Malbranque
F Keane — F Berbatov

G STAR GOALKEEPER
PAUL ROBINSON: He fired a goal over England rival Foster's head to score but Spurs' defence was leaky

Average goals per game conceded by club	1.42
Goals per game conceded when player on pitch	1.42
Points per game club won when player on pitch	1.58
Minutes played	3420	Clean sheets	6

D STAR DEFENDER
LEDLEY KING: His performances for Spurs were limited by injury but he was still a regular in the England squad.

Goals per game conceded when player on pitch	1.29
Points per game club won when player on pitch	1.81
Goals scored by player	0
Minutes played	1880	Clean sheets	4

M STAR MIDFIELDER
AARON LENNON: The pacy and versatile winger lost his England spot to Beckham but is always improving.

Goals per game conceded when player on pitch	1.67
Goals per game club scored when player on pitch	1.84
Goals scored by player	3
Minutes played	1974	Assists	12

F STAR FORWARD
DIMITAR BERBATOV: He scored 23 goals in all competitions and set up 13 for colleagues in a stellar season.

Average goals per game scored by club	1.50
Goals per game scored when player on pitch	1.73
% of club goals scored by player	21.1
Minutes played	2716	Assists	13

2006-07 RESULTS ROUND-UP

□ Premiership ■ League Cup ■ FA Cup ■ UEFA Cup □ Champions League

Bolton	A	0-2
Sheff Utd	H	2-0
Berbatov 8, Jenas 18		
Everton	H	0-2
Man Utd	A	0-1
Slavia Prague	A	1-0
Jenas 37		
Fulham	H	0-0
Liverpool	A	0-3
Slavia Prague	H	1-0
Keane 80		
Portsmouth	H	2-1
Murphy 1, Defoe 35 pen		
Aston Villa	A	1-1
Angel 76 og		

Besiktas	A	2-0
Ghaly 31, Berbatov 63		
West Ham	H	1-0
Mido 45		
MK Dons	A	5-0
Mido 36, 59, Defoe 44, 51, Keane 90		
Watford	A	0-0
Club Brugge	H	3-1
Berbatov 17, 73, Keane 63		
Chelsea	H	2-1
Dawson 25, Lennon 52		
Port Vale	H	3-1
Huddlestone 80, 99, Defoe 107		
Reading	A	1-3
Keane 23 pen		
Blackburn	A	1-1
Defoe 61 pen		

B Leverkusen	A	1-0
Berbatov 36		
Wigan	H	3-1
Defoe 43, Berbatov 44, Lennon 90		
Arsenal	A	0-3
Middlesbrough	H	2-1
Berbatov 48, Keane 83		
Charlton	H	5-1
Berbatov 31, 66, Tainio 33, Malbranque 55, Defoe 63		
Din Bucharest	H	3-1
Berbatov 16, Defoe 39, 50		
Man City	A	2-1
Davenport 16, Huddlestone 24		
Southend	H	1-0
Defoe 115		
Newcastle	A	1-3
Murphy 15		

Aston Villa	H	2-1
Defoe 58, 77		
Liverpool	H	0-1
Portsmouth	A	1-1
Malbranque 50		
Cardiff	A	0-0
Newcastle	H	2-3
Defoe 14, Berbatov 54		
Cardiff	H	4-0
Lennon 27, Keane 30, Malbranque 41, Defoe 81		
Fulham	A	1-1
Chimbonda 88		
Arsenal	H	2-2
Berbatov 12, Baptista 20 og		
Southend	H	3-1
Keane 12, Jenas 50, Mido 76		

Arsenal	A	1-3
Mido 83		
Man Utd	H	0-4
Sheff Utd	A	1-2
Jenas 2		
Fulham	A	4-0
Keane 6, 68, Berbatov 77, 90		
Everton	A	2-1
Berbatov 35, Jenas 88		

Bolton	H	4-1
Keane 11, 22, Jenas 19, Lennon 90		
West Ham	A	4-3
Defoe 50 pen, Tainio 63, Berbatov 89, Stalteri 90		
Braga	A	3-2
Keane 57, 90, Malbranque 72		
Chelsea	A	3-3
Berbatov 5, Essien 28 og, Ghaly 36		
Braga	H	3-2
Berbatov 28, 42, Malbranque 76		
Watford	H	3-1
Jenas 41, Robinson 63, Ghaly 85		
Chelsea	H	1-2
Keane 79 pen		
Reading	H	1-0
Keane 36		

Seville	A	1-2
Keane 2		
Chelsea	A	0-1
Seville	H	2-2
Defoe 65, Lennon 67		
Wigan	A	3-3
Berbatov 4, Keane 35 pen, 68		
Arsenal	H	2-2
Keane 30, Jenas 90		
Middlesbrough	A	3-2
Keane 12, 83, Berbatov 47		
Charlton	A	2-0
Berbatov 7, Defoe 90		
Blackburn	H	1-1
Defoe 67		
Man City	H	2-1
Keane 10, Berbatov 32		

WATFORD

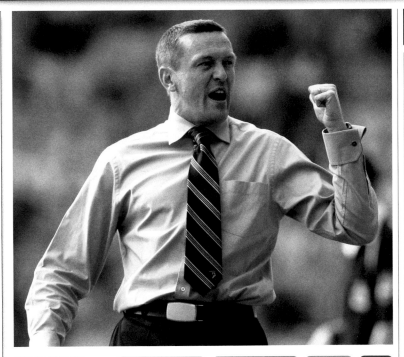

WATFORD FACTS

MANAGER	CAPTAIN
ADRIAN BOOTHROYD	**GAVIN MAHON**

CLUB

Stadium: Vicarage Road

Capacity: 20,800

Average Attendance 2006-07: 18,750

Pitch Size: 105m x 68.5m

Website: www.watfordfc.com

STRIP

Home: Yellow shirts with scarlet trim, scarlet shorts

Away: All black with gold cuffs to sleeves

SPONSORS

Shirt: Beko (appliances)

Kit Partner: Diadora

CHEAPEST TICKET PRICES

Adult: £20.00

Junior: £10.00

RECORDS

Record Home Attendance: 34,099 v Manchester United (FA Cup) February 3, 1969

Record Victory: 10-1 v Lowestoft Town (FA Cup) November 27, 1926

Record Defeat: 0-10 v Wolves (FA Cup) Jan 24, 1912

Most League Goals: Luther Blissett (158)

Most League Apps: Luther Blissett (415)

Most Capped Player: John Barnes, 31 (England); Kenny Jacket, 31 (Wales)

HONOURS

Division Two: 1998

Division Two: 1969

Division Four: 1978

COCA-COLA CHAMPIONSHIP PLAY-OFF WINNERS 2006
WATFORD F.C.

SQUAD RECORD 2006-07

	CLUB				INTERNATIONAL			POSITIONAL RANKING		OVERALL RANKING
	Mins	Goals	Mins per goal	% played	Country	Games	Goals	Domestic	World	All positions
GOALKEEPERS		CONCEDED					CONCEDED			
BEN FOSTER	2564	44	58	75%	England	1	1	14	54	333
RICHARD LEE	855	15	57	25%	England	0	0	31	175	2221
DEFENDERS		CONCEDED					CONCEDED			
JAY DEMERIT	2758	50	55	81%	United States	4	4	120	576	1566
JAMES CHAMBERS	1314	20	66	38%	England	0	0	161	843	2500
DANNY SHITTU	2343	38	62	69%	Nigeria	0	0	141	662	1889
LLOYD DOYLEY	1621	29	56	47%	England	0	0	170	891	2678
JORDAN STEWART	2681	46	58	78%	England	0	0	114	555	1512
ADRIAN MARIAPPA	1558	32	49	46%	England	0	0	183	944	2870
MALCOLM MACKAY	1182	18	66	35%	Scotland	0	0	146	738	2140
MIDFIELDERS		SCORED					SCORED			
GARETH WILLIAMS	1228	1	1228	36%	Scotland	0	0	146	737	2102
TOMMY SMITH	3002	2	1501	88%	England	0	0	76	361	997
ALHASSAN BANGURA	1087	0	0	32%	Sierra Leone	0	0	172	922	2636
GAVIN MAHON	2937	1	2937	86%	England	0	0	88	428	1181
DAMIAN FRANCIS	2481	4	620	73%	England	0	0	122	583	1646
FORWARDS		SCORED					SCORED			
DARIUS HENDERSON	2196	3	732	64%	England	0	0	104	623	2665
MARLON KING	1122	4	281	33%	Jamaica	0	0	56	314	1578
HAMEUR BOUAZZA	2348	5	470	69%	Algeria	2	0	84	437	1986
TAMAS PRISKIN	755	2	378	22%	Hungary	3	0	92	502	2254

KEY: *Club stats are all for the 2006-07 season. Mins = Minutes played in the league for club; Goals conceded = goals let in when the player is on the pitch; Goals scored = scored by the player; Mins per goal = number of minutes on average between each goal conceded or scored; % played = the percentage of the league season the player played; Domestic = player ranking by position in domestic league; World = player ranking by position in World; Overall Position = player ranking in world across all positions.*

THE STARS OF LAST SEASON

TEAM OF THE SEASON

- G Foster
- D Doyley | D Shittu | D DeMerit | D Stewart
- M Smith | M Mahon | M Bangura | M Francis
- F King | F Bouazza

G STAR GOALKEEPER

BEN FOSTER: The loan star caught McClaren's eye and often stood between Watford and an avalanche of goals.

Average goals per game conceded by club	1.55
Goals per game conceded when player on pitch	1.53
Points per game club won when player on pitch	0.79
Minutes played 2654	Clean sheets 6

D STAR DEFENDER

DANNY SHITTU: The former Nigerian international had his ups and downs but was Watford's most consistent defender.

Goals per game conceded when player on pitch	1.44
Points per game club won when player on pitch	0.82
Goals scored by player	1
Minutes played 2433	Clean sheets 7

M STAR MIDFIELDER

TOMMY SMITH: The winger had easily the best assists record in a season where goals were a rarity.

Goals per game conceded when player on pitch	1.55
Goals per game club scored when player on pitch	0.84
Goals scored by player	1
Minutes played 2597	Assists 6

F STAR FORWARD

MARLON KING: A former Jamaican international, he was injured early on and with him went Boothroyd's best hope.

Average goals per game scored by club	0.76
Goals per game scored when player on pitch	0.88
% of club goals scored by player	13.8
Minutes played 1122	Assists 1

2006-07 RESULTS ROUND-UP

■ Premiership ■ League Cup ■ FA Cup ■ UEFA Cup □ Champions League

Everton	A	1-2	
Francis 90			
West Ham	H	1-1	
King 63			
Man Utd	H	1-2	
Francis 34			
Bolton	A	0-1	
Aston Villa	H	0-0	
Accrington	H	6-5*	
*(*on penalties)*			
Wigan	A	1-1	
Bouazza 63			
Fulham	H	3-3	
King 23, Young 46, 89			
Arsenal	A	0-3	

Charlton	A	0-0	
Hull City	H	2-1	
Young 2, Priskin 54			
Tottenham	H	0-0	
Middlesbrough	H	2-0	
Woodgate 6 og, Young 60			
Newcastle	H	4-5*	
*Francis 69, Shittu 108 (*on penalties)*			
Chelsea	A	0-4	
Portsmouth	A	1-2	
DeMerit 32			
Sheff Utd	H	0-1	
Man City	A	0-0	
Reading	H	0-0	

Newcastle	A	1-2	
Bouazza 57			
Liverpool	A	0-2	
Arsenal	H	1-2	
T.Smith 23			

Fulham	A	0-0	
Stockport	H	4-1	
Mackay 30, 76, T.Smith 48, Ashikodi 82			
Liverpool	H	0-3	

Aston Villa	A	0-2	
Blackburn	H	2-1	
Emerton 12 og, DeMerit 70			
West Ham	A	1-0	
McNamee 42			
Man Utd	A	0-4	
Bolton	H	0-1	
West Ham	A	1-0	
Henderson 12 pen			
Ipswich	H	1-0	
Francis 88			
Wigan	H	1-1	
Henderson 24			
Everton	H	0-3	

Charlton	H	2-2	
Bouazza 15, Francis 21			
Plymouth	A	1-0	
Bouazza 21			
Tottenham	A	1-3	
Henderson 89			
Chelsea	H	0-1	
Middlesbrough	A	1-4	
Francis 23			
Portsmouth	H	4-2	
Bouazza 28 pen, 72, Mahon 45, Priskin 51			
Man Utd	H	1-4	
Bouazza 26			
Blackburn	A	1-3	
Rinaldi 21			

Man City	H	1-1	
Priskin 75			
Sheff Utd	A	0-1	
Reading	A	2-0	
Shittu 60, King 85			
Newcastle	H	1-1	
King 52 pen			

WEST HAM

WEST HAM FACTS

MANAGER	CAPTAIN
ALAN CURBISHLEY	**NIGEL REO-COKER**

CLUB

Stadium: Boleyn Ground (Upton Park)

Capacity: 35,657

Average Attendance 2006-07: 34,719

Pitch Size: 103m x 66m

Website: www.whufc.co.uk

STRIP

Home: Claret shirts, with pale blue sleeves, white shorts

Away: White shirts with claret trim, claret shorts

SPONSORS

Shirt: Jobserve (£400,000)

Kit Partner: Reebok

CHEAPEST TICKET PRICES

Adult: £27.00

Junior: £14.00

RECORDS

Record Home Attendance: 43,322 v Tottenham (league) October 17, 1970

Record Victory: 10-0 v Bury (League Cup) October 25, 1983

Record Defeat: 2-8 v Blackburn Rovers (league) December 26, 1963

Most League Goals: Vic Watson (298)

Most League Apps: Billy Bonds (663)

Most Capped Player: Bobby Moore, 108 (England)

HONOURS

Division Two: 1958, 1981

FA Cup: 1964, 1975, 1980

European Cup Winners Cup: 1965

SQUAD RECORD 2006-07

	CLUB				INTERNATIONAL			POSITIONAL RANKING		OVERALL RANKING
	Mins	Goals	Mins per goal	% played	Country	Games	Goals	Domestic	World	All positions
GOALKEEPERS		CONCEDED					CONCEDED			
ROBERT GREEN	2340	39	60	68%	England	0	0	13	50	310
ROY CARROLL	1080	20	54	32%	N Ireland	2	1	28	137	1763
DEFENDERS		CONCEDED					CONCEDED			
LUCAS NEILL	2700	43	63	79%	Australia	3	1	14	34	101
ANTON FERDINAND	2647	41	65	77%	England	0	0	36	110	294
JAMES COLLINS	1360	19	72	40%	Wales	7	7	66	309	831
GEORGE MCCARTNEY	1456	22	66	43%	N Ireland	0	0	76	366	1002
JONATHAN SPECTOR	1787	26	69	52%	United States	5	1	83	389	1054
PAUL KONCHESKY	1964	39	50	57%	England	0	0	96	447	1227
DANIEL GABBIDON	1553	27	58	45%	Wales	7	12	105	495	1345
MIDFIELDERS		SCORED					SCORED			
NIGEL REO-COKER	3082	1	3082	90%	England	0	0	24	57	178
MARK NOBLE	1882	3	627	55%	England	0	0	32	81	264
YOSSI BENAYOUN	2268	3	756	66%	Israel	7	2	58	240	701
LUIS BOA MORTE	1877	1	1877	55%	Portugal	0	0	64	296	848
MATTHEW ETHERINGTON	2018	0	0	59%	England	0	0	74	348	963
NIGEL QUASHIE	2150	0	0	63%	Scotland	2	0	139	692	1969
FORWARDS		SCORED					SCORE			
BOBBY ZAMORA	2149	11	195	63%	England	0	0	28	104	612
CARLOS TEVEZ	1696	7	242	50%	Argentina	2	0	31	122	725
MARLON HAREWOOD	1757	3	586	51%	England	0	0	47	246	1277

KEY: Club stats are all for the 2006-07 season. Mins = Minutes played in the league for club; Goals conceded = goals let in when the player is on the pitch; Goals scored = scored by the player; Mins per goal = number of minutes on average between each goal conceded or scored; % played = the percentage of the league season the player played; Domestic = player ranking by position in domestic league; World = player ranking by position in World; Overall Position = player ranking in world across all positions.

TEAM OF THE SEASON

- **G** Green
- **D** Spector
- **D** Collins
- **D** Ferdinand
- **D** Konchesky
- **M** Benayoun
- **M** Reo-Coker
- **M** Mullins
- **M** Etherington
- **F** Zamora
- **F** Tevez

G STAR GOALKEEPER

ROBERT GREEN: Won the gloves from Roy Carroll and had a great game against United but still hasn't convinced Curbishley.

Average goals per game conceded by club	1.55
Goals per game conceded when player on pitch	1.50
Points per game club won when player on pitch	1.31
Minutes played	2340	Clean sheets	9

D STAR DEFENDER

JAMES COLLINS: The Welsh international got stronger as the season went on and was a regular in West Ham's late escape run.

Goals per game conceded when player on pitch	1.26
Points per game club won when player on pitch	1.67
Goals scored by player	0
Minutes played	1360	Clean sheets	6

M STAR MIDFIELDER

YOSSI BENAYOUN: The classy Israeli international had more goals and assists than any other midfielder at the club last season.

Goals per game conceded when player on pitch	1.55
Goals per game club scored when player on pitch	0.96
Goals scored by player	3
Minutes played	2268	Assists	3

F STAR FORWARD

BOBBY ZAMORA: Tevez may have stolen the headlines but Zamora outscored him and made 32 appearances for the side.

Average goals per game scored by club	0.92
Goals per game scored when player on pitch	1.14
% of club goals scored by player	31.4
Minutes played	2149	Assists	3

2006-07 RESULTS ROUND-UP

■ Premiership ■ League Cup ■ FA Cup ■ UEFA Cup ■ Champions League

Charlton	H	3-1
Zamora 52, 66, C.Cole 90		
Watford	A	1-1
Zamora 65		
Liverpool	A	1-2
Zamora 12		

Aston Villa	H	1-1
Zamora 51		
Palermo	H	0-1
Newcastle	H	0-2
Man City	A	0-2
Palermo	A	0-3
Reading	H	0-1
Portsmouth	A	0-2
Tottenham	A	0-1
Chesterfield	A	1-2
Harewood 4		
Blackburn	H	2-1
Sheringham 21, Mullins 80		

Arsenal	H	1-0
Harewood 89		
Middlesbrough	A	0-1
Chelsea	A	0-1
Sheff Utd	H	1-0
Mullins 36		

Everton	A	0-2
Wigan	H	0-2
Bolton	A	0-4
Man Utd	H	1-0
Reo-Coker 75		

Fulham	A	0-0
Portsmouth	H	1-2
Sheringham 81		
Man City	H	0-1
Reading	A	0-6
Brighton	H	3-0
Noble 49, Cole 58, Mullins 90		
Fulham	H	3-3
Zamora 28, Benayoun 46, 64		
Newcastle	A	2-2
Cole 18, Harewood 22		
Watford	H	0-1
Liverpool	H	1-2
Blanco 77		
Aston Villa	A	0-1

Watford	H	0-1
Charlton	A	0-4
Tottenham	H	3-4
Noble 16, Tevez 40 fk, Zamora 84		
Blackburn	A	2-1
Tevez 71 pen, Zamora 75		
Middlesbrough	H	2-0
Zamora 2, Tevez 45		
Arsenal	A	1-0
Zamora 45		
Sheff Utd	A	0-3
Chelsea	H	1-4
Tevez 35		
Everton	H	1-0
Zamora 13		

Wigan	A	3-0
Boa Morte 30, Benayoun 57, Harewood 83		
Bolton	H	3-1
Tevez 10, 21, Noble 29		
Man Utd	A	1-0
Tevez 45		

WIGAN ATHLETIC

WIGAN FACTS

MANAGER	CAPTAIN
PAUL JEWELL	**ARJAN DE ZEEUW**

CLUB

Stadium: JJB Stadium

Capacity: 25,000

Average Attendance 2006-07: 18,168

Pitch Size: 110m x 60m

Website: www.wiganlatics.co.uk

STRIP

Home: Blue and white stripe shirts, blue shorts

Away: Grey shirts, black shorts

SPONSORS

Shirt: JJB (£300,000 per year)

Kit Partner: JJB Sports

CHEAPEST TICKET PRICES

Adult: £27.00

Junior: £16.00

RECORDS

Record Home Attendance: 27,325 v Hereford (league) October 12, 1953

Record Victory: 7-1 v Scarborough (league) March 11, 1997

Record Defeat: 1-6 v Bristol Rovers (league) March 3, 1990

Most League Goals: Andy Liddell (70)

Most League Apps: Kevin Langley (317)

Most Capped Player: Roy Carroll, 9 (Northern Ireland)

HONOURS

Division Three: 1997

SQUAD RECORD 2006-07

	CLUB				INTERNATIONAL			POSITIONAL RANKING		OVERALL RANKING
	Mins	Goals	Mins per goal	% played	Country	Games	Goals	Domestic	World	All positions
GOALKEEPERS		CONCEDED				CONCEDED				
CHRIS KIRKLAND	2295	42	55	67%	England	1	0	17	82	630
JOHN FILAN	900	14	64	26%	Australia	0	0	24	126	1555
DEFENDERS		CONCEDED				CONCEDED				
LEIGHTON BAINES	3116	59	53	91%	England	0	0	30	86	228
EMMERSON BOYCE	3020	54	56	88%	England	0	0	40	131	354
ARJAN DE ZEEUW	1763	26	68	52%	Holland	0	0	77	370	1009
FITZ HALL	1822	38	48	53%	England	0	0	99	456	1247
RYAN TAYLOR	1110	18	62	32%	England	0	0	111	539	1473
MATT JACKSON	1531	30	51	45%	England	0	0	94	445	1222
MIDFIELDERS		SCORED				SCORED				
DENNY LANDZAAT	2519	2	1260	74%	Holland	10	0	39	104	325
KEVIN KILBANE	2450	1	2450	72%	Rep of Ireland	9	2	41	113	346
PAUL SCHARNER	2053	3	684	60%	Austria	0	0	57	237	687
LEE MCCULLOCH	2306	4	577	67%	Scotland	4	0	54	184	568
JOSIP SKOKO	2159	0	0	63%	Australia	2	0	72	322	900
LUIS ANTONIO VALENCIA	1375	1	1375	40%	Ecuador	0	0	92	458	1264
GARY TEALE	1495	1	1495	44%	Scotland	5	0	69	317	894
FORWARDS		SCORED				SCORED				
EMILE HESKEY	2695	9	299	79%	England	0	0	26	96	549
HENRI CAMARA	1617	6	270	47%	Senegal	0	0	45	217	1151
CALEB FOLAN	692	2	346	20%	England	0	0	66	366	175

KEY: Club stats are all for the 2006-07 season. Mins = Minutes played in the league for club; Goals conceded = goals let in when the player is on the pitch; Goals scored = scored by the player; Mins per goal = number of minutes on average between each goal conceded or scored; % played = the percentage of the league season the player played; Domestic = player ranking by position in domestic league; World = player ranking by position in World; Overall Position = player ranking in world across all positions.

THE STARS OF LAST SEASON

TEAM OF THE SEASON

- G Kirkland
- D Hall
- D Boyce
- D De Zeeuw
- D Baines
- M McCulloch
- M Landzaat
- M Scharner
- M Kilbane
- F Camara
- F Heskey

G STAR GOALKEEPER

CHRIS KIRKLAND: Won his first England cap before getting injured and being unable to influence the team's slide to 17th in the table.

Average goals per game conceded by club	1.55
Goals per game conceded when player on pitch	1.62
Points per game club won when player on pitch	0.96
Minutes played	2385	Clean sheets	7

D STAR DEFENDER

ARJAN DE ZEEUW: Struggled with injuries but the former club captain added defensive stability when he was there.

Goals per game conceded when player on pitch	1.31
Points per game club won when player on pitch	1.05
Goals scored by player	0
Minutes played	1853	Clean sheets	6

M STAR MIDFIELDER

PAUL SCHARNER: The final game of the season showed his ability – poaching a goal before switching to a vital defensive role.

Goals per game conceded when player on pitch	1.55
Goals per game club scored when player on pitch	1.18
Goals scored by player	3
Minutes played	2053	Assists	1

F STAR FORWARD

EMILE HESKEY: He top-scored with ten goals to repay Jewell's faith but too often he was more of a handful than a real goal threat.

Average goals per game scored by club	0.97
Goals per game scored when player on pitch	0.91
% of club goals scored by player	27.0
Minutes played	2695	Assists	2

2006-07 RESULTS ROUND-UP

☐ Premiership ☐ League Cup ☐ FA Cup ☐ UEFA Cup ☐ Champions League

Newcastle	A 1-2	*McCulloch 59*	
Reading	H 1-0	*Heskey 38*	
Portsmouth	A 0-1		
Everton	A 2-2	*Scharner 62, 68*	

Crewe	A 0-2	
Watford	H 1-1	*Camara 29*
Blackburn	A 1-2	*Heskey 2*
Man Utd	H 1-3	*Baines 4*
Man City	H 4-0	*Heskey 2, Dunne 4 og, Camara 65, Valencia 67*
Fulham	A 1-0	*Camara 83*
Bolton	A 1-0	*McCulloch 79*
Charlton	H 3-2	*McCulloch 13, Camara 41, Jackson 78*

Aston Villa	H 0-0	
Tottenham	A 1-3	*Camara 25*
Liverpool	H 0-4	

West Ham	A 2-0	*Cotterill 51, Spector 58 og*
Middlesbrough	A 1-1	*Camara 24 pen*
Arsenal	H 0-1	

Sheff Utd	H 0-1	
Chelsea	H 2-3	*Heskey 45, 75*
Man Utd	A 1-3	*Baines 90 pen*
Blackburn	H 0-3	
Portsmouth	A 1-2	*McCulloch 83*
Chelsea	A 0-4	
Everton	H 0-2	
Reading	A 2-3	*Heskey 3, Landzaat 90*
Portsmouth	H 1-0	*McCulloch 68*

Arsenal	A 1-2	*Landzaat 35*
Watford	A 1-1	*Folan 40*
Newcastle	H 1-0	*Taylor 40*
Man City	A 1-0	*Folan 18*
Fulham	H 0-0	
Charlton	A 0-1	
Bolton	H 1-3	*Heskey 32*
Aston Villa	A 1-1	*Heskey 21*
Tottenham	H 3-3	*Heskey 1, Baines 30, Kilbane 60*

Liverpool	A 0-2	
West Ham	H 0-3	
Middlesbrough	H 0-1	
Sheff Utd	A 2-1	*Scharner 14, Unsworth 45 pen*

There are four quiz pages in the 2008 MOTD Annual. Fill in the answers below to test your football knowledge against the experts from the world's best TV football programme!

QUIZ 1
FROM PAGE 21

GOAL OF THE MONTH WORD SEARCH

S	C	A	S	H	E	V	C	H	E	N	K	O	N	P	B	A	C	Y
O	A	G	G	E	R	E	P	J	A	G	E	L	N	A	E	T	A	
L	L	O	U	N	I	T	R	O	U	G	C	O	L	I	T	U	M	
M	U	A	Z	Z	I	T	S	E	Y	H	J	P	O	H	V	P		
A	N	O	U	M	A	M	U	M	C	D	F	O	E	N	A	R	E	
R	A	M	A	R	A	G	O	R	I	O	M	M	R	A			B	
R	O	B	A	I	S	R	T	L	Z	O	N	Q	X	O	O	L	L	S
Y	E	R	K	N	L	A	M	B	A	R	D	R	S	A	I	H	L	
A	R	T	E	T	A	R	I	C	M	E	O	S	T	O	B	E		
S	C	H	L	A	M	T	A	D	E	Y	N	R	U	I	S	L		
E	V	H	G	S	K	E	Y	L	S	O	B	R	G	E	P	I		
A	N	E	K	A	R	A	R	B	P	T	Q	S	J	S				
R	O	B	L	E	T	A	S	C	R	R	E	K	Q	A	O	E		
Z	S	H	E	V	E	C	H	N	K	T	N	B	R	I	D	A		
R	O	B	I	N	S	O	N	U	B	N	G	O	R	D	A	L	M	
O	C	H	R	A	T	I	M	O	T	E	A	R	B	A	I	N	E	S
B	A	R	T	P	V	W	T	A	Y	O	R	A	W	H	I	E		
S	E	C	H	K	F	G	E	R	O	N	P	I	C	T	A	I	N	L
K	R	A	N	C	J	A	R	X	O	U	O	W	A	R	D	O	E	T

OUT OF 35 POINTS I SCORED

NAME THE YEAR

1.
2.
3.
4.
5.

1. 2002. 2. 2006. 3. 1999. 4. 1993. 5. 1994

2006-07 SEASON

1.
2.
3.
4.
5.
6.
7.
8.
9.
10.
11.
12.

1 Aidy Boothroyd; 2. John Terry; 3 Old Trafford, Emirates Stadium and St James' Park;
4 David Colthill of Wigan; 5 Emirates Stadium; 6 True; 7 Ryan Giggs; 8 Liverpool;
9 Scottish Third Division; 10 Gareth Southgate; 11 Sevilla; 12 Roma

GUESS THE PUNDIT

1.

1. Les Ferdinand

WHO CAPTAINS WHO?

1.
2.
3.
4.
5.
6.
7.
8.

1.B; 2.F; 3.E; 4.A; 5.G; 6.H; 7.D; 8.C

GETTING SHIRTY

1.
2.
3.
4.
5.
6.

1. Cristiano Ronaldo; 2. James Beattie; 3. Joe Cole; 4. Dave Kitson; 5. Thierry Henry; 6. Ledley King

QUIZ 2
FROM PAGE 35

THE CARDIFF CUPS!

1.
2.
3.
4.
5.
6.
7.
8.
9.
10.

1. Jamie Carragher; 2. Chelsea; 3. Liverpool; 4. Ruud van Nistelrooy; 5. Arsenal; 6. Robert Pires;
7. Manchester United; 8. Michael Owen; 9. Steven Gerrard; 10. Chelsea & Manchester United

FOREIGN LEGION

1.
2.
3.
4.
5.

1. Spain; 2. Czech Republic; 3. Belarus; 4. Holland; 5. Ivory Coast

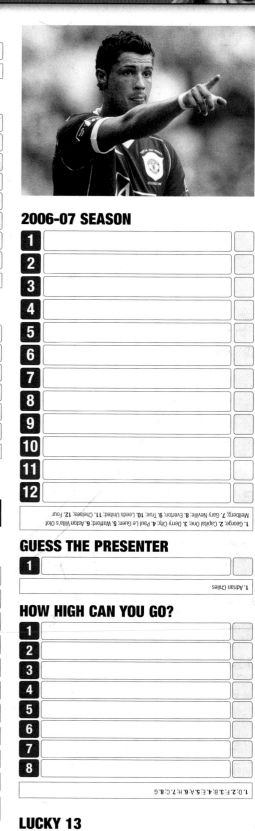

2006-07 SEASON

1.
2.
3.
4.
5.
6.
7.
8.
9.
10.
11.
12.

1. George; 2. Capital One; 3. Derry City; 4. Paul Le Guen; 5. Watford; 6. Aston Villa's Olof
Mellberg; 7. Gary Neville; 8. Everton; 9. True; 10. Leeds United; 11. Chelsea; 12. Four

GUESS THE PRESENTER

1.

1. Adrian Chiles

HOW HIGH CAN YOU GO?

1.
2.
3.
4.
5.
6.
7.
8.

1. D; 2. F; 3. B; 4. E; 5. A; 6. H; 7. C; 8. G

LUCKY 13

1.
2.
3.
4.
5.
6.

1. Park Ji-Sung; 2. Chris Kirkland; 3. Alexander Hleb; 4. Michael Ballack; 5. Danny Murphy;
6. Tomasz Radzinski